The Saving Life of Christ
— AND —
The Mystery of Godliness

Clarion Classics

The Christlike Christian, an unknown Christian
The Complete Green Letters, Miles J. Stanford
Fairest Girlhood, Margaret E. Sangster
Fox's Book of Martyrs, W. B. Forbush, editor
The Glory Christian, an unknown Christian
How to Live the Victorious Life,
  an unknown Christian
In His Steps, Charles M. Sheldon
The Kneeling Christian, an unknown Christian
Our Daily Walk, F. B. Meyer
The Power of Prayer, Reuben A. Torrey
The Power of the Blood of Jesus, Andrew Murray
The Prayers of Susanna Wesley, W. L. Doughty,
  editor
Robert Murray McCheyne, A. A. Bonar
The Spirit of Prayer, Hannah More
They Found the Secret, V. Raymond Edman
With Christ in the School of Prayer, Andrew Murray

The Saving Life of Christ
— AND —
The Mystery of Godliness

Major W. Ian Thomas

ZondervanPublishingHouse
Grand Rapids, Michigan

A Division of HarperCollins*Publishers*

Requests for information should be addressed to:
Zondervan Publishing House
Grand Rapids, Michigan 49530

Library of Congress Cataloging in Publication Data

Thomas, W. Ian.
 The saving life of Christ; and, The mystery of godliness.

 (Clarion classics)
 1. Christian life—1960— . I. Title: Saving life of Christ. II.
Title: Mystery of Godliness.
BV4501.2.T48   1988   248.4   88-100
ISBN 0-310-33261-3

Designed by Anne Cherryman

Printed in the United States of America

08 09 10 • 28 27 26 25 24 23 22

Contents

The Saving Life
of Christ

Meet the Major

**An Introduction* by Dr. V. Raymond Edman,
President, Wheaton College**

Some Christians learn that the Lord can make life an adventure. Major W. Ian Thomas of England is one of them.

The major is every inch a soldier. With his infantry battalion he served in the British Expeditionary Forces in Belgium at the outset of World War II and took part in the evacuation at Dunkirk. Often in combat, in France, Italy, Greece, and elsewhere during that long war, he found the Lord Jesus to be his complete sufficiency. The major is likewise a soldier of the Cross, faithful to the Captain of our salvation. He has found life an adventure with God and for Him, a pageant of triumph in Christ.

Reared in a "respectable" middle-class English home, he was taken to church and taught its precepts. He learned little or nothing of the Bible, however, either at home or in the church attended by the family. At the age of twelve he was invited to a Bible study group of the Crusaders' Union by a lad of thirteen who, during that year, had received Christ as his Saviour. The Bible began to be meaningful to young Ian, and the following summer, still twelve years old, he was converted to Christ at a Crusaders' Union camp. That decision was made when he was alone and simply by praying earnestly, "Lord Jesus, please be my Saviour!"

---

*This Introduction was taken from a chapter in Dr. Edman's book, *They Found the Secret*.

At the age of fifteen, he felt convinced that he should devote all of his life to the service of the Lord Jesus. He told God that he would become a missionary. He began to preach, out in the open air at Hampstead Heath, at that early age. He was also actively engaged in Sunday school work, as well as in the Crusaders' Bible class. Life began to be a round of ceaseless activity. . . .

Speaking of his youthful decision to become a missionary, he said: "I began to consider the best area in which I could become a missionary, and the best means I could employ to be most effective—perfectly sincere and genuine questions." The first missionary influence upon young Ian's life came through a doctor serving in Nigeria, in the Housa Band. "First impressions are often the strongest," related Major Thomas, and so it became his ambition one day to go and join the Housa Band in Nigeria, West Africa. He thought the best thing for him to do was to become a doctor. . . .

At the university Ian became a leader in the Inter-Varsity Fellowship group. If ever there was any evangelistic activity going on, this youthful zealot was "buzzing around the place, every holiday, every spare moment!" He started a slum club down in the East End of London. "Out of a sheer desire to win souls, to go out and get them, I was a windmill of activity until, at the age of nineteen, every moment of my day was packed tight with doing things. . . .

"Thus by the age of nineteen, I had been reduced to a state of complete exhaustion spiritually, until I felt that there was no point in going on. . . .

"Then, one night in November, that year, just at midnight . . . I got down on my knees before God, and I just wept in sheer despair. I said, 'Oh, God, I know that I am saved. I love Jesus Christ. I am perfectly convinced that I am converted. With all my heart I have wanted to serve Thee. I have tried to my uttermost and I am a hopeless failure!' . . . That night things happened.

"I can honestly say that I had never once heard from the lips of men the message that came to me then. . . . but God, that night simply focused upon me the Bible message of *Christ Who is our Life*. . . . The Lord seemed to make plain to me that night, through my tears of bitterness: 'You see, for seven years, with utmost sincerity, you have been trying to live *for* Me, on My behalf, the life that I have been waiting for seven years to live *through* you."

That night, all in the space of an hour, Ian Thomas discovered the secret of the adventurous life. He said: "I got up the next morning to an entirely different Christian life, but I want to emphasize this: I had not received one iota more than I had already had for seven years! . . . "

Thus step by step the Most High led His trusting and obedient servant into paths that he neither foresaw nor chose, but they were pathways of service eminently satisfying and always adventurous. Instead of medical school and the mission field, the ministry was evangelism throughout Britain, especially among young people. Before World War II broke out, he had six wonderful years of ever-expanding ministry in sharing the secret of the life that is Christ.

"I found that it is anything but inactivity (standing back and saying, 'I thank Thee, Lord, this is Thy situation!'). Since the war alone I have traveled a quarter of a million miles, 45,000 this year. . . . It has been my joy to preach in Norway and Denmark, in Germany, Austria, Switzerland, the United States, and Canada, apart from the British Isles, . . . It is not inactivity; it is simply His activity, and that is what makes the difference."

Foreword

I have known the author of this book for many years. He and I have been closely associated from time to time in the ministry of the Word of God, and I have often received personal blessing in my own life through his ministry.

I am sure that the emphasis of this book is something that is urgently needed in this country today and indeed in every area where the message of saving faith in Christ is made known. To so many people, the Lord is in danger of being no more than a patron of our systematic theology instead of the Christ Who is our life. There is such a tendency to departmentalize Christian living and to regard our devotions as one department and then to live for the rest of our time almost as religious pagans.

This book strikes home at that attitude and presents to us the triumphant life of our risen Lord indwelling us by His Spirit as the one vital essential for Christian living.

It will be my earnest prayer that this book receives the attention and interest that it deserves and that its message may be a rich blessing to many thousands of readers.

—Alan Redpath
Pastor, Moody Church, Chicago

Chapter I

The Saving Life of Christ

There is something which makes Christianity more than a religion, more than an ethic, and more than the idle dream of the sentimental idealist. It is this something that makes it relevant to each one of us right now as a contemporary experience. It is the fact that Christ *Himself* is the very life content of the Christian faith. It is He who makes it "tick." "Faithful is he that calleth you, who also will do it" (1 Thess. 5:24). The One who calls you is the One who does that to which He calls you. "For it is God which worketh in you both to will and to do of his good pleasure" (Phil. 2:13). He is Himself the very dynamic of all His demands.

Christ did not die simply that you might be saved from a bad conscience or even to remove the stain of past failure, but to "clear the decks" for divine action. You have been told that Christ died to save you. This is gloriously true in a very limited, though vital sense. In Romans 5:10 we read, "If, when we were enemies, we were reconciled to God by the death of his Son, much more, being reconciled, we shall be saved by his life." The Lord Jesus Christ therefore ministers to you in two distinct ways—He reconciles you to God by His death, and He saves you by His life.

I would like to examine with you what this implies. The

very first word of the gospel is a word of reconciliation, so that "we are ambassadors for Christ, as though God did beseech you by us: we pray you in Christ's stead, be ye reconciled to God" (2 Cor. 5:20). This is a call to the sinner to be at peace with God Himself. How is this possible? Only by virtue of the fact that "God was in Christ, reconciling the world unto himself" (2 Cor. 5:19a).

God in righteousness has no option but to find you guilty as a sinner—by nature dead in trespasses and sins—and to pass upon you the sentence of death, the forfeiture of His Holy Spirit, and alienation from the life of God. But more than nineteen hundred years ago, God in Christ stepped out of eternity into time, and there are extended to you today the nail-pierced hands of One who suffered, "the just for the unjust," to bring you back to God (1 Peter 3:18a). He bore "our sins in his own body on the tree" (1 Peter 2:24a).

This is what makes the gospel at once so urgent! Mental assent is not enough—a moral choice is imperative! Christ is God's last word to man and God's last word to you, and He demands an answer.

Your response to Jesus Christ will determine your condition in the sight of God—redeemed or condemned!

This, however, is but the beginning of the story, "for if, when we were enemies, we were reconciled to God by the death of his Son, much more, being reconciled [*now an accomplished fact*] we shall be saved [*as a continuing process*] . . . by his life" (Rom. 5:10). The glorious fact of the matter is this—no sooner has God reconciled to Himself the man who has responded to His call, than He reimparts to him, as a forgiven sinner, the presence of the Holy Spirit, and this restoration to him of the Holy Spirit constitutes what the Bible calls regeneration, or new birth. Titus 3:5—6: "Not by works of righteousness which we have done, but according to his mercy he saved us, by the washing of regeneration, and the renewing of the Holy Ghost; which he shed on us abundantly through Jesus Christ our Saviour."

On the third morning after His crucifixion, the Lord Jesus Christ rose from the dead and appeared to His disciples. He instructed them for some forty days and then ascended to the Father. On the first day of Pentecost He returned, not this time to be *with them* externally—clothed with that sinless humanity that God had prepared for Him, being conceived of the Holy Spirit in the womb of Mary—but now to be *in them* imparting *to them* His own divine nature, clothing Himself with *their* humanity, so that they each became "members in particular" of a new, corporate body through which Christ expressed Himself to the world of their day. He spoke with their lips. He worked with their hands. This was the miracle of new birth, and this remains the very heart of the gospel!

"Faithful is he that calleth you, who also will *do it.*" The One who calls you to a life of righteousness is the One who by your consent lives that life of righteousness *through* you! The One who calls you to minister to the needs of humanity is the One who by your consent ministers to the needs of humanity *through* you! The One who calls you to go into all the world and preach the gospel to every creature, is the One who by your consent, goes into all the world and preaches the gospel to every creature *through* you!

This is the divine genius that saves a man from the futility of self-effort. It relieves the Christian of the burden of trying to pull himself up by his own bootstraps! If it were not for this divine provision, the call to Christ would be a source of utter frustration, presenting the sorry spectacle of a sincere idealist, constantly thwarted by his own inadequacy.

If you will but trust Christ, not only for the death He died in order to redeem you, but also for the life that He lives and waits to live through you, the very next step you take will be a step taken in the very energy and power of God Himself. You will have begun to live a life which is essentially supernatural, yet still clothed with the common humanity of your physical body, and still worked out in the things that inevitably make up the lot of a man who, though his heart may be with Christ in heaven, still has his two feet firmly planted on the earth. *WOW!*

You will have become *totally dependent* upon the life of Christ within you, and never before will you have been so *independent*, so *emancipated* from the pressure of your circumstances, so *released* at last from that self-distrust which has made you at one moment an arrogant, loud-mouthed braggart, and the next moment the victim of your own self-pity—and, either way, always in bondage to the fear of other men's opinions.

You will be free from the tyranny of a defeated enemy within. You will be more than conqueror, for even death itself is conquered by His life. Christ through death destroyed "him that had the power of death, that is, the devil" (Heb. 2:14b). This indeed is victory!

You will be restored to your true humanity—to be the human vehicle of the divine life. Your faith will open the windows of heaven, for God will move in to do the impossible—and this is the speciality of creative deity. Your friends will be baffled, for in reality you will have become a new creature—old things will have passed away, all things will have become new (2 Cor. 5:17). Through peace *with* God you will have found the peace *of* God, which "passeth all understanding."

Now if it is true that the Lord Jesus Christ will live His life through you on earth today, as He lived His life once in His own body on earth more than nineteen hundred years ago, it is both interesting and necessary to discover *how* He lived *then* so that you may know how He will live through you *now*. Let us look at Scriptures that show us how He lived.

In John 6:56 it says, "He that eateth my flesh, and drinketh my blood, dwelleth in me, and I in him." From the context of this passage, we understand that the Lord Jesus Christ here uses the expression "to eat and to drink" as representing "to come and to believe," so that those that come *to* Him and believe *on* Him enter into a unique relationship *with Him*—they dwell *in Him* and He dwells *in them*.

Verse 57 continues, "As the living Father hath sent me, and I live by the Father: so he that eateth me, even he shall live by me." As He lived by the Father, so you are to live by Him. How then did Jesus Christ live by the Father? Once you know the answer to this question, you will know thereafter how you are to live by Him, and at first the answer is surprising.

In John 5:19, Jesus said, "Verily, verily, I say unto you, The Son can do *nothing* of himself" (emphasis added). "Then said Jesus unto them, When ye have lifted up the Son of man, then shall ye know that I am he, and that I do *nothing* of myself" (John 8:28a, emphasis added). Here we see Jesus Christ as man, living in total, unquestioning dependence upon the Father. Thus He fulfilled His true vocation as man, for He came in His sinless humanity to be what man through sin had ceased to be—the willing vehicle of the Divine Presence, allowing the Father to express Himself in action through His humanity.

Although Jesus Christ was Himself the Creative Deity, by whom all things were made, *as man* He humbled Himself—set aside His divine prerogatives and walked this earth *as man*—a perfect demonstration of what God intended man to be—the whole personality yielded to and occupied by God for Himself.

So the Lord Jesus prayed in John 17 verse 19—"For their sakes I sanctify myself, that they also might be sanctified [set wholly apart] through the truth." That is to say, as He lived in unbroken dependence upon the Father, taking no step except in recognition of the fact that apart from the Father, He could do nothing, so He calls upon you to live in the same total dependence upon Him—taking no step except in recognition of the fact that apart from Him, Christ, *you* can do nothing.

"I am the vine, ye are the branches: He that abideth in me, and I in him, the same bringeth forth much fruit: for *without me* ye can do *nothing*" (John 15:5, emphasis added). In other words, you can do no more without Him than He could do without the Father. But how much could the Father do through the Son? Everything! For He was available to all that the Father made available to Him. "Jesus, knowing that the Father had given all things into his hands" (John 13:3a). "It pleased the Father that in him should all fullness dwell" (Col. 1:19).

How much then can Jesus Christ do through you and through me? Everything! He is limited only by the measure of our availability to all that He makes available to us, for "in him dwelleth all the fullness of the Godhead bodily. And ye are complete in him" (Col. 2:9–10a). What then is the faith that releases divine action? How may you be saved by His life, as you have already claimed to be redeemed by His death? This is the critical question of Christian experience, and the answer is simple—"The just shall live by faith" (Rom. 1:17c).

Faith in all its sheer simplicity! Faith that takes God precisely at His Word! Faith that simply says, "Thank You."

If you are to know the fulness of life in Christ, you are to appropriate the efficacy of *what He is* as you have already appropriated the efficacy of *what He has done*. Relate everything, moment by moment as it arises, to the adequacy of *what He is in you*, and assume that His adequacy will be operative; and on this basis in 1 Thessalonians 5:16 you are exhorted to "rejoice evermore!" You are to be incorrigibly cheerful, for you have solid grounds upon which to rejoice!

Again, "Pray without ceasing" (1 Thess. 5:17), and here the word "pray" does not mean to beg or to plead as if God were unwilling to give—but simply to expose by faith every situation as it arises, to the all-sufficiency of the One who indwells you by His life. Can any situation possibly arise, in any circumstances, for which He is not adequate? Any pressure, promise, problem, responsibility, or temptation for which the Lord Jesus Himself is not adequate? If He be truly God, there cannot be a single one! "And [He is] declared to be the Son of God with power, according to the Spirit of holiness, by the resurrection from the dead" (Rom. 1:4)—and of this, His resurrection life, we are made partakers!

This being so, applying His adequacy by faith to every situation as it arises, will leave you with no alternative but to obey the injunction of 1 Thessalonians 5:18—"In everything give thanks!" In how many things? In *everything*—without exception, "for this is the will of God in Christ Jesus concerning you."

If there is any situation from which you are not prepared to step back, in recognition of the total adequacy of Christ who is in you, then you are out of the will of God. You are asserting by your action and by your attitude that He has nothing to give you for that situation, which you do not have in yourself. This is the very negation of dependence, and you disobey the injunction of verse 19—"Quench not the Spirit," for the office of the Holy Spirit is to make known to you, and to make experiential to you, all that Christ is in you.

This, of course, is what it means to be filled with the Holy Spirit—to allow the Holy Spirit to occupy the whole of your personality with the adequacy of Christ. This is the sublime secret of drawing upon the unlimited resources of Deity. "Speaking to yourselves in psalms and hymns and spiritual songs, singing and making melody in your heart to the Lord; giving thanks always for all things unto God and the Father in the name of our Lord Jesus Christ" (Eph. 5:19–20).

How stupid it would be to buy a car with a powerful engine under the hood and then to spend the rest of your days pushing it! Thwarted and exhausted, you would wish to discard it as a useless thing! Yet to some of you who are Christians, this may be God's word to your heart. When God redeemed you through the precious blood of His dear Son, He placed, in the language of my illustration, a powerful engine under the hood—nothing less than the resurrection life of God the Son, made over to you in the person of God the Holy Spirit. Then stop pushing! Step in and switch on and expose every hill of circumstance, of opportunity, of temptation, of perplexity—no matter how threatening—to the divine energy that is available.

With what magnificent confidence you may step out into the future when once you have consented to die to your own self-effort and to make yourself available as a redeemed sinner to all that God has made available to you in His risen Son!

To be *in Christ*—that is redemption; but for Christ to be *in you*—that is sanctification! To be *in Christ*—that makes you fit for heaven; but for Christ to be *in you*—that makes you fit for earth! To be *in Christ*—that changes yours destination; but for Christ to be *in you*—that changes your destiny! The one makes heaven your home—the other makes this world His workshop.

I may wish to return to my home in England, and I stand in New York, but ever since I was born, I have been bound to this earth by a law that I have never been able to break—the law of gravity. I am told, however, that there is another law, a higher law, the law of aerodynamics, and if only I will be willing to commit myself in total trust to this new law, then this new law will set me free from the old law. By faith I step into the plane, I sit back in the *rest* of faith, and as those mighty engines roar into life, I discover that the new law of aerodynamics sets me free from the law of gravity.

So long as I maintain by faith that position of total dependence, I do not have to *try to be free* from the law of gravity—I am *being set free* by the operation of a new and a higher law. Of course, if I am stupid enough, way out across the Atlantic, I may decide that the cabin of the plane is too stuffy and may step out through the emergency window—but the moment I discard my position of faith in the new and higher law that is setting me free, I discover that the old down-drag is still fully in operation, and I am caught again by the law of gravity and plunged into the water!

I must maintain my attitude of dependence if I am to remain airborne!

So you too are called upon by God to *walk* by faith, to *walk* in the Spirit, resting the whole weight of your personality upon the living Christ who is in you; and as by faith you walk in the Spirit, so God declares you will not fulfill the lusts of the flesh. You will be liberated, emancipated, set free from the down-drag of that inbred wickedness, which Christ alone can overcome. You will be made more than conqueror through "Christ, who is our life" (Col. 3:4a).

I wonder how it is with you? Have you ever put your trust in the Lord Jesus as your Redeemer? Have you been reconciled to God by the death of His Son? I wonder, if reconciled, whether you are at this moment being saved by His life? Have you learned to step out of every situation and relate it wholly to *what He is in you,* and by faith say "Thank You"?

Lord Jesus, how I thank Thee that Thou hast not only redeemed me with Thy precious blood, reconciled me to God, and established peace between my guilty soul and

God my Maker, but I thank Thee that Thou art risen from the dead, that at this very moment Thou dost indwell me in the person and power of Thy divine Spirit; that Thou hast never expected of me anything but failure, yet Thou hast given to me Thy strength for my weakness, Thy victory for my defeat, Thyself for all my bankruptcy! I step out now, by faith, into a future that is limited only by what Thou art! To me to live is Christ! For Thy name's sake. Amen.

Chapter II

A New Principle

We have begun to see that victorious Christian living is not a method or technique; it is an entirely different, revolutionary principle of life. It is the principle of an *exchanged* life—"not I, but Christ liveth in me" (Gal. 2:20b).

This is all part of our gospel—it is not the gospel *plus!* We must not get our terminology wrong. To divorce the behavior of the Christian from the gospel is entirely false and is not true to the Word of God, yet all too often such is the characteristic of gospel preaching.

I would like to explore with you what is the true spiritual content of our gospel—not just heaven *one day*, but Christ *right now!* Christ *in you*, on the grounds of redemption—this is the gospel! To preach anything less than this must inevitably produce "Evan-jellyfish"—folk with no spiritual vertebrae, whose faith does not "behave"!

Do you remember what James says in his epistle? "As the body without the spirit is dead, so faith without works is dead also" (James 2:26). The "spirit" there means breath, and a body without breath is dead. Stop breathing—and folk will bury you! In other words a *living body* breathes, and a *living faith* breathes, and a living faith breathes with *divine action*. A living faith breathes with the activity of

Jesus Christ. That is why the Lord Jesus, in John 6:29, said, "This is the work of God, that ye believe on him whom he hath sent."

That is the work of God. It is your living faith in the adequacy of the One who is *in you*, which releases His divine action *through you*. It is the kind of activity that the Bible calls "good works," as opposed to "dead works."

"Good works" are those works that have their origin in Jesus Christ—whose activity is released through your body, presented to Him as a living sacrifice by a faith that expresses total dependence, as opposed to the Adamic independence (Rom. 12:1–2).

There are two very simple illustrations given to us in the Old Testament of these two facets of the truth—"you in Christ" and "Christ in you." We will glance at them briefly because there is no better Bible commentary in all the world than the Bible itself! If you want to know what the Bible means, then turn to the Bible and it will tell you—and you are not likely to be confused!

> So Moses brought Israel from the Red Sea, and they went out into the wilderness of Shur; and they went three days in the wilderness, and found no water. And when they came to Marah, they could not drink of the waters of Marah, for they were bitter: therefore the name of it was called Marah [a word that means bitterness]. And the people murmured against Moses, saying, What shall we drink? And he cried unto the Lord; and the Lord showed him a tree, which when he had cast into the waters, the waters were made sweet; there he made for them a statute and an ordinance, and there he proved them, and said, If thou wilt diligently hearken to the voice of the Lord thy God, and wilt do that which is right in his sight, and wilt give ear to his commandments, and keep all his statutes, I will put none of these diseases upon thee, which I have brought upon the Egyptians: for I am the Lord that healeth thee. (Exod. 15:22–26)

The incident concerns God's divine intervention in bringing His people out of Egypt. We will not pause to consider that now as we shall be doing so later. Suffice it to recognize that this particular incident is just an underlining, an emphasis of the redemptive principle. This is the first picture—bitter waters in which there was only death, and they cried to God, and God showed them a tree.

The meaning, of course, is obvious, for there had come a day when Adam fell into sin, and how dark and how deep and how bitter had the waters become within the soul of man! All the tears and all the anguish and all the sorrow and all the death and all the crying and all the dying—this has been the consequence of that first Adamic repudiation of man's true relationship to God, of which you and I today are still the heirs, in this poor, sin-sick world!

The waters indeed are dark and deep and bitter within the soul of man, but the Spirit of God moves upon the face of the waters, and they are stirred, and the soul is awakened, and at last the soul, convicted of its sin, cries out to God, and He says, "Behold the Lamb of God, which taketh away the sin of the world" (John 1:29).

He showed them a *tree*, "which when he had cast into the waters, the waters were made sweet." He bore our sins "in His own body on the tree" (1 Peter 2:24a). This was the *second* tree, the place of *second choice*, for as Adam had repudiated his relationship to God at that first tree, and said "No" to God, and stepped out of life into death, out of dependence into independence—so may you and I at that second tree, the place of second choice, say our "Yes" where he said "No." Step back out of death into life! Be raised from the dead—out of our self-will and independence, into a childlike *dependence*—the obedience of faith.

"I am the Lord that healeth thee." This is the beginning of our salvation! This is to be reconciled to God by the death of His Son.

It is "the tree for bitterness"—the precious blood of the Lord Jesus that cleanses us from all sin, and though our sins be as scarlet, they shall be as white as snow; though they are red like crimson, they shall be as wool. This is the beginning of our faith, and this is where we must begin— for if we have not begun here, we have not begun at all. But it would be a very sad thing to stop there!

That is why we have this other very valuable picture. It is found this time in 2 Kings 2:19: "And the men of the city said unto Elisha, Behold, I pray thee, the situation of this city is pleasant, as my lord seeth: but the water is naught, and the ground barren." This is a different picture.

Here is a beautiful city, enchantingly situated. The casual passerby, the stranger, the traveler, the merchant—they would be glad to sojourn awhile, to spend the night, or, if possible, the weekend. They would like to come back for their vacation with the family! They would congratulate the inhabitants on the good fortune that was theirs to live in such attractive surroundings; and yet, beneath all this charming exterior, there was heartbreak, a sickening load within the breasts of those who lived there.

They showed a brave face when folk congratulated them; and when folk admired their beautiful city, they displayed a sweet smile; they tried not to give their inner sorrow away, yet every time somebody admired and flattered the place where they lived, it hurt them! They knew the inner secret: "The water was naught, and the ground was barren."

When it says "the water was naught," it does not mean that there was no water, as we shall discover; but it was stale and stagnant, producing sterility! When it says "the ground was barren," it does not mean to say that nothing grew—otherwise the place would not have looked so charming. The word "barren" means "causing to miscarry."

Had you been there in early spring, you would have seen all the early evidences of coming harvest. You would have seen the tiny, tender shoots bursting through the soil. You would have seen the leaves beginning to pop out of the buds on the trees and bushes, and a week or two later you would have seen the blossom fashion, fade, and fall, to leave the promise of a bumper crop. You might well have congratulated the people on all that they had, seemingly, to look forward to.

That was the tragedy of it! Maybe there still lurked in the hearts of the inhabitants the feeble hope that this year things would be different—that maybe they had turned the corner and that everything was now to be all right—yet something, heavy as lead, deep down in their hearts, kept saying, "No! it will always be just the same! You know exactly what is going to happen!" And it did! It always happened! The fruit, just about to ripen, ready to be plucked, fell suddenly to the ground—premature and immature—to rot and never to reproduce. This was the heartbreak of that beautiful city! So deceptive! So impressive to everybody except to those who lived there! Of what is this a picture?

It may, of course, be a picture of *you!* Do not be shocked when I say it—it is the picture of a carnal Christian. You say, "I thought a carnal Christian was a backslider—somebody, for instance, who used to go to church but has run off with somebody else's wife!" Oh no! That is only one kind of carnal Christian, and I would not suggest that you were that kind of carnal Christian.

No, no! I am talking about some Sunday school teachers. I am talking about some Sunday school superintendents. I am talking about some pastor in his pulpit. I am talking about some missionary on the field. I am talking about many ordinary, average, earnest Christians. They are wonderful people. You would love to meet them. They talk all the language of salvation and they mean every word they say. They are not hypocrites! They are tired, many of them—

desperately tired! God knows how tired they are, but they are not hypocrites.

They are overwhelmed inwardly with a sense of defeat and frustration and futility and barrenness—but when you meet them, they will smile sweetly and they will mean the smile they give you. They will grip you by the hand and they will say, "God bless you for passing my way!" They will thank you for all the encouragement that you have given them; yet, as you thank them for the message you have just heard from their lips, your very words of thanks will hurt them, because they know what you do *not* know—that for years they have labored in vain!

The fruit that has appeared to others has fallen—oh, so often, so *cruelly* often—to the ground—premature, immature—only to rot and never to reproduce.

Story after story could be told of men and women who bravely, doggedly, out of a sense of duty, love, and devotion go on and on and on—yet deep down in their hearts they are tired, almost beyond endurance! Again and again they have got down by their bedside and cried out to God, with tears in their eyes: "God, You know how barren I am. You know how empty I am. You know how stale I am. You *know* it!"—and yet they do not know the answer.

I wonder, are you like that?

At last the burden became intolerable. The men of the city came to the man of God, and they poured out the whole story. "He said, Bring me a new cruse, and put salt therein. And they brought it to him. And he went forth unto the spring of the waters, and cast the salt in there, and said, Thus saith the Lord, I have healed these waters; there shall not be from thence any more death or barren land. So the waters were healed unto this day, according to the saying of Elisha which he spake" (2 Kings 2:20–22). He went to the spring of the waters—for there *were* waters—and he placed salt at the source. What does salt represent?

Salt speaks of the risen life of the glorified Saviour, imparted by the indwelling of the Holy Spirit to the redeemed sinner. It is the *tree* for bitterness! It is the *salt* for barrenness! As you have been reconciled to God by His *death*, so you are constantly to be saved by His *life*.

It is only the life of the Lord Jesus—His activity, *clothed* with you and *displayed* through you, that ultimately will find the approval of God. As a forgiven sinner, you are a member of "a holy priesthood, to offer up spiritual sacrifices, acceptable to God by Jesus Christ" (1 Peter 2:5b). It is the Lord Jesus Christ alone who makes your sacrifices acceptable to God. Only what He does in you and through you merits His approval, and God can, and will, accept nothing less!

"And every oblation of thy meat-offering shalt thou season with salt; neither shalt thou suffer the salt of the covenant of thy God to be lacking from thy meat offering: with all thine offerings thou shalt offer salt" (Lev. 2:13). *Under no circumstances*, God said in His law given to Moses, were any offerings to be brought to Him, or sacrifices made, that were not seasoned with salt. Without the salt they would not be acceptable, no matter how sincerely brought, no matter at how great a cost, no matter how lofty the motive, no matter how noble the ideal; without the salt they would not be acceptable.

This was the practice, as suggested in Ezekiel 43:24. "Thou shalt offer [these offerings] before the LORD, and the priests shall cast salt upon them, and they shall offer them up for a burnt offering unto the LORD." It was salt that made the offering acceptable.

Now the Lord Jesus, in Luke 14:33, tells us the minimum demands that He makes for true discipleship. He says, "Whosoever he be of you that forsaketh not all that he hath [literally, *all that he hath*—himself and all that he possesses], he cannot be my disciple." He has got to recognize his bankruptcy, so that his sole wealth is vested in the One whom God has credited to him in the person and by the presence of His divine Spirit. This is the condition for discipleship.

"Salt," He goes on to say, "is good: but if the salt have lost his savour, wherewith shall it be seasoned? It is neither fit for the land, nor yet for the dunghill; but men cast it out. He that hath ears to hear, let him hear" (Luke 14:34–35). There is a substitute salt that has lost its savor. In the Middle East, salt is at a premium. I served there in the army during the war, and we did good business! For some reason, salt is scarce, and the Arabs would give anything for a pinch of salt. You could get a dozen eggs, you could buy a chicken, you could have bought their shirt for a pinch of salt! I do not think you would have wanted the shirt, as you would not have known which holes to put your arms through! But salt was everything to them, because with salt they preserved their meat and their fish.

Salt was scarce, so there were substitutes on the market—good to the taste, all right for immediate consumption, but the moment they tried to preserve their food with these substitutes, to keep it pure and healthy and edible, within a matter of hours, or at most a matter of days in that hot, sultry climate, it went putrid and bad and stank! It was not even fit for the dunghill!

As in the case of substitute salt, there is a *form of activity* that is all right for immediate consumption. It impresses everybody. Your stock goes high—but it will always leave a stink behind it, if it stems from the flesh, if it is self-activity! It will always produce the kind of fruit that drops, both premature and immature—to rot and never to reproduce.

This is the work of God, that you believe, and maintain unrelentingly, total dependence upon the One whom God has sent to fill you with Himself. He is the true Salt, through whom you are made the salt of the earth.

Here is another, fascinating reference to salt. It is described in Leviticus 2:13 as the "salt of the covenant," the token of God's unfailing pledge and purpose in the lives of redeemed sinners, who are "accepted in the beloved. In whom we have redemption through his blood, the forgiveness of sins, according to the riches of his grace" (Eph. 1:6b–7). That is the tree for bitterness! "In whom ye also trusted ... in whom also after that ye believed, ye were sealed with that Holy Spirit of promise, which is the earnest [or guarantee] of our inheritance" (Eph. 1:13–14a). That is the salt of the covenant—the salt for barrenness! The resurrection life of the Lord Jesus imparted to the true believer by the presence of the Holy Spirit!

The Lord Jesus said, "He that believeth on me, as the scripture hath said, out of his [innermost being] shall flow rivers of living [*not stagnant!*] water. (But this spake he of the Spirit, which they that believe on him should receive: for the Holy Ghost was not yet given; because that Jesus was not yet glorified)" (John 7:38–39). That is to say, salt at the source! Salt at "the spring of the waters" (2 Kings 2:21).

"This Ezra went up from Babylon; and he was a ready scribe in the law of Moses, which the LORD God of Israel had given: and the king granted him all his request, according to the hand of the LORD his God upon him" (Ezra 7:6). It is a wonderful thing to be in such a relationship to God that everything you need, for any circumstance, is always yours, by the good hand of your God upon you! "For Ezra had prepared his heart to seek the law of the LORD, and to do it, and to teach in Israel statutes and judgments" (Ezra 7:10). He had said in his heart, "I am going to seek the mind of God in the Word of God, do the will of God, and teach the ways of God," and for this reason he was among those whom God raised up to rebuild, cleanse, and fill the temple with the worship of God.

The king gave him a letter. He said, "I, even I Artaxerxes

the king, do make a decree to all the treasurers which are beyond the river, that whatsoever Ezra the priest, the scribe of the law of the God of heaven, shall require of you, it be done speedily" (Ezra 7:21). What had Ezra asked for, that pure worship might be re-established in the cleansed House of God? "Unto a hundred talents of silver, and to a hundred measures of wheat, and to a hundred baths of wine, and to a hundred baths of oil, *and salt without prescribing how much!*" He said, in so many words, "King Artaxerxes, I want a hundred of this, I want a hundred of that, and I want a hundred of the other; but I must have *unlimited quantities of salt!* I must never run out of salt—because no matter how costly, no matter how sacrificial, no matter how sincere, God will accept *nothing* that is not seasoned with salt! I must have *unlimited quantities of salt!*"

Now is that not a wonderful picture? And God has given you unlimited quantities of salt! "And God is able to make *all* grace abound toward you; that ye, *always* having *all* sufficiency in *all* things, may abound to *every* good work" (2 Cor. 9:8, emphasis added).

Is it this Salt that you need? Then prepare your heart, with Ezra of old, "to seek the law of the Lord and to do it," and know that Jesus Christ Himself is all you need, in death and resurrection, to cleanse and fill you, and hear Him say, "Thus saith the Lord, I have healed these waters; there shall not be from thence any more death or barren land" (2 Kings 2:21b).

Chapter III

Three Categories of Men

One of the most remarkable episodes in the Bible is the story of how God brought His people Israel out of Egypt, through the wilderness, and into the land of Canaan. It is as though the Holy Spirit gave us here a master key, a point of reference, a framework into which are woven all the mighty-colored threads of truth. It will be my purpose to examine with you what it means to be in the land of Egypt, what it means to be in the wilderness, and what it means to be in Canaan. Over four hundred years the children of Israel had been enslaved by the Egyptians, suffering bitterly beneath burdens inflicted by their taskmasters, helpless to save themselves, hopeless but for the fact that four hundred years before, God had promised Abraham that He would act to redeem them. This is the picture God gives us of the unforgiven sinner.

At the fall of man, when Adam sinned, God withdrew His Holy Spirit from the human spirit, and although man retained his animal body and possessed still a functioning soul of mind, emotion, and will, he was empty of God. Spiritually bankrupt, man was destitute of that spiritual life which could be his only by virtue of God's presence, through His Holy Spirit, within the human spirit. God had left him!

This was the consequence of sin—the absence of all spiritual life. As the absence of all physical life means physical death, so the absence of all spiritual life means spiritual death. This is the wages of sin; not the ultimate consequence of sin *one day*, but that which has been the consequence of sin ever since man fell and that which is now the consequence of sin to all who have not as yet been saved from this condition, for it is in this condition of spiritual death that we are all born, easy prey to the ravages of a sin principle that came into the human heart in the day that God went out.

This sin principle is called in the Bible "the flesh." This is not the human body, which in itself is not sinful, but the flesh in this biblical sense speaks of an evil bias, a satanic agency from which springs all man's own inbred wickedness, so that in Mark 7:20–23, the Lord Jesus said, "That which cometh out of the man, that defileth the man. For from within, out of the heart of men, proceed evil thoughts, adulteries, fornications, murders, thefts, covetousness, wickedness, deceit, lasciviousness, an evil eye, blasphemy, pride, foolishness: All these evil things come from within, and defile a man."

Here the Lord Jesus Christ is speaking about "the flesh," this satanic agency, this sin principle, and just as the land of Egypt represents our natural condition of spiritual death, so the Egyptian taskmasters represent the flesh in its tyrannical control over human behavior, so that Paul, in Romans 7:19–20, writes, "For the good that I would I do not: but the evil which I would not, that I do. Now if I do that I would not, it is no more I that do it, but *sin* that dwelleth in me" (emphasis added). "Sin," in this sense, as a singular word, is the same thing as "the flesh"—the root that bears the fruit. And in this our flesh dwells no good thing! It is "enmity against God: for it is not subject to the law of God, neither indeed can be" (Rom. 8:7b).

It is quite obvious that it is no more God's purpose for you to remain in this condition of spiritual destitution and defeat than it was God's purpose for His earthly people, Israel, to remain in the land of Egypt, tyrannized by Egyptian taskmasters. It is not surprising, therefore, that in this story there is great stress laid upon the means which God employed to get His people *out* of Egypt.

God raised up Moses, and through him He commanded the people to take a little lamb without blemish and to slay it—but without breaking a bone thereof. The blood of this little lamb was then to be painted on the doorposts and on the lintel of every home, and this was to be known later as the Passover, for in the night that the lamb was slain, God executed judgment upon the Egyptians, so that all the firstborn in the land of Egypt died, from the firstborn of Pharaoh that sat upon his throne, to the firstborn of beasts. God's plan for Israel was this:

> The blood shall be to you for a token upon the houses where ye are: and when I see the blood, I will pass over you, and the plague shall not be upon you to destroy you, when I smite the land of Egypt. And this day shall be unto you for a memorial; and ye shall keep it a feast to the LORD throughout your generations; ye shall keep it a feast by an ordinance for ever. (Exod. 12:13–14)

This picture foreshadowed the death of Christ upon the Cross, for He was declared by John the Baptist to be "the Lamb of God which taketh away the sin of the world" (John 1:29), or as in 1 Corinthians 5:7b—"Christ our passover is sacrificed for us."

Just as the little lamb bore the judgment in the place of the firstborn in the house of Israel, so Jesus Christ bore our sins in His own body on the tree at Calvary. First Peter 3:18b tells us that He suffered "the just for the unjust, that he might bring us to God." This is God's plan of redemption. When the Lord Jesus Christ died upon the Cross, God executed judgment upon *your* sin in *His* person. Of His own free will He took your place in death, that you might be reconciled to God, a forgiven sinner.

All that God asked His people Israel to do was to apply the blood to the doorposts and to the lintels *by faith* and then *rest* in God's promise. All that God asks *you* to do is to apply the death of Christ to your own need as a guilty sinner by faith and then rest in God's promise of forgiveness and humbly say, "Thank You."

The story goes on to tell us that as God's judgment descended upon Egypt that night, God, by the hand of Moses, led His people out from Egypt and through the Red Sea. Because of God's miraculous intervention, the Israelites went through the Red Sea on dry land, but when the Egyptians tried to follow, they were drowned. So the enemy was buried in the place of death, while God's people passed on *through* the place of death into a new land and on to a new life.

There is a significant passage in 1 Corinthians 10. In the first two verses we read, "Moreover, brethren, I would not that ye should be ignorant, how that all our fathers were under the cloud, and all passed through the sea, and were all baptized unto Moses in the cloud and in the sea." Here Paul describes the children of Israel as having been baptized into Moses, for on that day they followed him into the Red Sea, which would have been a place of death had not God divided the waters and brought them miraculously out of this place of death, on to dry land. This must be compared with Romans 6, for there we read in the third verse, "Know ye not, that so many of us as were baptized into Jesus Christ were baptized into His death? Therefore we are buried with Him by baptism into death; that like as Christ was raised up from the dead . . . even so we also should walk in newness of life."

In other words, just as the Egyptian taskmasters were left

buried in the place of death, from which the children of Israel had been raised miraculously by God, so you and I identify ourselves by faith with Jesus Christ. In God's economy we go with Him, spiritually, into the place of death, leaving this old sin nature called the flesh buried with Him there.

We may understand again, therefore, from this picture that God's purpose in the Cross of Jesus Christ was twofold: first that we might be forgiven, being saved from sin's penalty because Christ died for *us;* and second, that we might be delivered from sin's power, because this old sinful nature, called the flesh, died *with Him.*

The question that must arise quite naturally now is this, "If in God's economy my old nature has been crucified with Christ, and I am to reckon upon this by faith as a fact, what is to take its place as the controlling principle of my life?" The Bible answer is to be found in Galatians 4:4–6: "When the fullness of the time was come, God sent forth his Son, made of a woman, made under the law, to redeem them that were under the law, that we might receive the adoption of sons. And because ye are sons, God hath sent forth the *Spirit of his Son into your hearts,* crying Abba, Father" (emphasis added). That is to say, no sooner are you redeemed, because you have put your faith in the One who died for you, than God restores to your human spirit the presence of the Holy Spirit, by whose presence you receive the very life of the Lord Jesus, risen from the dead, and become in Him a partaker of the divine nature.

In 2 Peter 1:3–4a, we read, "According as his divine power hath given unto us all things that pertain unto life and godliness, through the knowledge of him that hath called us to glory and virtue: Whereby are given unto us exceeding great and precious promises, that by these ye might be partakers of the divine nature."

I may say to a glove, "Glove, pick up this Bible," and yet,

somehow, the glove cannot do it. It has got a thumb and fingers, the shape and form of a hand, and yet it is unable to do the thing I command it to do. You may say, "Well, of course not. You have never told the glove how!" But I may preach to and instruct that glove until my patience is exhausted, but the glove, try as it will, still cannot pick up that Bible. Yet I have a glove at home that has picked up my Bible dozens of times—but never once before I put my hand into it! As soon, however, as my hand comes into that glove, the glove becomes as strong as my hand. Everything possible to my hand becomes possible to that glove—but only in the measure in which the glove is prepared simply to clothe the activity of my hand.

That is what it is to have Christ, by His Spirit, dwelling within your redeemed humanity. You are the glove, Christ is the Hand! Everything that is possible to Him becomes possible to you, and with Paul you may say, "I have strength for all things in Christ Who empowers me—I am ready for anything and equal to anything through Him Who infuses inner strength into me, [that is, I am self-sufficient in Christ's sufficiency]" (Phil. 4:13 AMPLIFIED NEW TESTAMENT). The presence of the living Christ, by His Spirit within you, imparts to you all the things that pertain to life and godliness, all that you need to live a life of righteousness and nobility of character.

It is this enjoyment of Christ's indwelling which is represented by the land of Canaan—the land of promise and of plentiful provision.

Canaan in the Bible is not heaven. It is not "pie in the sky when I die." It is *Christ Himself*, and *right now*, living His victorious life through me. Indeed, it is only the Lord Jesus Christ Himself who is capable of living the Christian life; as Romans 5:10 declares, He not only reconciles you to God by His death, but He saves you moment by moment by His life; that is to say, He died not only for what you *have done*, but

He rose again to live in you, to take the place of *what you are*. His strength for your weakness! His wisdom for your folly! His drive for your drift! His grace for your greed! His love for your lust! His peace for your problems! His joy for your sorrow! His plenty for your poverty! *This* is Canaan!

> *Out of my bondage, sorrow, and night . . .*
> *Into Thy freedom, gladness, and light . . .*
> *Out of my sickness into Thy health,*
> *Out of my want and into Thy wealth,*
> *Out of my sin and into Thyself,*
> *Jesus, I come to Thee!*

This is Canaan! Brought *out* to be brought *in!*

This was God's purpose for His people *then*, and this is God's purpose for His redeemed people *now*. He desires that the natural man—destitute of divine life, the Devil's plaything, destined for hell—might become the *spiritual man*— filled with the Spirit of Christ, alive unto God as an instrument of righteousness, destined for heaven!

Why then the wilderness?

This is the tragedy of Christendom today, as it was the tragedy of God's people Israel then, for forty years in the wilderness. A people who lived in self-imposed poverty! Every day they spent in the desert was a day they could have spent in Canaan—for God had given them the land! They would not believe, however, that the God who brought them out was the God who could bring them in!

The wilderness is a picture of what the New Testament describes as a carnal Christian. If you are a carnal Christian, it means that you have been redeemed by faith in Christ through His reconciling death; you have received the gift of the Holy Spirit by whose gracious presence Christ lives within you, but you live, in spite of this, in self-imposed poverty, under the subtle influences of a defeated foe, the flesh, which Christ took with Him into the grave. You are just like the children of Israel who lived for forty years, plagued by the memories and the subtle influences of an enemy whom God buried to the last man in the depths of the Red Sea. You, as they, enjoy neither the fleshpots of Egypt nor the golden corn of Canaan—you are dumped in the desert!

The unbelief of the children of Israel cheated them of that for which they had been brought out of Egypt. They lived only to discredit the good name of the One who had redeemed them. In the same way, there is nothing quite so pathetic as a Christian who has been vested with "all the fulness of the Godhead bodily" in Christ, and to whom has been made available all the illimitable resources of heaven, yet who in ignorance, or in defiance of this fact, scratches out a mere existence in the meager resources which he brings with him out of the Egypt of his unbelief, with no sense of direction or finality of purpose—for he will not take what God has *given!*

Forty weary years it took before God was able, through Joshua, to teach His people that to *get in* takes precisely the same kind of faith that it takes to *get out*—the faith that trusts God and says "Thank You"! When once they stood by faith with their feet in the waters of Jordan, the God who divided the Red Sea divided the Jordan also and brought them through on dry land to possess at last their possessions.

The carnal Christian is the one who has received the Holy Spirit and all the fulness of Christ, yet ignores His presence and struggles to live the Christian life as though Christ were not there. He is the one who constantly begs and pleads for all that God has already given him but which he will not take. He is the one who will not step out by faith upon the glorious fact that Christ is his life and therefore his victory!

The Christian life is an exchanged life. "I am crucified with Christ: nevertheless I live; *yet not I,* but Christ liveth in me" (Gal. 2:20a, emphasis added). "To me to live is Christ"

(Phil. 1:21a). Three categories of men! In Egypt, in the wilderness, or in Canaan. I wonder—in which category are you?

Are you still in Egypt? Then trust Christ *now* as your Saviour! By faith, *now*, apply the precious blood that He shed upon the Cross, to the doorposts and lintel of your own heart, and thank Him like a child that you are redeemed!

Are you still in the wilderness? Then repudiate your unbelief! Start right now trusting the Lord Jesus for that for which His blood was shed—that He might live His resurrection life in and through you, even while you are still on earth in the body, and thank Him that He *is* your victory, that He *is* your strength, that He *is* your future, that He is *all* that you can *ever* need at *any* time, in *any* circumstances, for "in him dwelleth all the fulness of the Godhead bodily, and ye are complete in him" (Col. 2:9–10a).

Are you in the Promised Land? Then your portion is to reign in life! To reign by One, Christ Jesus, and to know joy unspeakable and full of glory, to know His peace that passeth all understanding, to know that every place that the sole of your foot shall tread upon has been given to you, that you may be strong and of a good courage, neither afraid nor dismayed, in the knowledge that the Lord your God is with you whithersoever you go, for this—*this* is your victory, even your faith (1 John 5:4).

Dear Lord Jesus Christ, I thank Thee for dying upon the Cross for me, a guilty sinner. I accept Thee gladly as my Saviour, to redeem me now—to cleanse and to forgive me now. Come by Thy gracious Holy Spirit to live in me, that I may be born again, a child of God—now! This is Thy promise, and that is enough for me. I know I am redeemed! Thou art my very life, all that I can ever need at any time! Thou wilt never leave me nor forsake me, but ever guide me and keep me—Christ my Saviour, my Lord, my God, my life—forever! Amen.

Chapter IV

A Day to Be Remembered

Having viewed in general in the preceding chapter, this "spiritual master key" as seen in the early history of Israel, I would like in these succeeding chapters to examine the story in closer detail. This must involve, inevitably, a certain amount of recapitulation.

In Exodus we read that the Lord spoke to Moses and said, "This month shall be unto you the beginning of months: it shall be the first month of the year to you. Speak ye unto all the congregation of Israel, saying, In the tenth day of this month they shall take to them every man a lamb, according to the house of their fathers, a lamb for a house" (Exod. 12:2–3).

This month would see the dawn of a day of such significance that it would herald an entirely new era in the lives of the children of Israel. It would be as though they had never lived before! It would be a day indeed to be remembered!

I hardly need explain to you that the day to be considered here is a picture of that day when a man enters into peace with God, becomes reconciled on God's terms, and finds salvation. He is redeemed!

Can you look back to the day when you were redeemed? Have you a day to be remembered?

I can look back to that day when, as a boy of twelve, I accepted Jesus Christ as my Saviour. I remember the hour! I could almost take you to the very spot! A quarter to nine, on a Saturday night, in a boys' camp in August. And nobody knew, apart from myself and the Christ who redeemed me! But I know that *that* day was the beginning of days for me; and *that* month was the first month of a new life! I can hardly remember anything that happened before my twelfth year—it was just as though I had only existed, and then suddenly I had begun to live, for it was the beginning of life as God intended life to be. It was a day to be remembered!

"Your lamb shall be without blemish, a male of the first year . . . and the whole assembly of the congregation of Israel shall kill it in the evening. And they shall take of the blood, and strike it on the two side posts and on the upper door post of the houses, wherein they shall eat it" (Exod. 12:5-7).

This is one of the most beautiful pictures of our redemption that we have in the Word of God. The Holy Spirit leaves us in no doubt as to the spiritual significance of the Passover lamb, for "Christ our passover is sacrificed for us" (1 Cor. 5:7b). He is "the Lamb of God that taketh away the sin of the world," and only those who are sheltered beneath His shed blood can ever escape the final judgment that God in His holiness must execute upon sin and the sinful seed of Adam.

The picture is clear. Recognizing your guilty condition before a holy God and humbly recognizing Jesus Christ, the One in whom your sin was executed once for all, you mix with faith this word of reconciliation, and cast yourself upon Him, and you are redeemed! By faith you apply the precious blood of the Lamb to the doorposts and the lintel of your heart, and the wrath of God passes over you. This represents the vicarious sacrifice of Jesus Christ, His substitutionary work whereby He was made sin for you, that you might be made the righteousness of God in Him (2 Cor. 5:21). This is the beginning of days! This is where life begins! Can you look back to that moment when, as a guilty sinner, you humbly confessed your need and claimed Jesus Christ as your Saviour, the One in whom alone you may find peace with a holy God?

Notice how the Passover was celebrated. "Thus shall ye eat it; with your loins girded, your shoes on your feet, and your staff in your hand; and ye shall eat it in haste . . ." (Exod. 12:11). In the day that the blood was applied, they had to be equipped for a journey, for that day was to be to them the threshold of a journey. It was not just to be a critical experience, one to be enjoyed and then forgotten, or something ecstatic which would become a fond memory of the past! The Passover was to be the *beginning*—the *means*, not the *end!* From this day they could never be the same again—they were to embark upon a journey!

Now this is vitally important, and in Romans 8, from verse 1 onward, there is the spiritual counterpart in the New Testament: "There is therefore now no condemnation to them which are in Christ Jesus, who *walk* not after the flesh but after the Spirit" (emphasis added). In other words, the New Testament definition of a man who is "in Christ Jesus," and who can claim that there is therefore now no condemnation for him, is a man who has been precipitated by the crisis of redemption into a *new walk*—"not after the flesh but after the Spirit."

The claim that you are in Christ Jesus and under no condemnation because you have been redeemed is valid only if it is vindicated by a walk that indicates your new relationship to God.

I know of no gospel in the Bible that offers you salvation from the condemnation of your sin, that does not at the same time demand a radical change of walk—a walk under entirely new management, revolutionized according to an entirely new principle of life. And this we see beautifully illustrated in the story that we are now considering.

In a Land to Be Possessed

They were to eat the Passover on this first occasion, girded for a journey—a journey which would take them *out* of Egypt and *into* Canaan. "And Moses said unto the people, Remember this day, in which ye came out from Egypt, out of the house of bondage; for by strength of hand the LORD brought you out from this place. . . . And it shall be when the LORD shall bring thee into the land of the Canaanites . . . which he sware unto thy fathers to give thee, a land flowing with milk and honey, that thou shalt keep this service in this month" (Exod. 13:3, 5). It was a day to be remembered—but *in a land to be possessed!*

Only in the *land* could the people celebrate the day intelligently! They came out from Egypt, which, as we have already seen, is the Bible picture of the unregenerate condition of the unforgiven sinner—the first category of men; but God brought them out that He might bring them into the land of Canaan, the Bible picture of the Spirit-filled, victorious Christian—the third category of men.

Do not be deceived by the false significance given to Canaan in so much popular hymnology composed, no doubt quite sincerely, but by those who have mistaken the issues and missed the point. Remember, Canaan is Christ *now*, not heaven *one day!*

There is only one place where you can intelligently celebrate your redemption through the death of Jesus Christ, and that is in the fulness of His resurrection life! This is a spiritual principle!

It was a day to be remembered in a land to be possessed!

"And thou shalt show thy son in that day saying, This is

done because of that which the LORD did unto me when I came forth out of Egypt" (Exod. 13:8). Can you imagine how unimpressed a small boy would be in the middle of the desert if his father told him, in answer to his question, that the Passover feast was in celebration of their deliverance out of Egypt?

Manna for breakfast, manna for lunch, manna for supper! This poor kid had had that for thirteen years or more, and everybody knew what he would get for breakfast the next morning! I think he would be inclined to say, "Dad, if this is all we are celebrating, isn't it time we got back into Egypt? I've heard what it was like in Egypt, and it sounds much more attractive to me than here in the desert!"

I wonder if this is why so many children grow up unconverted in Christian homes? I wonder if it is because so many Christian parents are living in the wilderness? They have demonstrated so little to their children of what it means to walk in the plenitude of the risen Christ that "the kids" inevitably glance back over their shoulders in search of relief from the monotony of a desert diet!

The Passover, together with two other feasts, was to be celebrated *yearly* from the day that God brought them out. "Three times thou shalt keep a feast unto me in the year. Thou shalt keep the feast of unleavened bread: (thou shalt eat unleavened bread seven days, as I commanded thee, in the time appointed of the month Abib; for in it thou camest out of Egypt)" (Exod. 23:14–15b). You are to remember the day that God redeemed you! "And the feast of harvest, the firstfruits of thy labors, which thou hast sown in the field: and the feast of ingathering, which is in the end of the year, when thou hast gathered in thy labors out of the field" (Exod. 23:16). These three feasts were to be celebrated yearly by God's redeemed people—the feast of unleavened bread (the Passover), the feast of harvest, and the feast of ingathering. The harvest of that "which they had sown in the field"—how much did they sow in the desert? Nothing! How much did they ingather in the desert? Nothing! How much corn had they in the desert with which to keep the feast of unleavened bread? None! How then could the people of Israel keep yearly these three feasts in the wilderness? They could not! Because it was a day to be remembered *in a land to be possessed!*

I can discover only one account of the Passover feast having been celebrated in the wilderness and that was in the second year. "The LORD spake unto Moses in the wilderness of Sinai, in the first month of the second year after they were come out of the land of Egypt, saying, Let the children of Israel also keep the passover at his appointed season" (Num. 9:1). That is the only record I find of their ever having celebrated the Passover in the wilderness, and with what did they celebrate it? Only with the corn that they must have brought with them out of Egypt! That is significant, because unless you go on into the fulness of what Christ is in you, you will only be able to celebrate your conversion with such meager, poverty-stricken resources as you brought with you out of your unregenerate condition— in other words, the "energy of the flesh." And this, you will discover, will last just about twelve months and then you will be exhausted!

Exodus 13:9—"It shall be for a sign unto thee upon thine hand"—the Passover is to represent that your redemption "out of Egypt" has changed the things you do. "It shall be for a memorial between thine eyes"—it is to represent the fact that your redemption "out of Egypt" has changed the things you think. "That the LORD's law may be in thy mouth: for with a strong hand hath the LORD brought thee out of Egypt"—it is to represent the fact that not only has your redemption changed the things you do and changed the things you think, but it has changed the things you say! In other words, it is to represent a complete, revolutionary change of character and conduct. That was to be the significance of the Passover.

It would, therefore, be interesting to examine what they *did* in the wilderness, what they *thought* in the wilderness, and what they *said* in the wilderness!

What They Did

Deuteronomy 12:1—"These are the statutes and judgments, which ye shall observe to do in the land which the LORD God of thy fathers giveth thee to possess it, all the days that ye live upon the earth." Notice that they are to enjoy the land and possess it all the days that they are *on the earth*— not in heaven! Deuteronomy 12:7—"And there ye shall eat before the LORD your God, and ye shall rejoice in all that ye put your hand unto, ye and your households, wherein the LORD thy God hath blessed thee." Everything you do will be a sheer delight! The whole of your activity will be bathed in joy! "Ye shall not do after all the things that we do here this day, every man whatsoever is right in his own eyes" (Deut. 12:8). That is what they were doing in the wilderness! Every man did whatsoever was *right in his own eyes.*

There was no sense of the sovereignty of God. Every man did what was right *in his own eyes.* His conduct was controlled by his own sincere convictions, maybe, but he knew nothing of the supreme direction of God in his soul.

A man in the wilderness, even though prompted by sincere motives, is subject to certain patterns of conduct to which he seeks to conform. His Christian activity and his Christian walk tend to be a drudgery rather than that sheer, pure joy that God purposes for His redeemed people, walking in the power and fulness and energy of God the Holy Spirit. "For ye are not as yet come to the rest and the inheritance which the LORD your God giveth you" (Deut. 12:9).

While you are still doing what is right in your own eyes,

you have not entered into rest nor your inheritance. "There remaineth therefore a rest to the people of God. For he that is entered into his rest, he also hath ceased from his own works" (Heb. 4:9–10). He has relinquished the right to do what is right in his own eyes and has submitted himself to the totalitarian dictatorship of Jesus Christ. He recognizes to be valid only that activity that stems from Him—that stems from the indwelling sovereignty of Jesus Christ, to whom he is sold out completely. This is the definition that God gives us of true spiritual rest.

What have *you* been *doing* since your redemption? Still what is right in your own eyes? Are you sold out for Jesus Christ? Do you still claim the right to choose your own career? You do not have that right! Do you still claim the right to choose the wife or husband you will marry? You do not have that right! Do you still claim the right to use your leisure hours as you please? You do not have that right! Do you still claim the right to spend your money as you please? You do not have that right! Do you still consider that you have the right to choose where you will spend your vacation? You do not have that right! Except in the wilderness!

Maybe that is precisely where you are right now—still doing what *you think* is right *in your own eyes,* because when you were redeemed by the blood of Jesus Christ and when God once and for all forgave you, you never realized that this experience of Jesus Christ was a *crisis* calculated, in God's economy of things, to precipitate a *process,* a walk no longer under the dictates of the flesh, however sincere, but under the dictates of the Spirit. "For as many as are led by the Spirit of God, they are the sons of God" (Rom. 8:14).

The moment a man, woman, boy, or girl gives to the Holy Spirit the right to re-establish the sovereignty of Jesus Christ within his soul, he does not even have the right to do what is *right* in his own eyes—let alone what is *wrong!*

What They Thought

Now what did they think about in the wilderness? For this was to be "a memorial between their eyes" to indicate that all their thinking had been changed. What did they think about in the wilderness? "And the mixed multitude that was among them fell a lusting; and the children of Israel also wept again, and said, Who shall give us flesh to eat? We remember the fish, which we did eat in Egypt freely; the cucumbers, and the melons, and the leeks, and the onions, and the garlic: but now our soul is dried away: there is nothing at all, beside this manna, before our eyes. And the manna was as coriander seed . . . and the taste of it was as the taste of fresh oil" (Num. 11:4–8).

Oil in the Bible is a beautiful picture of the Holy Spirit, and, as we shall see more fully in a later chapter, the daily manna demonstrated constantly, supernaturally, the unrelenting presence of the living God in the midst of His redeemed people. But they got bored with it!

Nothing but manna! Manna for breakfast, manna for lunch, manna for supper, and manna for breakfast again—it gets a bit tedious after a bit, doesn't it? "Manna, manna, manna," they said, "seven days a week, fifty-two weeks in the year; manna, manna—we're sick and tired of manna!" But God never intended them to eat manna for forty years. God had prepared Canaan for them, but they stayed in the wilderness and dreamed of Egypt!

Maybe you say, "Oh, my Christian life is dull and boring to me. I read my Bible only out of a sense of duty." I tell you that if the Christian life has become dull and boring to you, it is simply because you will not go in to possess what God has given you in Jesus Christ. You have never tasted the thrill and adventure of being totally abandoned to the One who will lead you through in glory and in victory. I would not change places with you for a million dollars, if you *must* stick to manna for breakfast, manna for lunch, and manna for supper! It was good for the purpose for which it was given, but it was never intended to be their diet for forty years.

Here was a redeemed people, brought out of Egypt and on their way to the "land of promise," but with their thoughts, their ambitions, their appetites, fed by the memory of that from which God had redeemed them! "We remember the fish of Egypt; the cucumbers, and the melons, and the leeks, and the onions, and the garlic." Enslaved to the memories of that from which they had been redeemed! Their whole thought-life was dominated by a defeated enemy whom God had buried to a man in the Red Sea, the place of death, into which, on the day of their redemption, they, with Moses, had been baptized, to be raised miraculously by God and poised upon the threshold of a new walk that would lead them on and into a new land—the land to be possessed!

The fish, the cucumbers, the melons, the leeks, the onions, and the garlic—these were the things that occupied their minds in the wilderness! "We remember, we remember . . ." they said—and with what did they remember? With their minds! In their imagination they were still living in Egypt!

What is it that preoccupies your imagination as a redeemed sinner! With what does your mind busy itself? What are your ambitions? What are your appetites? Where do you go, what company do you keep, and what do you do—in your mind? Have you been weaned from the things of Egypt?

Fish! Fish in a hot climate! Something particularly unsavory! Cucumbers! Twelve inches of indigestion! Then the melons! Ninety-five percent water and five percent pits! And the onions and the garlic—things which speak for themselves!

It was with *these* things that they occupied their minds. With what do you occupy *your* mind? What is it that has captured the imagination of your heart since you were redeemed?

Sin is conceived in the imagination. First there comes the suggestion—the satanic suggestion—and that suggestion becomes a desire; and if it is allowed to conceive and mature and be brought to birth within the area of your imagination, the desire will become an intent that you have already sinned, whether your circumstances allow you to implement your intent or not. That is why the Lord Jesus Christ said: "Whosoever looketh on a woman to lust after her hath committed adultery with her already in his heart" (Matt. 5:28).

Where suggestion becomes desire, desire becomes intent, and the intent becomes an act—the act becomes a memory and that memory is hung like a picture upon the wall of your imagination, in the picture gallery of your mind. When later in your thoughts you wander through the picture gallery, you see the memory on the wall, and this memory itself becomes a suggestion, and this suggestion becomes desire, and this desire may become intent, and if this intent becomes an act, you will then have hanging on the wall *two* memories, and the process can begin all over again with double force!

Do you see the principle? That is why every time you commit sin, you make it easier to commit another sin, because every time you commit sin, you are making "an altar to sin" (Hos. 8:11a). Every sinful memory stimulates sinful desire, encourages sinful intent, and another sinful act which will become yet another sinful memory, until your mind is polluted.

Now we know what they were thinking about in the wilderness. They only had memories of that *from* which they had been redeemed, because they had never gone on and in, and so had no memories of that *to* which they had been redeemed.

What memories had they of Canaan in the wilderness? None! They had only heard sermons *about* Canaan! They only had secondhand talk about Canaan! They had no personal, vital, individual experience of Canaan; it was language, but not life, and nature abhors a vacuum!

I want to tell you this, that if you do not walk in the power of God the Holy Spirit, if your life is not abandoned to the indwelling sovereignty of Jesus Christ, then all the promises of victory in the Bible, all the promises of power by the Holy Spirit and of divine vocation will simply be texts, printed on so much paper—impersonal and irrelevant! Your mind will be filled only with memories of that which has been true to your experience in the bitterness of defeat.

No wonder they had nothing to celebrate in the wilderness!

What They Said

What did they say in the wilderness? This people who knew nothing of the sovereignty of God in their lives, to whom God gave such unrelenting evidence of His presence by the daily manna, but who never acted as though He mattered, who had received such lavish promises of a land to be possessed, yet could feed only upon their miserable memories of the past—what did this people have to say?

"They gathered themselves together against Moses and against Aaron, and said unto them, Ye take too much upon you, seeing all the congregation are holy, every one of them, and the Lord is among them: wherefore then lift ye up yourselves above the congregation of the Lord?" (Num. 16:3). That is what they said in the wilderness! They had become acclimatized to their circumstances in the desert and resisted any suggestion that their unhappy lot could be bettered in "the land." In their own estimation, they were all holy, "every one of them!" How holy? Holy enough!

How holy are you? Holy enough?

Nursing memories of Egypt, are you perfectly content to call yourself converted? Recognizing the witness of God's Spirit to your spirit that a wonderful thing has happened, you can remember the day you were redeemed, and yet are you perfectly content to live a self-centered life that renounces and repudiates the lordship of Christ? Are you holy *enough?*

They resented every suggestion on the part of Moses and Aaron that they were missing God's purpose for their lives, on the ground that they were holy enough—but by whose standards? God's or their own?

Is that how holy you are? You can always be holy enough *by your own standards!* In the day that Moses came down from the mountain with the tables of stone in his hands, the law of righteousness inscribed by the finger of God, he found the people half-drunken, half-naked, dancing round the golden calf—a redeemed people! Holy *enough* by their *own* standards!

It may well be that as you began to read this book, you were firmly convinced that you were holy enough—ready still to resist the idea that you should be anything other than what you already are. Then do not miss that purpose for which this message comes to you, for redemption is a "day to be remembered" in a "land to be possessed"—and only there have you the legitimate right to celebrate the fact that the blood of Jesus Christ was shed that you might have peace with God.

Would you like to pray?

Dear Lord Jesus Christ, I thank Thee for Thy Word, quick and powerful, and sharper than any two-edged sword, piercing to the dividing asunder of soul and spirit, laying bare the thoughts and the intents of the heart, opening up to the glare of Thy righteousness the picture gallery of the mind. I bow before Thee as one who is naked before the eyes of Him with whom I have to do.

All my wanderings in the wilderness have not passed unnoticed. Every secret thought of my mind as I have meditated upon the fleshpots of Egypt has been recorded in heaven. All my rebellious talk has been heard by God! I have despised my birthright and I have neglected so many tokens that Thou hast given me of my inheritance. I can look back to a history of failure and of superficial dedication, in which I have boosted up my self-importance and bitterly complained at every demand that God has made upon me.

I am heartily sick of this imitation of the real thing—the counterfeit Christian life, and I do not want it anymore! I want to get in as I once got out and to have something to celebrate in the land!

I know that Thou art the living God in the midst of Thy people. Do Thou Thine ancient work in me, for Thy name's sake. Amen.

Chapter V

Any Old Bush Will Do!

By God's miraculous intervention, Moses had been saved as a little baby out of the bulrushes, but Moses did not have any say in that! The best he could do at that stage in his career was to squeak! God had foreshadowed these things.

Over four hundred years before, God had told Abraham that He was going to raise up a deliverer for His people and save them from the tyranny of a wicked Pharaoh, and now God's hour had struck.

Preserved from death, Moses was introduced by God's divine providence into Pharaoh's household, adopted by his daughter, and nourished as her own son. With all the privileges of royalty, he received a magnificent education. He was trained as a statesman, a soldier, and an administrator, and by the age of forty he was a polished, scholarly man who could have taken his place in any society. In the words of Acts 7:20, 22: "[Moses was] exceeding fair. . . . And Moses was learned in all the wisdom of the Egyptians, and was mighty in words and in deeds."

This is the portrait that God gives us of the man in the prime of life, highly qualified and filled with a sense of urgency, yet in his humility seemingly indifferent to his own intellectual stature—poised, it would seem, upon the threshold of a brilliant career. In point of fact, he was a man only a few hours away from a tragic blunder that would bring to frustration all his noblest ambitions and make him useless to God or man for forty years in the backside of the desert.

"And when he was full forty years old, it came into his heart to visit his brethren the children of Israel. And seeing one of them suffer wrong, he defended him, and avenged him that was oppressed, and smote the Egyptian: for he supposed his brethren would have understood how that God by his hand would deliver them: but they understood not" (Acts 7:23–25). On the basis of what he was, and on the basis of what he knew, Moses took it for granted that he would be accepted in the ministry for which he believed God had called him: "He *supposed* his brethren would have understood . . . but they understood not" (emphasis added). With a strong sense of mission, he was baffled at his own impotence!

Maybe this is the dilemma into which you too have fallen. You have felt the surge of holy ambition. Your heart has burned within you. You have dreamed dreams and seen visions, but only to awaken again and again to a dull sense of futility, as one who beats the air or builds castles in the sky.

We need to turn to the record itself to discover how Moses lost the way. "And it came to pass in those days, when Moses was grown, that he went out unto his brethren, and looked on their burdens: and he spied an Egyptian smiting a Hebrew, one of his brethren" (Exod. 2:11).

You can imagine the natural impulse of a man moved with compassion for his own kith and kin. There was nothing evil, there was nothing implicitly sinful or wrong in the thoughts that filled his mind—that natural feeling of resentment against a tyrannical people, mercilessly whipping one of his own defenseless brethren—but it was just at that stage that he allowed sincerity and genuine compassion to rob him of his true vocation.

It says in verse 12, "And he looked this way and that way, and when he saw that there was no man, he slew the Egyptian, and hid him in the sand." The enormity of the need knocked him off balance, and in a false sense of dedication he committed himself to the task instead of to God—"He looked this way and that way. . . ." The one way he did not look was up! "And when he saw that there was no *man*, he slew the Egyptian." In his sensitivity to the presence of man, Moses became strangely insensitive to the presence of God. How easy it is for us to do just that and relate our actions to the approval or disapproval of men. Are you "man-conscious" or "God-conscious"?

Had Moses been overwhelmingly confident that his actions merited God's complete approval, he would have been indifferent to other men's reactions—their opinions would have been irrelevant. Spiritual pioneers, consciously in the center of God's will, can afford to be lonely in the face of public opinion, whether it be Nehemiah building the wall, Peter taking the gospel to the house of a Gentile, or Wilberforce and Livingstone campaigning for the abolition of slavery.

Paul loved to preface his epistles by introducing himself as "an apostle, (not of men, neither by man, but by Jesus Christ, and God the Father, who raised him from the dead)" (Gal. 1:1). Yes, "by the will of God"! That was his mandate, that was all he needed to know, and so he could say, "The Holy Ghost witnesseth in every city, saying that bonds and afflictions abide me. But none of these things move me, neither count I my life dear unto myself, so that I might finish my course with joy, and the ministry, which I have received of the Lord Jesus, to testify the gospel of the grace of God" (Acts 20:23–24). He had become invulnerable; he had a God-given sense of vocation.

Moses lost his sense of God, and maybe you have lost your sense of God for the same reason. You are not called upon to commit yourself to a need or to a task or to a field. You are called upon to commit yourself to God! It is He then who takes care of the consequences and commits you where *He* wants you. He is the Lord of the harvest! He is the Head of the body—and He is gloriously competent to assume His own responsibilities! Man is not indispensable to God. God is indispensable to man!

I sometimes have an uneasy feeling about certain missionary conventions and the missionary challenge to which we have become accustomed. You hear one speaker after another committing you to the *task*, claiming your life for this mission field or for that. "The need," all too often it is said, "constitutes the call"! There are a *thousand* needs, but you are not committed to these. You are committed to Christ, and it is *His* business to commit you where *He* wants you. No man or woman on earth has the right to commit any member of the body of Jesus Christ to any task or to any field; that is to usurp the authority of the head of the body, Jesus Christ Himself. "But now hath God set the members every one of them in the body, as it hath pleased him" (1 Cor. 12:18). The moment I claim the right to commit a man or a woman or a boy or a girl to some field of service, I blaspheme His sovereign place as Lord of the harvest.

God is perfectly capable of taking care of His own affairs, and the reason so little is being accomplished by the church of Jesus Christ today is that we have all too often organized God out of business. Millions of man-hours and countless millions of dollars are being misspent on man's promotional activity, unasked, on God's behalf.

This is not to challenge the sincerity of those who are thus employed, but we so often confuse bustle for business and plant for power and perspiration for inspiration. What an embarrassment it would be to you if you had a pair of hands that always tried to demonstrate how busy they were! Do you expect your fingers to tell you each morning what their program is for the day, and then demonstrate their enthusiasm by a vigorous show of uncontrolled activity? Do you think you would be successful in playing the piano on that basis? I would not like to ask a barber who had hands like that to shave me!

Surely, what the head demands of every member of the body is *restful availability*, and prompt response to every impulse of the head in instant obedience, producing the coordinated activity of the whole and the orderly fulfillment of that purpose to which each, as a member of the team, has been committed in particular.

The challenge we hear so often today in the name of consecration is "Do more! Give more! Be more!" Go! Go! Go! But God says, "Be *still*, and know that *I* am God"! In other words, quit the panic! Just let God be God!

Moses had not learned that lesson when he saw the Egyptian smiting one of his brethren. He rolled up his sleeves and said in so many words, "If ever there was a time when I was on call, it is now!" and he blundered in like a bull in a china shop, smote the Egyptian, and tried unsuccessfully to bury him. With the best intentions in the world, he became a murderer instead of a missionary!

"And when he went out the second day, behold two men of the Hebrews strove together: and he said to him that did the wrong, Wherefore smitest thou thy fellow? And he said, Who made thee a prince and a judge over us? Intendest thou to kill me, as thou killedst the Egyptian? And Moses feared, and said, Surely this thing is known" (Exod. 2:13–14). Yes, the thing was known. When Moses tried to tackle the job, he could not even bury one Egyptian successfully. Maybe he left his toes sticking out of the sand! When *God* tackled the job,

He buried the whole lot of them in the Red Sea! That is how competent God is to deal with His own business.

Moses fled, for "when Pharaoh heard this thing, he sought to slay him"—and for forty years he was in the land of Midian. A man whom God had specifically raised up for a particular task, but who on the basis of his own sincerity and on the basis of his own enthusiasm, neutralized his usefulness because he committed himself to a need instead of to God. He tried to do God's work man's way, and he had to learn that it is not scholarship but relationship, not just his *ability* but his *availability* that qualifies a man for God.

One can imagine the awful sense of futility that must have overwhelmed Moses again and again during those forty years of uselessness, unrecognized and unknown in the backside of the desert. Maybe you too have found your Christian service unrewarding. You are converted, you can look back to the day when you put your trust in Jesus Christ as your personal Saviour, but you imagined that the Christian life was just conforming to certain patterns of Christian conduct—patterns which had been projected upon you—and that your spirituality would be judged in terms of your conformity. That is not spirituality, that is "copyism," and Christian service that stems solely from conformity to the demands of an organizational machine will always be lacking in spiritual luster and characterized by the absence of divine unction. You will waste away with Moses in the wilderness of Midian.

Poor Moses—soldier, scholar, and statesman! Born to be a leader, caring for a handful of sheep, his wife's husband, with a job on her father's farm! Hope must have seemed to wither at the roots, when "the angel of the Lord appeared unto him in a flame of fire out of the midst of a bush: and he looked, and, behold, the bush burned with fire, and the bush was not consumed" (Exod. 3:2).

When Moses saw that bush, he was amazed! It was a

phenomenon—something that immediately attracted his attention. Here was a bush that burned and burned and burned, and went on burning. As far as he could see, it could burn on for eternity, and he could not help but compare himself with that bush! In his heart he must have said something like this: "I have never seen a bush like that before. I'm not like that bush! Forty years ago I burned myself out in twenty-four hours, and I have been a heap of ashes for forty years since. There must be something very unusual about that bush, something very unique! It must be a very wonderful bush!" "And Moses said, I will now turn aside and see this great sight, why the bush is not burnt" (Exod. 3:3). Aroused within his heart there was a holy curiosity, and he did a very wise thing—he made intelligent inquiry and, in consequence, he made a very wonderful discovery!

So often there is aroused within us a holy curiosity, but it is unmatched by intelligent inquiry, and that is why we do not make the same wonderful discovery!

We are tutored in these days to hero worship. In every walk of life we become "fans," and that is not less true in the area of Christian activity. There are those in whose lives there is manifestly evident the mighty unction and power of God. They are transparently genuine. The hand of God is upon them. They speak with an authority that God honors. Lives are transformed. Those spiritually dead are raised to life again. Defeated, helpless, useless, barren Christians are transformed into useful vehicles of divine life. Wherever they go it seems that there is a touch of glory about their path, and we admire them and applaud—but we stand back as though this were to be the monopoly of the few, as though they have a special call upon the grace of God, and as though this were something not for the common run of men. We say in our hearts, "*There* is a bush that burns! I would like to be a bush like that, but I am just a heap of ashes!" And that is as far as it gets.

You discuss the burning bush with others! You admit that it is an amazing thing, and maybe you invite others to come and look at the phenomenon, but you have resigned yourself to be nothing more than what you are—a heap of ashes! It has never dawned on you that you could be anything different, so you have to make the best of a bad job in your own little desert! You resign yourself to sit on the balcony among the spectators, just to be average, a spiritual nonentity!

This is the attitude that Paul sought above everything else to avoid in those of whom it had been his privilege to lead to the Lord Jesus Christ. That is the significance of his words to the Philippians when he wrote, "Work out your own salvation with fear and trembling. For it is God which worketh in you both to will and to do of his good pleasure" (Phil. 2:12c—13).

To the Philippians, who were tempted to lean upon Paul as their spiritual crutch, as though God had a particular interest in him that He did not have in them, he said, in so many words, "All that God has given to me, He has given to you! The Lord Jesus Christ who dwells in my humanity is the same Lord Jesus Christ who dwells in your humanity. What I have, you have! What *I* can be by the grace of God, *you* can be by the grace of God! Work out your *own* salvation! It is yours as much as mine. It is *God*, not Paul the apostle, who works in you, both to will and to do of His good pleasure. Recognize that all the illimitable resources that God has vested in me in the person of His own dear Son are the same illimitable resources that He has vested in you!"

This is the message of the Bible, that God has chosen the weak and the base, the nothing and the things that are not to confound the things that are. All God demands of a man is his availability—to be what man was created to be, the human vehicle of the divine life, inhabited *by* God *for* God. That God may be *Himself*—*His* size in terms of what you are on earth, in your availability to Him. What *you are* is totally irrelevant—nationality-wise, money-wise, education-wise, personality-wise, and any other wise, if only you will recognize the principle that it is God that works in you, to will and to do of His good pleasure.

The only ultimate source of divine activity in all spiritual life is God Himself—"Christ in you the hope of glory" (Col. 1:27c). The church is so slow to learn. It admires and seeks to emulate the example of the mighty, but so seldom takes the trouble "to turn aside and see" the reason why. You read the lives of men like Hudson Taylor, George Mueller, Dwight L. Moody, A. B. Simpson—men whose lives have made spiritual history. You would like to be like them and do the things they did, and yet maybe you have never taken the trouble to find out *why* it was they were what they were or *how* it was they did what they did! Instead, you mobilize your own resources and seek to emulate the example they set and are constantly buffeted by a sense of frustration because of your hopeless failure in the endeavor.

As some have sought to introduce you to the principle that made these men what they were and enabled them to do what they did, you have been impatient, and said, "Don't interfere! I'm too busy trying to be like them, and I don't have time to listen to you!" Now is that not stupid? Why was Hudson Taylor what he was, and how could he do what he did? Why was A. B. Simpson what *he* was, and how could he do what *he* did? Were they God's favorites? Of course they were not! They were simply men who had qualified in the school of failure and despair. They were men who came to the end of themselves and discovered that what they were apart from God was nothing!

Moses began by being a failure! That was the school from

which he qualified! Abraham began by being a failure! That was the school from which *he* qualified! Jacob was a hopeless failure! David was a hopeless failure! Elijah was a hopeless failure! Isaiah was a hopeless failure and a "man of unclean lips," but it is in the school of destitution—the bitter school of self-discovery—that finally you graduate into usefulness, when at last you discover the total bankruptcy of what you are apart from what God is! These men made this discovery and were blessed!

Moses had to discover this, and you will have to discover it! He had to discover that a fine physique, noble ambitions, royal breeding, and Egyptian scholarship could never be a substitute for that for which man was created—God Himself!

Moses said, "I will now turn aside and see this great sight, why the bush is not burnt. And when the LORD saw that he turned aside to see, God called unto him out of the midst of the bush, and said, "Moses, Moses" (Exod. 3:3–4b). God called him by name! *When* did God call him? While he stood admiring at a distance? No, God never said a word then—but "when he turned aside to see," God called!

Maybe you are wondering why it is that you have never had an urgent sense of call; why in your Christian life there is no real driving sense of direction; why you do not have a deep spirit-born conviction of the purpose for which you have been redeemed; why it is you drift, and live with no target in view! Maybe it is because you never took time out to find the reason why! When Moses turned aside to see, God called him—by name!

Judged by purely human standards, you may be highly qualified for Christian service, and yet you go out into the oblivion of spiritual uselessness. No matter to what distinction you may attain in this world, no matter how much you may be acclaimed by your fellow men, no matter how gifted you may be, it is tragically possible for you to go down in the annals of spiritual history as one of those who did not count, either for God or man—and do you know why? Because you never took time out to find the reason why God uses men! You have been too busy, and you never turned aside to see, and God was silent. He never called you by your name!

And as God called, Moses said, "Here am I. And [God] said, Draw not nigh hither: put off thy shoes from off thy feet, for the place whereon thou standest is holy ground. Moreover he said, I am the God of thy father, the God of Abraham, the God of Isaac, and the God of Jacob. And Moses hid his face; for he was afraid to look upon God" (Exod. 3:4c–6). God had something to say to Moses, and I think that it must have been something like this: "Moses, you have done a wise thing in making intelligent inquiry, for you thought that this was a very remarkable bush. You thought that there must be something about it at once peculiar and wonderful, something unique, that it could burn and burn and burn, and go on burning, and yet not burn itself out. But you are wrong—you are *quite* wrong! Do you see that bush over there? That scruffy, scraggy looking thing—*that* bush would have done! Do you see this beautiful looking bush, so shapely and fine—*this* bush would have done! For you see, Moses, any old bush will do—*any* old bush—if only *God* is in the bush! The trouble with you, Moses, is this: forty years ago, learned in all the wisdom of the Egyptians, mighty in word and deed, you admired your own foliage! You thought you were some bush! But you burned yourself out in twenty-four hours, and you have been a heap of ashes for forty years! If this bush that you have admired were depending upon its own substance to sustain the flame, it too would burn itself out in twenty-four hours; it too would be a heap of ashes like you. But it is not the *bush* that sustains the flame, it is God *in* the bush; and *any old bush* will do!"

Did you ever make this discovery? Have you ever come to

the place where you realized that all you can produce, at your best, is ashes? Did you ever come to the place where you presented yourself for what you are—*nothing*—to be filled with what He is—*everything*—and to step out into every new day, conscious that the eternal I AM is all you need, for all His will!

This is the forgotten tense of the church of Jesus Christ today. We live either in the *past* tense or in the *future* tense. We say either "Ebenezer—hitherto hath the Lord helped us," or we comfort ourselves with "Maranatha—behold the Lord cometh." But we forget that He is the eternal I AM, the eternal *present* tense, adequate right *now* for every need!

If you are born again, all you need is *what you have,* and what you have is *what He is!* He does not *give* you strength—He *is* your strength! He does not give you victory—He *is* your victory!

Do you understand the principle? Christ is in you— nothing less than that! You cannot have *more,* and you do not need to have *less.* Every day can be the glorious fulfillment of the divine end—"proving what is that good, and acceptable, and perfect, will of God," as you present your body a living sacrifice, holy and acceptable unto God, which is your reasonable service (Rom. 12:1–2).

Only remember this—any old bush will do!

Chapter VI

The Church in the Wilderness

It is plainly indicated to us in the Bible that the earthly Israel and God's dealings with them are a picture of a greater spiritual Israel, "For they are not all Israel, which are of Israel: neither, because they are the seed of Abraham, are they all children: but, In Isaac shall thy seed be called. That is, They which are the children of the flesh, these are not the children of God: but the children of the promise are counted for the seed" (Rom. 9:6b–8).

Paul, in this passage, is simply stating the fact that it is not their natural affiliation to Israel that makes them the true Israel of God, but faith that appropriates the promise of redemption. "For he is not a Jew, which is one outwardly; neither is that circumcision, which is outward in the flesh: but he is a Jew, which is one inwardly; and circumcision is that of the heart, in the spirit, and not in the letter; whose praise is not of men, but of God" (Rom. 2:28–29). It is to this spiritual significance of circumcision to which Paul refers again in Colossians 2:11–12 when he writes, "In whom also ye are circumcised with the circumcision made without hands, in putting off the body of the sins of the flesh by the circumcision of Christ: buried with him in baptism, wherein also ye are risen with him through the faith of the operation of God, who hath raised him from the dead." Here, this circumcision made without hands in the experience of the spiritual Israel of God is representative of the believer's identity with the Lord Jesus in His death and resurrection, and this of course is fully in keeping with the vivid picture that God gives us in the historical record of the earthly Israel.

God made a covenant with Abraham: "And I will give unto thee, and to thy seed after thee, the land wherein thou art a stranger, all the land of Canaan, for an everlasting possession; and I will be their God. . . . Every man child among you shall be circumcised. . . . and it shall be a token of the covenant betwixt me and you" (Gen. 17:8, 10b–11). Circumcision was to be the hallmark of a redeemed people destined for the plenitude of Canaan, and yet in Joshua 5:5 we read that "all the people that were born in the wilderness by the way as they came forth out of Egypt, them they had not circumcised." For this was the Church in the Wilderness, a people who had come out, but who had not gone in—dumped in the desert! Circumcision in Egypt was a confession of faith, but circumcision in the wilderness could only have been a confession of failure.

In the picture language of the Bible, they had gone through all the motions, but in common with all too much of Christendom today, they had "a form of godliness, but denying the power thereof'" (2 Tim. 3:5b).

All had been "baptized unto Moses in the cloud and in the sea" (1 Cor. 10:2) and one might almost describe Moses as pastor of the First Baptist Church in the Wilderness! We have seen already in an earlier chapter that as they were baptized unto Moses, so we have been baptized into Christ. They went with him into the place of death, to be raised with him into newness of life on the other side of the Red Sea. In God's purpose we too have gone with Christ into the place of death, to be raised with Him into newness of life—

"For by the death He died, He died to sin [ending His relation to it] once for all, and the life that He lives He is living to God—in unbroken fellowship with him. Even so consider yourselves also dead to sin *and* your relation to it broken, but [that you are] alive to God—living in unbroken fellowship with Him—in Christ Jesus" (Rom. 6:10–11 AMPLIFIED NEW TESTAMENT).

This is your spiritual baptism into Christ. It is quite obvious that you can be baptized outwardly without being baptized inwardly. The rite of baptism cannot make us true Christians. If there is no spiritual content to the outward exercise, baptism becomes no more than an empty superstition. That, of course, is obvious, and there is only spiritual content where *faith* has been exercised, in *obedience* to the truth.

Not only were they baptized into Moses, however, but they "did all eat the same spiritual meat; and did all drink the same spiritual drink: for they drank of that spiritual Rock that followed them: and that Rock was Christ" (1 Cor. 10:3–4).

We have also touched upon the spiritual significance of the manna—the "spiritual meat" upon which the Church in the Wilderness fed throughout their forty weary years of wandering—but I would like to examine this now a little more closely.

"And when the children of Israel saw it, they said one to another, It is manna." What the children of Israel said when they saw the manna may be translated "What is this?" for "they wist not what it was" (Exod. 16:15). This was something new, something that they had never tasted before; it was God's gift to a redeemed people, and it represents for you and for me the gift of God's Holy Spirit, to those who have been redeemed in the precious blood of Christ.

No man, woman, or child can ever receive, taste, or know

this heavenly gift until he has put his trust in Christ "in whom also," wrote Paul to the Ephesians, "after that ye believed, ye were sealed with that Holy Spirit of promise, which is the earnest of our inheritance" (Eph. 1:13b–14a), and of whom the Lord Jesus said, "even the Spirit of truth; whom the world cannot receive, because it seeth him not, neither knoweth him: but ye know him; for he dwelleth with you, and shall be in you" (John 14:17).

The presence of the Holy Spirit is the birthright of forgiven sinners, and the miracle of regeneration is a new and novel experience, introducing the newborn child of God into a quality of life of which, until then, he has lived in total ignorance.

The taste of the manna was "as the taste of fresh oil" (Num. 11:8), speaking, as we have already mentioned, of the presence of the Holy Spirit, and yet the role played by the manna in the Church in the Wilderness was not representative of His full, gracious ministry. It was but a foretaste of better things to come! It is significant that in Exodus 16:31 we read that "the taste of it was like wafers made with honey." Oil and honey! The Holy Spirit, reminding God's people of a day to be remembered in a land to be possessed! Not just a dry thin wafer, but a *land* flowing with milk and honey! There is not much substance in a wafer—just enough to stimulate the salivary juices and make the hungry cry for more!

The twofold taste of the manna speaks of the dual role of the Holy Spirit in the Church in the Wilderness. The taste of oil speaks of His witness to the presence of the living God in the human spirit of the forgiven sinner, and the taste of honey speaks of His constant incentive to the wilderness Christian to get on and get in, to live in the land, to be filled with the Spirit.

I am fully aware that very often the daily manna is used as a picture of your daily Bible reading, and it makes quite a good picture in that they went out every morning and they gathered. However, the more they gathered of it, the more they got sick of it, and complained, "But now our soul is dried away: there is nothing at all, beside this manna, before our eyes" (Num. 11:6). It has become dull and monotonous and boring. Should this be true of your daily Bible reading?

I cannot feel that this picture presents a very happy precedent, and I am sure that we should not accept it as the norm of Christian experience. Your daily Bible reading is designed to allow the Holy Spirit to lead you into all truth, so that you may increasingly "become a body wholly filled and flooded with God Himself!" (Eph. 3:19c AMPLIFIED NEW TESTAMENT). It is designed to show you the wealth and heritage that is yours in Christ, but the more *they* had of manna, day after day, week after week, month after month, year after year, the more they disliked it!

Mind you, even in relation to your daily Bible reading, this could be equally true of you! If you will not respond to the Holy Spirit and the incentive that He constantly gives you through His Word to holiness of life, nor be enticed by the taste of the honey, then the wafer will remain stubbornly thin and dry and uninteresting—and your quiet time will degenerate into a mechanical performance that may conform to pattern, but provide you with little pleasure or profit. You *may* be sustained, but you will hardly be satisfied!

The witness of the Spirit to the redeemed sinner living in disobedience is an extremely unpleasant experience, and for the Christian who gets out but who refuses to get in, the things of the Spirit will become increasingly monotonous. The pastor in the pulpit, the missionary on the field, the teacher in his Bible class who belong to the Church in the Wilderness, and who by force of circumstance must go on going through the motions of Christian service, will become increasingly bored in all they do and increasingly boring to those for whom they do it!

That is why there are so many boring preachers and boring Sunday school teachers. They are as boring as they are bored themselves!

There were some who belonged to the Church in the Wilderness who were living in willful rebellion and disobedience; they would gladly have escaped any conscious sense of God's presence, for it constantly reminded them that they were a redeemed people. To such the daily witness of the manna was, paradoxically enough, at one and the same time both a source of aggravation and of relief. On the one hand it disturbed a conscience already ill at ease, and yet upon the other they were strangely aware that they could not live without it! They were spoiled for Egypt and were not enjoying Canaan! This is the paradox of the carnal Christian.

Perhaps you too, with them and with Jonah of old, have been trying to run away from God—and yet you cannot! You resist His claims and yet are fearful lest He should forsake you! You are still a soul in conflict—you belong to the Church in the Wilderness!

But if the daily presence of the manna was a source of discomfort to some, it was a source of untold comfort to others!

Caleb and Joshua were men who never ceased to believe that the God who brought them out was the God who could bring them in, and I sometimes feel that when they saw the wickedness, the idolatry, the grumbling, and the unbelief of God's people in the wilderness, they must have turned to each other and said, "God will leave us! God *must* leave us!" Then through the long watches of a restless night, they would wait fearfully for the dawn, to see if God had left them! At the first hint of daylight they would scan the ground at their feet and would see the manna and would be comforted! God had not left them—there was His witness!

While Moses was away in the mountain speaking with God and receiving the law, Aaron yielded to the pressure of the people and, half naked in their shame, they worshiped the golden calf which he had made. What despair and what misgivings must have filled the hearts of the faithful few, and yet the next morning, mingled with the shattered fragments of those tables of stone, which had been written upon with the finger of God—there was manna on the ground! This is the amazing patience of God! This is a love that will not let you go! "Where sin abounded, grace did much more abound" (Rom. 5:20b), and God has said, "I will never leave thee, nor forsake thee" (Heb. 13:5c).

There is no mandate here for disobedience, nor does it make sin less serious, but I want you to know that when all seems lost, mercy can shine through judgment, and the rainbow of God's promise tells of One who "shall not fail nor *be discouraged,* till he have set judgment in the earth" (Isa. 42:4b, emphasis added). When every hope is dashed, when every noble dream and every holy ambition written with the finger of God Himself upon your heart is shattered, hope can rise again and grace can chase away the gloom—*there is manna on the ground!* He has not left you—nor left you comfortless! Then "Grieve not the Holy Spirit of God, whereby ye are sealed unto the day of redemption" (Eph. 4:30).

God said to the prophet Haggai, "According to the word that I covenanted with you when ye came out of Egypt, so my spirit remaineth among you: fear ye not" (Hag. 2:5). God might well have said to His people of old, "For forty years you grieved my Spirit, and yet I never left you! I never left you!" The daily manna tells us of a Holy Spirit who seals us until the day of redemption. You may grieve Him, you may quench Him, and if you do, He will let you know it—for "whom the Lord loveth he chasteneth" (Heb. 12:6a)—but He will never leave you! This is the amazing grace of God!

However, while God was *feeding* His people in the wilderness—He let them *hunger*. "And thou shalt remember all the way which the LORD thy God led thee these forty years in the wilderness, to humble thee, and to prove thee, to know what was in thine heart, whether thou wouldest keep his commandments, or no. And he humbled thee, and suffered thee to hunger, and fed thee with manna" (Deut. 8:2–3a). All those forty years, in other words, they were never satisfied, for the manna was given only to sustain life, but never to satisfy, because God never *intended* them to be satisfied in the wilderness!

Where did God intend to satisfy His people? In the land! God refuses to satisfy His people in the wilderness, when He has spread the table with good things in Canaan!

God will never satisfy *you* in the wilderness. You are no good to anybody in the wilderness! Basically you will never change in the wilderness! There will be no glow to your testimony, and the first enthusiasm of Christian service, the novelty of being on the mission field, of being the pastor of a church, or teaching a Bible class in Sunday school will soon wear off when you get accustomed to the new sights and sounds and the people you have to live with in the wilderness. The vision will grow dim, and the light of battle will vanish from your eyes. Ignoring what you *need*, you will begin to clamor for what you *want*, and if you are not careful, God will give it to you!

The people "lusted exceedingly in the wilderness, and tempted God in the desert. And he gave them their request; but sent leanness unto their soul" (Ps. 106:14–15). The quails God sent them rotted in their mouths, and they lived in self-imposed poverty, carnally fat and spiritually thin!

It is a sad thing to be impoverished by the things you *want*, while God is waiting to give you the things you *need*.

Hezekiah clamored for another fifteen years of life, and he got what he wanted! But he "rendered not again according to the benefit done unto him; for his heart was lifted up: therefore there was wrath upon him . . ." (2 Chron. 32:25). He lived to beget one of the wickedest kings who ever reigned over Judah—Manasseh, who was twelve years old when Hezekiah died fifteen years too late! Manasseh "built again the high places which Hezekiah his father had broken down. . . . [and] made Judah and the inhabitants of Jerusalem to err, and to do worse than the heathen, whom the LORD had destroyed before the children of Israel" (2 Chron. 33:3, 9). What a pity Hezekiah did not die on schedule! He got what he wanted, *and died too old!*

No, the Church in the Wilderness was not a happy church—but what a transformation on the day they got into the land! "And the children of Israel encamped in Gilgal, and kept the passover on the fourteenth day of the month at even in the plains of Jericho" (Josh. 5:10). The first time for thirty-eight years! "And they did eat of the old corn of the land on the morrow after the passover, unleavened cakes, and parched corn in the selfsame day. And the manna ceased on the morrow after they had eaten of the old corn of the land; neither had the children of Israel manna any more; but they did eat of the fruit of the land of Canaan that year" (Josh. 5:11–12). For they bore *witness* of the Spirit, now they enjoyed the *fulness* of the Spirit. Not just sustained— now they were satisfied! Not just the thin, dry wafer—a foretaste of good things to come—but the *land itself* flowing with milk and honey; and for the monotonous diet of the desert, they had all the abundance of Canaan!

Are you bored? Are you suffering from leanness of soul? Have the things of God become monotonous? Are you more tempted to grumble than rejoice? Are the things you want more important than the things you need? Are you spiritually thin? Perhaps you are still living on manna! Maybe you got out but you never got in! Maybe you still belong to the Church in the Wilderness!

Oh, our God, may we enter increasingly into the good of Thy rich provision, that the memories of Canaan may soon banish the memories of Egypt, and the fulness of Thy Spirit flood our souls with the light of the knowledge of the glory of God in the face of Jesus Christ. Every horizon beckons us, bright with the promise of Thy blessing; we must and we will go on and in, to explore and to possess the land! In Jesus' name. Amen.

Chapter VII

Then Came Amalek!

In the preceding chapter we have seen something of the significance of the manna, and we need now to turn for a moment to Exodus 17, that we may understand to what Paul referred when he wrote in 1 Corinthians 10, not only of the "spiritual meat" (verse 3), but also of "the same spiritual drink: for they drank of that spiritual Rock that followed them: and that Rock was Christ" (verse 4).

As the children of Israel journeyed from the Wilderness of Sin, to pitch their tents in Rephidim, there was no water for the people to drink, and as became increasingly their characteristic in the wilderness, the people murmured against Moses and chided with him. And "Moses cried unto the LORD, saying, What shall I do unto this people? They be almost ready to stone me" (Exod. 17:4). In answer to his cry, God told Moses to take the rod in his hand, with which he smote the river, and said, "Behold, I will stand before thee there upon the rock in Horeb; and thou shalt smite the rock, and there shall come water out of it, that the people may drink" (Exod. 17:6). This Moses did, and water flowed from the smitten rock. The people drank and their thirst was quenched.

The picture here is clear. Water from the smitten rock in a

thirsty land represents the gift of eternal life through the crucified Lord Jesus Christ, for in the words of Paul, the apostle, "that Rock was Christ."

As we shall discover later, this does not tell the whole of the story, but it does represent its beginning, for here indeed is the only place where the story of man's redemption can begin—at the place where the Rock was smitten.

> Beneath the cross of Jesus
> I fain would take my stand,
> The shadow of a mighty rock,
> Within a weary land;
> A home within the wilderness,
> A rest upon the way,
> From the burning of the noontide heat,
> And the burden of the day.
>
> O safe and happy shelter!
> O refuge tried and sweet!
> O trysting-place where heaven's love
> And heaven's justice meet!
> As to the holy patriarch
> That wondrous dream was given,
> So seems my Saviour's cross to me,
> A ladder up to heaven.

Here then is the threefold portrait which God gives of a redeemed people living in the wilderness: They were baptized unto Moses—the believer identified with Christ and taken with Him through death into resurrection life. They were partakers of the daily manna—the believer experiencing the *witness* of the Holy Spirit to his heart, that he is a child of God, sealed unto the day of redemption, but having only a foretaste of all that Christ can be to those who enjoy the *fulness* of His Spirit. They were refreshed with water from the smitten rock—the believer receiving the gift of eternal life, on the basis of redemption through the precious blood of the crucified Lord Jesus Christ. But in spite of all this, "with many of them God was not well pleased."

Returning to Exodus 17, we see that no sooner had God given water to this people from the rock that Moses smote than "then came Amalek and fought with Israel in Rephidim." Amalek here is a picture of the flesh, seeking at all costs to bar the onward journey of God's redeemed people, through the wilderness, into the land of promise.

It was not God's purpose that His people should remain at the place where the rock was smitten. Moses reminded Israel in Deuteronomy 1:6: "The LORD our God spake unto us in Horeb, saying, Ye have dwelt long enough in this mount." How long had they dwelt in the Mount in Horeb? Long enough! "Turn you, and take your journey and go. . . . Behold, I have set the land before you: go in and possess the land which the LORD sware unto your fathers, Abraham, Isaac, and Jacob, to give unto them and to their seed after them" (Deut. 1:7−8). In other words, "Get down, get on, and get in!" But this, it was Amalek's business and ambition to prevent!

Amalek presents us with a most fascinating study and illustrates the relentless consistency of the Holy Spirit in the language which He uses in His revelation of truth throughout the whole of the Bible. He may use several types or symbols to illustrate the same spiritual principle, but such types or symbols as He may choose, He will use with complete consistency throughout the whole of Scripture.

This is one of the most remarkable evidences of the miraculous inspiration of the Bible. You will discover that the Bible will come to life in a new way, and the Old Testament in particular will become very much richer, a book charged with spiritual significance, if you will allow the Holy Spirit to teach you the meaning of the language that He uses.

We have already seen that just as soon as the Holy Spirit is restored to your human spirit as a forgiven sinner, His office is to re-invade your soul, there to re-establish the sovereignty of the Lord Jesus in the area of your mind, of your emotions, and of your will—so that your whole human personality may become available to Him, who has come to re-inhabit your redeemed humanity, and that your body might become the temple of the living God.

There is, however, immediate resistance on the part of the flesh, "For the flesh lusteth against the Spirit, and the Spirit against the flesh" (Gal. 5:17a). The flesh contests every attempt of the Spirit of God to lead you on into spiritual maturity. Standing across your pathway from the very outset of your Christian life is Amalek!

"And Moses said unto Joshua, Choose us out men, and go out, fight with Amalek: tomorrow I will stand on the top of the hill with the rod of God in mine hand. So Joshua did as Moses had said to him, and fought with Amalek" (Exod. 17:9–10a). So Joshua was on the battlefield, and Joshua engaged the enemy; yet the outcome of the battle did not rest with him, for "when Moses held up his hand, Israel prevailed: and when he let down his hand, Amalek prevailed" (Exod. 17:11). The principle is plain. Victory over Amalek is God given; it cannot be *won*, it can only be *received*, and that by the appropriation of faith.

We see that after God commissioned Moses to be the means in His hands of bringing His people out of Egypt, Moses answered and said,

Behold, they will not believe me, nor hearken unto my voice: for they will say, The Lord hath not appeared unto thee. And the Lord said unto him, What is that in thine hand? And he said, A rod. And he said, Cast it on the ground. And he cast it on the ground, and it became a serpent; and Moses fled from before it. And the Lord said unto Moses, Put forth thine hand, and take it by the tail. And he put forth his hand, and caught it, and it became a rod in his hand. (Exod. 4:1–4)

This was the sign that God gave to Moses of a victory already won, a victory that God gives to those who trust Him. As Moses fled before the serpent, God said in so many words, "Don't run away from it! Turn round! Face it! Put out your hand and take it by the tail!" And the moment Moses put out his hand and took it, the serpent became as helpless and harmless as a rod.

What is the serpent in your life before which you have been fleeing? As a Christian, what is it that has been chasing you? Of what are you afraid? God says, "Stop running away—there is victory for you too! Turn round, put out your hand, and *take* the victory that I will give you!" When Moses let his hand down, Amalek prevailed, and Joshua was fighting a battle already lost. When Moses held his hand high, Joshua prevailed—and he enjoyed the victory already won!

There are countless Christians fighting a battle that is already lost, trying in their own strength to overcome the subtleties of sin. That is a battle you can fight all your days, but I tell you now, you cannot win! It is a battle already lost, lost in the first Adam, who was made a living soul, and died; but the last Adam, Jesus Christ, has already defeated sin and death and hell, and Satan himself! Why not accept in Him the victory that He has already won? Victory over the flesh is not to be attained—it is to be received.

"Walk in the Spirit, and ye shall not fulfill the lusts of the flesh" (Gal. 5:16b). No matter what it is that threatens you, if you walk in the Spirit, you can turn around and face your enemy. You can "take him by the tail" and find him helpless and harmless in your hands, for God has already bruised the serpent's head! (Gen. 3:15; Heb. 2:14). In other words, to walk in the Spirit is to *assume* by faith the victory with which He credits you, and God will vindicate your assumption and make it real in your experience.

Now the Devil loves to invert truth and turn it into a lie,

and probably what he has been saying to you is this: "Try not to fulfill the lusts of the flesh, and *then* you will walk in the Spirit," as though the latter were a reward for the former. He knows that in this way, he will keep you preoccupied with yourself, instead of being preoccupied with Christ.

There is nothing quite so nauseating or pathetic as the flesh trying to be holy! The flesh has a perverted bent for righteousness—but such righteousness as it may achieve is always self-righteousness; and self-righteousness is always self-conscious righteousness; and self-conscious righteousness is always full of self-praise. This produces the extrovert, who must always be noticed, recognized, consulted, and applauded. On the other hand, when the flesh in pursuit of self-righteousness fails, instead of being filled with self-praise, it is filled with self-pity, and this produces the introvert. A professional "case" for professional counsellors!

The Devil does not mind whether you are an extrovert or an introvert, whether you succeed or whether you fail in the energy of the flesh, whether you are filled with self-pity or self-praise, for he knows that in both cases you will be preoccupied with yourself, not Christ. You will be "ego-centric" (self-centered) and not "Deo-centric" (God-centered)!

So Satan will seek to persuade you that "walking in the Spirit" is simply the *consequence* of your pious endeavor not to fulfill the "lusts of the flesh," of which he himself is the author, and thus by subtly confusing the means for the end, he will rob you of what he knows to be your only possibility of victory.

Is that not what you have been trying to do? You have been trying not to fulfill the lust of the flesh, *in order* to walk in the Spirit—fighting a battle already lost. What God has said to you is this, "Walk in the Spirit," in an attitude of total dependence upon Him, exposing everything to Him, "and you will not fulfill the lusts of the flesh"—for you will then be enjoying through Him the victory that Christ has already won. To walk in the Spirit is not a *reward*—it is the means! It is to enjoy the Saving Life of Christ!

As you take every step in an attitude of total dependence upon the Lord Jesus Christ who indwells you by His Spirit, He celebrates in you the victory He has already won over sin and death and Satan. As Moses held his hand high—a picture of the appropriation by faith of God-given victory—Joshua prevailed.

> [He] discomfited Amalek and his people with the edge of the sword. And the LORD said unto Moses, Write this for a memorial in a book, and rehearse it in the ears of Joshua: for I will utterly put out the remembrance of Amalek from under heaven. And Moses built an altar, and called the name of it Jehovah-nissi [the Lord my banner]: For he said, Because the LORD hath sworn that the LORD will have war with Amalek from generation to generation. (Exod. 17:13–16)

There will never come a day when God will be at peace with Amalek!

God says of you that in your flesh dwells no good thing, and no flesh will ever glory in His presence (Rom. 7:18; 1 Cor. 1:29). Remember what the flesh is—"that spirit that now worketh in the children of disobedience," which first found expression at the fall of Satan when he said in his heart, "I will ascend into heaven, I will exalt my throne above the stars of God: I will sit also upon the mount of the congregation, in the sides of the north: I will ascend above the heights of the clouds; I will be like the most High" (Isa. 14:13b–14).

He wanted to *have* something, to *do* something and *be* something, apart from God, and it is this satanic ambition which the flesh seeks to perpetuate in you. The flesh is all that you become in seeking to *have* and to *do* and to *be*, apart from what Christ is—and God is at war from generation to generation with this satanic principle which makes you what you are, apart from what Christ is.

Is there any good reason why Amalek should represent the flesh? What is the characteristic of Amalek that gives to us a legitimate, scriptural reason for seeking in him the picture of the fallen nature of a fallen man?

We must turn to a significant passage in Genesis 25, the relevance of which may not at first seem apparent, but we read:

> And Jacob sod [boiled] pottage: and Esau came from the field, and he was faint: And Esau said to Jacob, Feed me I pray thee, with that same red pottage; for I am faint: therefore was his name called Edom . . . And Jacob said, Swear to me this day; and he sware unto him: and he sold his birthright unto Jacob. Then Jacob gave Esau bread and pottage of lentils; and he did eat and drink, and rose up, and went his way: thus Esau despised his birthright. (Gen. 25:29–30, 33–34)

What was the birthright that Esau despised and that Jacob was to inherit? The birthright was this—the promise that God had given to Abraham that in his seed all the families of the earth should be blessed, not, as Paul points out in Galatians 3:16b, "seeds, as of many; but as of one, and to thy seed, which is Christ." That is to say, the birthright involved the birth of Christ—the Seed of Abraham in particular, through the seed of Abraham in general, the One who would redeem man from his lost condition and restore him to his true relationship to God, making him dependent once more upon the One whose presence is life and who alone can enable man to behave as man, as God intended man to be.

This was the birthright: that God was prepared in the person of His incarnate Son, to make man man again and to restore him to his true humanity—and Esau despised the birthright! Esau said in his heart, "Sunday school talk! I don't need this kind of kid's stuff! I have all that it takes to be man—apart from God!" There was perpetuated in him the basic lie perpetuated by Satan in Adam: "You are what you are, by virtue of what you are and not by virtue of what God is. You can lose God and lose nothing!"

In Esau the spirit of Satan was incarnate. "What do I need of a birthright restoring me to dependence upon God? I am independent, and I am self-sufficient, and I will be what I am, by virtue of what I am!"

Mind you, in a worldly context, some might have described Esau as a man's man. He was a hunter, with hair on his chest; he could go out into the forest and carve his own dinner! Jacob, on the other hand, was what we all might have described as a "sissy." He was his mother's pet! He stayed home and helped her with the cooking! He was tied to her apron strings; and she did not even let him look for a girlfriend until he was seventy years of age! That was Jacob! His name meant "twister" or "cheat," and he was as good as his name! He was a liar, and he was crooked. He lied to his aged father, and he double-crossed his brother.

Jacob was a sneak, and purely from a human point of view, Esau had no time for his twin brother! He could *have* his birthright! Esau had persuaded himself that religion was the weakling's crutch, and if ever there was a man who needed a crutch, it was Jacob!

Esau had no time for any birthright that was calculated to leave him anything other than completely self-sufficient and completely independent; and God can do nothing for a man like that.

The burden of the word of the LORD to Israel by Malachi. I have loved you, saith the LORD. Yet ye say, Wherein hast thou loved us? Was not Esau Jacob's brother? saith the LORD: yet I loved Jacob, and I hated Esau, and laid his mountains and his heritage waste for the dragons of the wilderness. Whereas Edom saith, We are impoverished, but we will return and build the desert places; thus saith the LORD of hosts, They shall build, but I will throw down; and they shall call them, The border of wickedness, and, The people against whom the LORD hath indignation for ever (Mal. 1:1—4).

Why did God hate Esau? Because God can do absolutely nothing with a man who will not admit that he needs anything from God. Esau rejected God's means of grace; he repudiated man's need of God's intervention; he *despised his birthright*—and God never forgave him! This is the basic attitude of sin—it makes God irrelevant to the stern business of living and gives to man a flattering sense of self-importance, an attitude portrayed by William Henley in the words of his poem "Invictus"—

> It matters not how straight the gate,
> How charged with punishment the scroll,
> I am the master of my fate,
> I am the captain of my soul.

God can do nothing for the man eaten up with the spirit of Esau. The sad thing is that even a Christian may be so impressed with himself and with his own ability that even though he gives lip service to the fact, he may still see no personal relevance in the indwelling presence of Christ. It will smack to him of mysticism; he will consider such teaching to be exaggeratedly subjective and will pride himself on being a practical man of action—and thus he too may despise his birthright.

But Jacob, the twister—God *could* do something for him! God could do something for Jacob when He could do nothing for Esau, for although men might legitimately despise Jacob, they did not despise him any more than he despised himself! There were times maybe, when in the darkness and when he was desperately lonely, the tears would course down his cheeks, and he would cry out in his heart, "God, if there is any kind of blessing that you can give to a person like me, that can make me different from what I am—that is what I need, and that is what I want!"

God can get in and God can begin with a man when he comes to the place of total despair, when he ceases to be impressed with what he is and jettisons all expectation in himself. God loved Jacob! He did not love him for what he was—He loved him for what He could make of him; and God never loved you for what you were. He loved you and He loves you still for what He can make of you.

God did not love Saul of Tarsus for standing by and consenting to the death of Stephen; He did not love Saul of Tarsus because he was on his way to Damascus, breathing out threatenings and slaughter, there to throw into jail men, women, and children who dared to call upon the name of the Lord Jesus. God did not love him for that; God loved Saul of Tarsus for what he could become—Paul, an apostle of Jesus Christ "by the will of God"!

God does not love you for what the flesh makes of your human personality, but He does love you for what Christ can make of your human personality—but God can only begin when you admit your need of Christ. Esau never admitted his need!

The vision of Obadiah. Thus saith the LORD God concerning Edom; We have heard a rumour from the LORD, and an ambassador is sent among the heathen, Arise ye, and let us rise up against her in battle. Behold, I have made thee small among the heathen: thou art greatly despised. The pride of thine heart hath deceived thee, thou that dwellest in the clefts of the rock, whose habitation is high; that saith in his heart, Who shall bring me down to the ground? Though thou exalt thyself as the eagle, and though thou set thy nest among the stars, thence will I bring thee down, saith the LORD. How are the things of Esau searched out! How are his hidden things sought up! (Obad. 1–4, 6)

This was the spirit of Esau—"I will set myself like God above the stars! Birthright? Who wants a miserable birthright? I have all that it takes to be a man—apart from God. God can keep His birthright!" So God kept it and gave it to Jacob, whom He loved!

Jacob wanted everything he could get from God, and although it was twenty weary years before he entered into the fulness of that purpose for which he had been called, God could at least *begin* with Jacob. He began first at Bethel, "the house of God," and continued twenty years later at Peniel, "the face of God," where, graduating from the school of despair, Jacob wrestled with a man who touched his thigh, and asked him, "What is your name?" And Jacob whispered hoarsely, "Cheat—Sneak—Twister—Thief—Supplanter—that is my name!" And God said, in effect, "Jacob, that is all I have been waiting for; I have been waiting for you to call yourself *by your own name*—and now I will change it! You shall be called Israel—Prince of God!"

Given the opportunity, God can take the most beggarly elements of humanity and make a prince out of them. Did you ever get down on your knees and tell God what you know yourself to be? Have you ever called yourself *by your own name*? If you have learned to do that, you have learned the secret of blessing—and God will *change your name!*

Chapter VIII

Know Your Enemy
(Amalek continued)

By now you are probably saying to yourself, "What has Esau to do with Amalek?" To discover this we need first to turn to Genesis 36. Let me remind you again of the relentless consistency of the Holy Spirit, so that wherever you see Esau or Mount Seir or Edom in the Word of God, you will know that He is referring to sin as a principle, to that satanic attitude of self-sufficiency and independence which is characteristic of the flesh, to the carnal mind that "is not subject to the law of God, neither indeed can be" (Rom. 8:7b). "Thus dwelt Esau in mount Seir: Esau is Edom. And these are the generations of Esau, the father of the Edomites in mount Seir. . . . And Timna was concubine to Eliphaz Esau's son; and she bare to Eliphaz Amalek" (Gen. 36:8–9, 12a).

Amalek was Esau's grandson! Malachi tells us that God was at war with Esau from generation to generation, and Exodus 17 tells us that God was at war with Amalek from generation to generation. Perpetuated in Amalek was the profanity of Esau, the man who refused the birthright.

It is interesting to note in Genesis 36:31: "And these are the kings that reigned in the land of Edom, before there reigned any king over the children of Israel." There were kings in Edom *before* there was a king in Israel, and this has interesting spiritual significance.

You were born by nature a child of wrath, and the flesh exercised the authority of the "king of Edom"—Satan—in your life, long before the Holy Spirit exercised the authority of the "King of Israel"—the Lord Jesus Christ. Chronologically, in fallen man, the flesh always precedes the Spirit, and this is consistently illustrated in the picture language of the Bible. Cain, "Who was of that wicked one" (1 John 3:12), was born before "righteous" Abel (Heb. 11:4). Ishmael, "born after the flesh," preceded Isaac, "born after the Spirit" (Gal. 4:29). Esau, that "profane person" whom God hated (Heb. 12:16–17), was born before Jacob, whom God loved. Saul, who "played the fool" (1 Sam. 26:21) and whom God rejected (1 Sam. 15:26), reigned before David, the neighbor better than he (1 Sam. 15:28) whom Saul feared, for God was with him (1 Sam. 18:12).

Notice too what is said of the kings that reigned in Edom, from verse 33 onward—"And Bela died, and Jobab . . . reigned in his stead. And Jobab died, and Husham . . . reigned in his stead. And Husham died, and Hadad . . . reigned in his stead. And Hadad died, and Samlah . . . reigned in his stead. And Samlah died . . . and Saul died . . . and Baal-hanan died. . . . And these are the names of the dukes that came of Esau . . . he is Esau the father of the Edomites." He died and he died and he died! The characteristic of the kings of Edom was that they died! They *all* died! The kings of Edom reigned *unto death*, as distinct from the One born later to be King of Israel, who reigns *unto life*— the promised seed of Esau's rejected birthright, whose kingdom shall have no end!

> If by one man's offence death reigned by one; much more they which receive abundance of grace and of the gift of righteousness shall reign in life by one, Jesus Christ. . . . That as sin hath reigned unto death, even so might grace reign through

righteousness unto eternal life by Jesus Christ our Lord. (Rom. 5:17, 21)

As I have already emphasized, you were born by nature a child of wrath, "dead in sins" (Eph. 2:5), "for to be carnally minded is death" (Rom. 8:6a), and to be carnally minded simply means that by nature, as the fallen seed of the fallen Adam, your human personality is dominated from birth by "the spirit that now worketh in the children of disobedience" (Eph. 2:2), the spirit that repudiates man's dependence upon God, whose presence alone is life, and whose absence is death.

On the other hand, "to be spiritually minded is life and peace" (Rom. 8:6b), for to be spiritually minded is to recognize always that all that makes you true man is Christ Himself—received, honored, and obeyed as King.

For in Him the whole fullness of Deity (the Godhead), continues to dwell in bodily form—giving complete expression of the divine nature. And you are in Him, made full and have come to fullness of life—in Christ you too are filled with the Godhead: Father, Son and Holy Spirit, and reach full spiritual stature. (Col. 2:9–10b AMPLIFIED NEW TESTAMENT)

It is the Devil's business to prevent your translation "from the power of darkness . . . into the kingdom of God's dear Son" and Amalek, imbued with the spirit of Satan, is unrelenting in his opposition to the prosperity of the Israel of God.

Balak, who was king of the Moabites at that time, sent a message to Balaam the prophet, saying, "Behold, there is a people come out from Egypt: behold, they cover the face of the earth, and they abide over against me: Come now therefore, I pray thee, curse me this people; for they are too mighty for me" (Num. 22:5b–6a). So Balak would have Balaam curse Israel, but in the next chapter we read that Balaam "took up his parable, and said, 'Balak the king of

Moab hath brought me from Aram, out of the mountains of the east, saying, Come, curse me Jacob, and come, defy Israel. How shall I curse, whom God hath not cursed? Or how shall I defy, whom the Lord hath not defied?' And he took up his parable, and said. . . . 'I shall see him, but not now; I shall behold him, but not nigh: there shall come a Star out of Jacob, and a Scepter shall rise out of Israel'" (Num. 23:7–8; 24:15, 17a).

This was the birthright! Speaking prophetically, Balaam foreshadowed the birth of the Lord Jesus Christ as the promised Seed of Abraham. "Out of Jacob shall come He that shall have dominion"—the message which was to be re-iterated upon the lips of the angel Gabriel: "Fear not, Mary: for thou hast found favour with God. And behold, thou shalt conceive in thy womb, and bring forth a son, and shalt call his name JESUS. He shall be great, and shall be called the Son of the Highest: and the Lord God shall give unto him the throne of his father David: And he shall reign over the house of Jacob for ever; and of his kingdom there shall be no end" (Luke 1:30–33).

But after this prophetic utterance, we read of Balaam the prophet: "And when he looked on Amalek, he took up his parable, and said 'Amalek was the first of the nations [that is to say, Amalek was the first of the nations to fight against Israel, the first to stand astride the path of God's redeemed people in their march onward into the land of Canaan] but his latter end shall be that he perish for ever'" (Num. 24:20).

Compromise with the flesh and you make an unholy alliance with that which is, and always will be, at enmity with God, and whose end is to perish forever—and this, God says, is something to remember!

Remember what Amalek did unto thee by the way, when ye were come forth out of Egypt; how he met thee by the way, and smote the hindmost of thee, even all that were feeble behind thee, when thou wast faint and weary. (Deut. 25:17–18b)

That is when Amalek hits you! It is when you are faint and weary. It is when you are one of the hindmost. When you are dragging your feet. When you are spiritually low and the sun is hidden and the skies are dark. When you have withdrawn yourself from the conflict, because you feel the pace is too much for you. When you think you are alone—but you are not alone, for Amalek will be there! With a little chuckle and a giggle, in his own slimy way, Amalek will be there! That is his business, and he will be up to no good thing! "And he feared not God" (Deut. 25:18c).

Amalek has no time for God. He is hostile to God. He "is not subject to the law of God, neither indeed can be" (Rom. 8:7b). He is profane! He despises the birthright!

Remember Amalek!

God says that there is something that you do not have the right to remember, because it is something that God forgets. God says, "Their sins and iniquities will I remember no more" (Heb. 10:17). It is not that God pretends that you have not sinned. He does not ignore your guilt. He says, "I will remember your sins," but in the light of the shed blood of His dear Son, having remembered your sins—every one of them—He says, "I will remember your sins *no more.*" He has put them away as far as the east is from the west (Ps. 103:12). He has put them behind His back (Isa. 38:17). He has placed them in the depths of the sea (Mic. 7:19). Though they were as scarlet, they have become as white as snow; red like crimson, they have become as wool (Isa. 1:18). God says that you do not have the right to remember what He forgets, and God says, "I will remember your sins— I will remember your sins, but I will remember them *no more!*"

I emphasize this in particular, because there are some who would seek to persuade you that true holiness comes only from rummaging into the background of your wicked past and in remembering the things that God has forgotten.

They make merchandise of your souls, and they glory in your shame. It is a masterpiece of satanic subtlety when the Devil persuades your flesh to take an unholy pride in the public confession of sin as the price of blessing. Victory, sanctification, revival, the fulness of the Spirit—these cannot be purchased at such a price, for the price has already been paid! To add anything is to repudiate the adequacy of the death of Christ.

Sin should and must be confessed to God, and restitution made where the Spirit of God demands it, but "the blood of Jesus Christ [God's] Son cleanseth us from all sin," and "if we confess our sins, he is faithful and just to forgive us our sins, and to cleanse us from all unrighteousness" (1 John 1:7, 9).

Satan is the accuser of the brethren, and he "accuses them before God day and night" (Rev. 12:10). Do not allow him to rob you of your joy or your peace or your assurance by a form of spiritual blackmail! *Christ* has been made unto you righteousness, and all that *He is* has been made over to you on the basis of what *He did*—"And they overcame him by the blood of the Lamb, and by the word of their testimony" (Rev. 12:11). The price has been paid, both for your redemption and for your sanctification, and when God forgives, God forgets!

If, however, you do not have the right to *remember* what God *forgets*—you do not have the right to *forget* what God *remembers*—and God remembers Amalek! Amalek is the dirty well! Amalek is the poisoned root! Amalek is "the mystery of lawlessness—that hidden principle of rebellion against constituted authority" (2 Thess. 2:7a AMPLIFIED NEW TESTAMENT) that is already at work in the world—"who opposeth and exalteth himself above all that is called God, or that is worshiped; so that he as God sitteth in the temple of God, showing himself that he is God" (2 Thess. 2:4). Amalek is that sin principle of satanic origin, which makes you what you are *apart* from what God is, and what you *do* (which God is willing to forgive and forget) stems from what you *are*—*this* you dare not and you must not forget!

Recognize the sinfulness of what you have *done*, and you will recognize the relevance, and your need, of what He did. Remember the sinfulness of what *you are*, and you will remember the relevance, and your need, of what *He is*. God says, "Remember Amalek"!

In the following chapter, we shall discuss together the tragedy of a man who *forgot to remember!*

Chapter IX

The Man Who Forgot To Remember

In the ninth chapter of the First Book of Samuel we are introduced to a promising, lovely young man—winsome, humble, courteous, conscientious, of unusually impressive physique, and one who had a solid sense of responsibility, the one who was ultimately to become the first king of Israel; and yet, at the same time, a young man who was to ruin his life and die a bitter, disappointed old man, because he forgot to remember!

> Samuel also said unto Saul, The LORD sent me to anoint thee to be king over his people, over Israel: now therefore hearken thou unto the voice of the words of the LORD. Thus saith the LORD of hosts, I remember that which Amalek did to Israel, how he laid wait for him in the way, when he came up from Egypt. (1 Sam. 15:1–2)

We have already seen in a previous chapter that sometimes the severest penalty that God can inflict upon His people who reject what they need is to give them what they want; and this was equally true when Israel clamored for a king: "that we also may be like all the nations; and that our king may judge us, and go out before us, and fight our battles" (1 Sam. 8:20).

God Himself was Israel's king, and it was never in the purpose of God that any other should usurp the place of the One to be born of Mary, who should reign over the house of Jacob forever. But the Lord said unto Samuel, "Hearken unto the voice of the people in all that they say unto thee: for they have not rejected thee, but they have rejected me, that I should not reign over them. . . . Now therefore hearken unto their voice: howbeit yet protest solemnly unto them, and show them the manner of the king that shall reign over them" (1 Sam. 8:7, 9). Thus it was that Saul, "a choice young man, and a goodly" (1 Sam. 9:2a) was anointed to be the first king of Israel.

In commissioning Saul to the task, however, Samuel solemnly warned him that if he was to be the earthly representative of Israel's heavenly King, it behooved him to know the mind of God and to do the will of God and to execute the judgments of God. And the very first thing that God had to say to Saul as king of Israel, was this: "I remember that which Amalek did to Israel, how he laid wait for him in the way, when he came up from Egypt. Now go and smite Amalek, and utterly destroy all that they have, and spare them not; but slay both man and woman, infant and suckling, ox and sheep, camel and ass" (1 Sam. 15:2–3).

God was at war with Amalek from generation to generation. There was no good thing in Amalek! There was absolutely no salvable content in Amalek! There was nothing in Amalek upon which God would look with favor. That was God's mind, God's will, and God's judgment concerning Amalek.

But Saul forgot to remember!

Though he smote the Amalekites, Saul "took Agag the king of the Amalekites alive"—a king of Edom, whom God had sentenced to death! He "utterly destroyed all the people with the edge of the sword. But Saul and the people spared

Agag and the best of the sheep, and of the oxen, and of the fatlings, and the lambs, and all that was good—they spared all that was good in what God had totally condemned as bad! ". . . and would not utterly destroy them: but everything that was vile and refuse, that they destroyed utterly" (1 Sam. 15:8–9). Saul presumed to find something good in what God had condemned. This was the sin of Saul.

He kept the *best* of what God hated!

This is the subtle temptation with which you too are confronted, for the Devil will come to you again and again and whisper in your ear that you are not as bad as the Bible makes you out to be, that there is always something good in what you are, apart from what Christ is—that there is always something salvable in human nature, no matter how bad a man may seem to be.

God, it seemed to them, was taking things too far. His judgment upon Amalek seemed to them to be unwarranted, a fanatical exaggeration of the issues; and so, in defiance of God's word, God's mind, God's will, and God's judgment, they tried to discern between good and bad in what God had wholly rejected.

It is comparatively easy to be sorry for what you have done and to recognize the sinfulness of sins committed, but we are by nature loathe to concede the natural depravity of what we are and the total spiritual bankruptcy of man without God. We fall again and again into the error of estimating ourselves without due regard to the ultimate origin of righteousness and the ultimate origin of sinfulness.

Let me remind you again that nothing is good or bad by virtue of what it is. It is good or bad only by virtue of its origin, and that is why you can be so easily deceived and impressed by the pseudo-righteousness and apparent virtue that stem from the self-life, with its perverted bent for simulating what is good.

The apostle voiced his complaint of the Hebrew Christians in the following language:

> Concerning this we have much to say which is hard to explain, since you have become dull in your [spiritual] hearing and sluggish, even slothful [in achieving spiritual insight]. For even though by this time you ought to be teaching others, you actually need some one to teach you over again the very first principles of God's Word. You have come to need milk, not solid food. For every one who continues to feed on milk is obviously inexperienced and unskilled in the doctrine of righteousness, [that is, of conformity to the divine will in purpose, thought and action], for he is a mere infant—not able to talk yet! (Heb. 5:11–13 AMPLIFIED NEW TESTAMENT)

The Hebrew believers had forgotten "first principles"; they were "sluggish in achieving spiritual insight"; they were "unskilled in the doctrine of righteousness." What was the measure of their spiritual immaturity that kept them "on the bottle"? Simply that milk is for babies, and that "strong meat belongeth to them that are of full age, even those who by reason of use have their senses exercised to discern both good and evil" (Heb. 5:14).

They could of course discern between what was obviously good and what was obviously evil—even the youngest child can do that—but because of their ignorance of the fundamental nature of sin (which is every attitude or activity that has its origin other than in God, no matter how pious its context), they were unable to discern between the *genuinely good*, with its origin in God, and the evil in the "good," which has its origin in Satan. "And no marvel; for Satan himself is transformed into an angel of light. Therefore it is no great thing if his ministers also be transformed as the ministers of righteousness; whose end shall be according to their works" (2 Cor. 11:14–15).

In other words, the fact that you are a preacher, the fact that you are a missionary, the fact that you are a Christian worker, the fact that you are a witnessing Christian, does not make *you* spiritual, nor your *activity* righteous—no matter how deep your sense of dedication or the sacrifice involved.

As far as God is concerned, Christ is the preacher, Christ is the missionary, Christ is the Christian worker, Christ is the witnessing Christian. Only what *He* is and what *He* does is righteousness—and what He is and what He does is released through you only by your unrelenting attitude of dependence. This is called faith—and "whatsoever is not of faith is sin" (Rom. 14:23c).

It is a shock to discover that you can go up into the pulpit with a Bible in your hand, preach a sermon entirely scriptural in its content, and yet if this be done in anything other than an attitude of total dependence upon Christ, in the very act of preaching you are committing sin.

This is not milk for babies but meat for the strong, who are "of full age," but "hard to be uttered" (Heb. 5:11), for we have become accustomed to the elaborate machinery of the church, as an organizational enterprise in which carnal activity on the part of Christians is not only tolerated, but solicited—often in sublime sincerity and with a false sense of dedication on the part of those involved, who, being ignorant of the "very first principles of God's Word," are "unskilled in the doctrine of righteousness."

The flesh does not take kindly to an exposure of the phony nature of its righteousness. It will be hurt, offended, indignant, and resentful, and will seek to justify itself.

> Then came the word of the LORD unto Samuel, saying, It repenteth me that I have set up Saul to be king: for he is turned back from following me, and hath not performed my commandments. And it grieved Samuel; and he cried unto the LORD all night. . . . And Samuel came to Saul: and Saul said unto him, Blessed be thou of the LORD: I have performed the commandment of the LORD. And Samuel said, What meaneth

then this bleating of the sheep in mine ears, and the lowing of the oxen which I hear? And Saul said, They have brought them from the Amalekites: for the people spared the best of the sheep and of the oxen, to sacrifice unto the LORD thy God; and the rest we have utterly destroyed. (1 Sam. 15:10–11, 13–15)

The bleating of the sheep and the lowing of the oxen did little to vindicate Saul's claim that he had performed the commandment of the Lord, but symptomatic of the man who "has forgotten to remember," Saul saw no inconsistency in this. Instead, assuming an air of offended innocence, he insisted that he had not only performed the commandment of the Lord, but had done so with *superior judgment*—the fact that the people had spared the best of the sheep and the best of the oxen and the best of the lambs was the only reasonable, sensible, logical, economical thing to do—but of course, only to sacrifice them to the Lord!

Saul said in so many words, "Don't get me wrong! Don't do us the injustice of misjudging our motives! The good that we have found in Amalek, we have kept to dedicate to God." It is a stroke of satanic genius, and one of his most ancient devices, to persuade you piously to dedicate to God all that you presume to find good in the flesh, which God has condemned.

This is the curse of Christendom! This is what paralyzes the activity of the church of Jesus Christ on earth today! In defiance of God's Word, God's mind, God's will, and God's judgment, men everywhere are prepared to dedicate to God what God condemns—the energy of the flesh!

All too characteristic of churchlife today is the bleating of the sheep in the pew and the lowing of the oxen in the pulpit!

No matter how much it may cost you, no matter how much sacrifice it may involve, and no matter how great your enthusiasm or your sincerity, the best that you can salvage from Amalek will be an offering unseasoned with salt, and will be repudiated by God as Saul himself was repudiated. "Then Samuel said unto Saul, Stay, and I will tell thee what the LORD hath said to me this night. . . . Behold, to obey is better than sacrifice, and to hearken than the fat of rams. For rebellion is as the sin of witchcraft, and stubbornness is as iniquity and idolatry. Because thou hast rejected the word of the LORD, he hath also rejected thee from being king" (1 Sam. 15:16a, 22b–23).

God rejected Saul because he forgot to remember!

Instead of the winsome, humble, courteous, thoughtful young man to whom we were first introduced in 1 Samuel 9, he became a bitter, murderous, wicked old man, who could only look back upon a wasted life and say, "I have sinned. . . . Behold, I have played the fool, and have erred exceedingly" (1 Sam. 26:21). He presumed to find good in what God had condemned, and God rejected him.

In his anguish of soul after the death of Samuel, he solicited the aid of a woman with a familiar spirit, and when Samuel appeared, Saul answered him:

> I am sore distressed; for the Philistines make war against me, and God is departed from me, and answereth me no more, neither by prophets, nor by dreams: therefore I have called thee, that thou mayest make known unto me what I shall do. Then said Samuel, Wherefore then dost thou ask of me, seeing the LORD is departed from thee, and is become thine enemy? Because thou obeyedst not the voice of the LORD, nor executedst his fierce wrath upon Amalek, therefore hath the LORD done this thing unto thee this day. (1 Sam. 28:15b–16, 18)

God had said, "Remember Amalek," and Saul forgot to remember! Saul had repudiated God's verdict on Amalek; now he was to learn the hard and bitter way that God's verdict was right. Though you may show mercy to Amalek, Amalek will never show mercy to you!

This, of course, is the key to the Book of Esther; for

Haman, the "enemy of the Jews" who hatched the murderous plot for their total annihilation, was an Agagite—a descendant of Agag, king of the Amalekites, whose life Saul spared (Esth. 3:1).

Saul attempted to commit suicide, but he did not succeed. Just how he died is described in 2 Samuel 1:2b–4: "A man came out of the camp from Saul with his clothes rent. . . . And David said unto him, From whence comest thou? . . . How went the matter? . . . And he answered, That the people are fled from the battle, and many of the people also are fallen and dead; and Saul and Jonathan his son are dead also."

David inquired of this young man how he could be so sure of his facts, and the young man replied, "As I happened by chance upon Mount Gilboa, behold, Saul leaned upon his spear; and, lo, the chariots and horsemen followed hard after him. And when he looked behind him, he saw me, and called unto me. And I answered, Here am I. And he said unto me, Who art thou? And I answered him, *I am an Amalekite*" (2 Sam. 1:6–8, emphasis added).

Oh yes, whenever you are down, there will always be an Amalekite around! In your hour of greatest temptation and despair, "faint and weary," you will always hear his sadistic whisper in your ear, "I am an Amalekite; I am always here when you *need* me! It is my job to hit a man when he is down—and it is my job to destroy him! I am an Amalekite! That is my business!"

Continuing his story to David, the Amalekite said, "He said unto me again, Stand, I pray thee, upon me, and slay me. . . . So I stood upon him, and slew him . . . and I took the crown that was upon his head" (2 Sam. 1:10). He slew him, *and he took his crown!*

You compromise with Amalek at your peril! In your flesh dwells *no good thing*. Spare it if you will, but it will never spare you! Presume to find something good in it, when God has wholly condemned it, and the day will come when it will destroy you and rob you of your crown! God says that no flesh will ever glory in His presence. It can only make your body the Devil's plaything, so that he can be incarnate in all you say and do, robbing Christ of His rightful sovereignty in your humanity, whose life alone constitutes the true and only source of genuine righteousness.

Are you still offering to God the *best* of what God has *condemned?*

With the Promised Land only eleven days' journey away, "then came Amalek," and for forty years they wandered in the wilderness, grieving God in self-imposed poverty, robbed of all that for which they had been redeemed!

Do not be deceived by Amalek! Resist him with the rod of God held high, appropriating the victory already won. Carve your way through his ranks, for this is your victory, even your faith! Go *on* and go *in,* thanking the Lord Jesus for his *life,* as you have learned to thank Him for His *death*—for what He *is,* as you have learned to thank Him for what He *did!* Christ is your Victory!

"Behold, I come quickly: hold that fast which thou hast, *that no man take thy crown!"* (Rev. 3:11, emphasis added).

Chapter X

The Man Who Died Too Young

The Book of Deuteronomy is in some senses one of the saddest books in the Bible, for it is the last will and testament of a disappointed man. It is the record of all that Moses had to say to the children of Israel, on the first day of the eleventh month of the fortieth year of their wanderings in the wilderness. "These be the words which Moses spake unto all Israel on this side Jordan in the wilderness, in the plain over against the Red Sea" (Deut. 1:1a).

On the wrong side of Jordan, and only just on the right side of the Red Sea! And this forty years after Moses had led his people out of Egypt.

Of those who died in the wilderness, it is written, "So we see that they could not enter in because of unbelief'" (Heb. 3:19), and it is a sobering thought to realize that Moses too died in the wilderness, numbered among the "unbelieving believers"—those who had faith enough to get out, but who did not have faith enough to get in.

Moses was a spiritual giant. "And there arose not a prophet since in Israel like unto Moses, whom the LORD knew face to face" (Deut. 34:10). He was unmatched for his sheer, moral integrity—unmatched in his selfless sense of duty, in his tireless concern for the people whom he served, in his nobility of character, and in his humble dedication to God. It would seem that if ever a man deserved to get into Canaan, it was Moses—but he died in the wilderness! "And Moses was an hundred and twenty years old when he died: his eye was not dim, nor his natural force abated" (Deut. 34:7).

There was no physical cause of death. Moses died *too young*, and he was buried *in the wrong place!* "So Moses the servant of the LORD died there in the land of Moab, according to the word of the LORD. And he buried him in a valley in the land of Moab, over against Bethpeor: but no man knoweth of his sepulchre unto this day" (Deut. 34:5–6).

It seems that the lesson that God would have us learn is of such supreme importance and so universal in its application that He purposely chose one of the choicest of His servants, lest any should consider himself to be excused. God loved Moses, and I cannot help but be convinced that he will be numbered among the aristocracy of heaven in the vast company of the redeemed—yet the very severity with which God dealt with him serves only to emphasize the importance that God attaches to the principle he violated.

Add to his nobility of character the fact that Moses was a great leader, a great preacher, a great administrator, a man of immense mental stature, and almost everything else that you or I might seek to emulate, embodying all our highest and holiest ambitions—and you have a man whom one cannot help but admire and respect. And yet in spite of all this, he died a disappointed man! He never entered the land! He was sick of his ministry, sick of the people to whom he ministered, and they were equally sick of him!

You will remember how at the outset of the journey, God had commanded Moses to smite the rock in Horeb, that water might flow for the children of Israel in the thirsty Wilderness of Sin, on the east of the Gulf of Suez. Then some thirty-eight years later, the children of Israel came to the desert of Zin, west of the south end of the Salt Sea, and there was no water for this congregation. In thirty-eight years, all that Moses had succeeded in doing was to lead the people from one geographical location in the desert to another, from the desert of Sin to the desert of Zin. He had changed an "S" into a "Z," and both are made out of a crooked "I"!

No matter how gifted you may be or how great your enthusiasm; no matter what kind of an orator or how dynamic your personality; no matter what your social standing; no matter how popular or famous you may become, the best that you can ever do in the wilderness, with your own life or with the lives of any others to whom you may minister, is to twist the crooked "I" into some new, crooked shape!

Some have imagined that the cure for their spiritual disability is a change of geographical location, a call to a new pastorate, or exchange of field or occupation, but if you are living in the wilderness, you will be as useless in one part of the desert as you are in another!

> And the people chode with Moses, and spake, saying, Would God that we had died when our brethren died before the Lord! And why have ye brought up the congregation of the Lord into this wilderness, that we and our cattle should die there? Wherefore have ye made us to come up out of Egypt, to bring us into this evil place? It is no place of seed, or of figs, or of vines, or of pomegranates; neither is there any water to drink. (Num. 20:3–5)

Having sat under Moses' preaching for nearly forty years, all that they could say of the place to which he had brought them was that it was an evil place—"no place of seed, or of figs, or of vines, or of pomegranates"—as dry and as thirsty as the place where the journey began. Is that the normal Christian life? Is that really all you may expect?

As a pastor or a missionary or a Sunday school teacher, would you like those to whom you have ministered to tell you after thirty-eight years that the place to which you have brought them is an evil place, that it has fallen completely short of anything that you gave them to believe?

The children of Israel knew all about Canaan in their heads, for Moses had preached about it until they were tired of the sound of it—the only thing he did *not* do was to take them there! It is a weary business preaching Canaan in the wilderness! It is language without life, sentiment without substance.

And the Lord came to Moses and said, "Take the rod and gather thou the assembly together, thou and Aaron thy brother, and speak ye unto the rock before their eyes" (Num. 20:8a). What was Moses told to do the first time in Horeb in the Wilderness of Sin? He was told to smite the rock—a picture of Jesus Christ and Him crucified.

What was he told to do now? He was told to *speak* to the rock—a picture of the Lord Jesus Christ risen from the dead and ascended to the Father, who "after He had offered one sacrifice for sins for ever, sat down on the right hand of God" (Heb. 10:12), whose body will never again be broken, and whose blood will never again be shed. "Speak ye unto the rock . . . and it shall give forth his water, and thou shalt bring forth to them water out of the rock."

God's instructions were explicit. The rock was not again to be smitten, for "by one offering he hath perfected for ever them that are sanctified" (Heb. 10:14). We may not now seek the living among the dead, for He is risen and glorified! God said, "Speak ye unto the rock"!

Moses, however, addressed his congregation, "Hear now, ye rebels. . . ." Is that how you would like to speak to *your* congregation, after nearly forty years of ministry? "Hear now, ye rebels; must *we* fetch you water out of this rock?"

No, God did not tell Moses to fetch water out of the rock.

God told Moses to *speak* to the rock, and the rock would *give* all the water that they needed. "For," said the Lord Jesus Christ, "He that believeth on me, . . . out of his [innermost being] shall flow rivers of living water; (but this spake he of the Spirit, whom they that believe on him should receive, for the Holy Ghost was not yet given; because that Jesus was not yet glorified)" (John 7:38–39).

Reconciled to God by His death—the smitten rock—you are to be saved by His life—the living Rock.

The Christian life is the life that the Lord Jesus Christ lived nineteen hundred years ago, *lived now by Him in you!* All things that pertain to life and godliness have been given to you in Him, as a partaker of the divine nature (2 Peter 1:3–4).

"And Moses lifted up his hand, and with his rod he smote the rock twice . . . " (Num. 20:11a)—the rock that might only be smitten once! He left Christ on the cross! In the language of the illustration, he was a man with only half a message. He declared the crucified Christ, but not the risen Lord! And a man with only half a message does only half a job! He got them out, but he did not get them in!

Moses preached his people to tears of repentance again and again—but he never got them in! He wooed and he threatened them, rebuked and encouraged them, and with tireless integrity, he stood in the gap and interceded for them; but they returned again and again to their backsliding. He never got them in!

This should be a solemn warning to each one of us, for we too, if we preach only half a message, will do only half a job. We too will be loaded with a bunch of spiritual babies, and with Moses, it will be our unhappy lot to fill their bottles and push them around in the wilderness! We may succeed in getting them out, but we shall never succeed in getting them in!

And the Lord said to Moses and Aaron, "Because ye

believed me not, to sanctify me in the eyes of the children of Israel, therefore ye shall not bring this congregation into the land which I have given them" (Num. 20:12).

"Because ye believed me not"—an "unbelieving believer." This was the sin of Moses, a man who died too young and who was buried in the wrong place.

It is almost disconcerting to witness the severity of God's judgment upon this mighty warrior; but he broke the type, he violated the first principle of victorious Christian living— *Christ in you*, the hope of glory! He never got beyond Jesus Christ and Him crucified. In the language of the Old Testament, his gospel was never more than "Come to Jesus and have your sins forgiven." It was a message of "heaven some day, but the wilderness now!" He left Christ on the cross! He knew nothing of the Saving Life of Christ.

It is our solemn responsibility, not only to present the Lord Jesus Christ as the One Who died historically to redeem sinners through His atoning sacrifice, but as a contemporary experience now—as the living Rock, the source of that "pure river of water of life, clear as crystal, proceeding out of the throne of God and of the Lamb" (Rev. 22:1).

I am deeply grateful to those who introduced me to the Lord Jesus Christ as my Redeemer, but the one thing that they did not make adequately clear to me (because in all probability it was inadequately clear to them) was that the Christ who died *for* me, rose again to live *in* me. So, knowing Christ experientially only as the Way, it took seven weary years to come to know Him as my Life.

At the age of nineteen, training at London University to become a doctor in order to serve as a missionary in Africa, I knew that my life as a Christian was ineffective. I did not know of one single soul whom it had been my privilege to lead to Christ. I engaged in more than my share of Christian activity, and with genuine enthusiasm, but I knew that if I ever went as a missionary to Africa, I would be just as useless there.

It was out of a deep sense of need, as I despaired of my Christian life, that I made the startling discovery that for seven years I had missed the whole point of my salvation, that Christ had not died just to save me from hell and one day get me to heaven, but that I might become available to Him—for Him to live His life through me.

For all those years I had known only the shadow of the smitten Rock in Horeb, but now at last in the bright light of day, I stepped out by faith to speak to the living Rock, and life for me as a Christian was transformed; the rivers of living water began to flow.

God gave me nothing new. I had simply discovered what I already had, Christ in all His fullness *in me*, "the hope of glory."

The sad thing is that it is all too possible to become accustomed to living in the wilderness, especially when we are surrounded by wilderness Christians, and it is almost with dismay that we read that Moses, who once told Joshua to go out and fight with Amalek, "sent messengers from Kadesh unto the king of Edom, Thus saith thy brother Israel" (Num. 20:14b).

It seems that after thirty-eight years Moses had come to terms with Amalek. But this is axiomatic, for it is the living, risen Lord who must take the place of that old Adamic nature; but if you know Him only as the smitten Rock, a crucified Redeemer, no matter how grateful you may be to Him, and no matter how strong the urge to follow in His ways, you will, like the foolish Galatians, "having begun in the Spirit," try to be "made perfect by the flesh." You will have to come to terms with Amalek and call him your brother, for you will know of nothing that can take his place.

However, although Moses' attitude toward Amalek had

changed, the attitude of Amalek toward Moses had not changed. "Edom said unto him, Thou shalt not pass by me, lest I come out against thee with the sword." In other words, said Amalek—"thirty-eight years ago I withstood you to your face, and I have not changed *my* mind—I withstand you still! Thou shalt not pass!" It was his business to keep God's people out of Canaan. "Thus Edom [Esau, Amalek] refused to give Israel passage through his border: wherefore Israel turned away from him" (Num. 20:21). Where was the rod held high? Where was their God-given victory? God had commanded them to go north—and they turned south! God said, "Go on"—and they went back!

> . . . We compassed mount Seir many days. And the LORD spake unto me, saying, Ye have compassed this mountain long enough: turn you northward. And command thou the people, saying, Ye are to pass through the coast of your brethren the children of Esau, which dwell in Seir; and they shall be afraid of you: take ye good heed unto yourselves therefore: Meddle not with them; for I will not give you of their land, no, not so much as a footbreadth; because I have given mount Seir unto Esau for a possession. (Deut. 2:1c–5)

There was to be no possession for Israel in the land of Edom, and they were not to meddle with the children of Esau. They were to go on northward, onward into the land which God had given them, and their enemies would be afraid of them. But alas, it was the children of Israel who were afraid, and they "journeyed from Kadesh, and came unto mount Hor. . . . And they journeyed from mount Hor by the way of the Red Sea, to compass the land of Edom: and the soul of the people was much discouraged because of the way" (Num. 20:22b; 21:4).

It was at this point that they crossed the brook Zered in the direction of Moab and Ammon, *on the wrong side* of Jordan, which now lay between them and the land of promise, and, said Moses, "The space in which we came from Kadesh-Barnea [from where the twelve spies were sent into Canaan], until we were come over the brook Zered, was thirty and eight years"—thwarted from start to finish by Amalek, who refused to give Israel passage through his borders.

Just suppose that, with the rod held high, Israel had obeyed God's word in Kadesh-Barnea, separated as it was from the Promised Land only by a small piece of the land of Edom! Just suppose that then they had listened to the "two," instead of to the "ten," and had gone on and gone in—there would have been no Jordan to cross!

There was no Jordan between Kadesh-Barnea and Canaan. Jordan lay to the east, and the crossing of the Jordan only became a necessity in the experience of Israel because instead of going *through*, they went *round* the land of Edom.

In forty years of compromise, of unbelief and disobedience, the children of Israel had forgotten what God had tried to teach them in their miraculous deliverance from Egypt, bringing them by faith through the place of death, the Red Sea, and raising them again into newness of life, so that this lesson had to be learned all over again in Jordan.

How true this is to Christian experience. If only we could grasp at the outset the deeper significance of the Cross, that Christ not only died for us, but that we died with Him, that He rose again to live in the power of His Holy Spirit within us, and that we are to be partakers of Christ now, as the children of Israel should have been partakers of the land then! (Heb. 3:14). Then we could get out and get out quickly, and we could get in and get in quickly, and begin to explore the land all at once, and we would never have to learn the true significance of the Cross a second time.

Unfortunately, because of the stubborn nature of the human heart, because of the deep roots of the flesh within the area of our human personality, it often takes months and years and sometimes a lifetime before a Christian is brought to the place where he can relearn at Jordan what he should have learned at the Red Sea.

Sometimes people talk about a second blessing, and I know what they mean, and I will not argue with them—but it is not really a second blessing. It is simply a rediscovery of the first blessing!

When you come to know Jesus Christ in the power of His resurrection, you receive absolutely nothing new from God; you simply discover and begin to enjoy experientially what you received from God the day that you were redeemed; the tragedy is that you can live for ten, twenty, or fifty years or more, having all that God can give you in Jesus Christ and yet live in self-imposed poverty—out, but not in—and that is why Jordan so often, unfortunately, is necessary.

It is the place where, under Joshua, God had to re-teach the children of Israel what, under Moses, the children of Israel had forgotten. "Now after the death of Moses the servant of the Lord it came to pass, that the Lord spake unto Joshua the son of Nun, Moses' minister, saying, Moses my servant is dead; now therefore arise, go over this Jordan, thou, and all this people, unto the land which I do give to them, even to the children of Israel" (Josh. 1:1–2).

The use of the word "therefore" implies the conclusion of an argument. It speaks of cause and effect, and God said to Joshua, "Moses my servant is dead; go, therefore . . . ." In other words, "*Because* Moses my servant is dead—*therefore* go!"

Can it really be true that the final obstacle to the onward march of God's people into their inheritance was Moses himself? That the man who *built* the Church in the Wilderness was the man who *buried* it in the wilderness? That there could be no spiritual change of climate until he was out of the way? This, it seems, is the inescapable conclusion to which we are forced.

You may think that I am being too rough on Moses, that it is not fair to blame him. You may argue in his defense that the children of Israel did not *want* to get in. I ask you a simple question. Did they want to get out?

> And when Pharaoh drew nigh, the children of Israel lifted up their eyes, and, behold, the Egyptians marched after them; and they were sore afraid: and the children of Israel cried out unto the LORD. And they said unto Moses, Because there were no graves in Egypt, hast thou taken us away to die in the wilderness? Wherefore hast thou dealt thus with us, to carry us forth out of Egypt? Is not this the word that we did tell thee in Egypt, saying, Let us alone, that we may serve the Egyptians? For it had been better for us to serve the Egyptians, than that we should die in the wilderness. (Exod. 14:10–12)

No, the record is clear—they did *not* want to get out. It was in spite of their protests that Moses led them out of Egypt. Had they had their way, they would have stayed there. "Let us alone," they said, "that we may serve the Egyptians," but somehow Moses knew how to teach them the kind of faith that gets out, though he did not know how to teach them the kind of faith that gets in. "And Moses said unto the people, Fear ye not, stand still, and see the salvation of the LORD, which he will show to you today: for the Egyptians whom ye have seen today, ye shall see them again no more for ever. The LORD shall fight for you, and ye shall hold your peace. . . . And the people feared the LORD, and believed the LORD, and his servant Moses (Exod. 14:13–14, 31b).

Why is it that a man who could lead an unwilling people out was unable to lead an unwilling people in? This is the problem that confronts so many who enjoy a measure of success in their evangelistic activity, but whose converts are of such poor spiritual caliber—who find it comparatively easy to precipitate the crisis of decision, but are baffled by the ensuing lack of spiritual substance in those who have made profession of faith.

It is to the solution of this problem that this book is dedicated.

Forgive me if I have seemed to be unduly severe in my treatment of Moses. Believe me, I have the deepest admiration for this mighty man of God, and it is evidence of the high esteem in which God held him that he was numbered among those who stood with the Lord Jesus upon the Mount of Transfiguration, when at last he was allowed into the land.

I believe that God deliberately chose this noble man, through whom to teach us this essential lesson, that all of us might be without excuse.

God would have us know without any shadow of ambiguity that no degree of human excellence can ever be a substitute for His dear Son. Moses did his best! His very, very best—but this was the mistake that Moses made! For God was waiting to do *God's* best, to *give* what only can be *given*, from the risen, living Rock.

The Rock that God smites once, let no man smite again!— or die too young! When God says speak, then speak! God will do the rest!

"This is the work of God *that ye believe* on him whom he hath sent" (John 6:29b, emphasis added).

"O come, let us sing unto the Lord: let us make a joyful noise to the rock of our salvation. Let us come before his presence with thanksgiving, and make a joyful noise unto him with psalms. For the Lord is a great God, and a great King above all gods" (Ps. 95:1–3).

Chapter XI

The Man With the Sword in His Hand

The fundamental characteristic of truth is its consistency.

In the face of every known and unknown fact, truth must remain inviolably consistent. It is final and absolute. Circumstance cannot change truth. If circumstance compels you to re-think previous conclusions, and if honesty, in the light of new information, compels you to change your convictions, it does not mean that the truth has changed—it simply means that you never knew the truth and that circumstance or additional information are compelling you to recognize the fact.

In His prayer to the Father for those who believe on Him, the Lord Jesus said, "Sanctify them through thy truth: thy word is truth" (John 17:17). Truth is not academic. It is the ultimate principle of life, and sanctification is this principle in action—truth in action!

This was the perfection of the Manhood of the Lord Jesus. He was The Truth—incarnate and its final exegesis.

Truth obeyed in the human heart identifies the believer instantly with Jesus Christ. He said, "Every one that is of the truth heareth my voice" (John 18:37c), and again, "If ye continue in my word, then are ye my disciples indeed; and ye shall know the truth, and the truth shall make you free" (John 8:31b–32).

Man's spiritual emancipation takes place when he returns to truth—that is to say, when he returns to basic first principles, and these have never changed.

We may miss them, we may depart from them, we may misinterpret them, but God's principles do not change. God does not need new methods. He does not need a new technique. He uses any means, any method, any technique. That is immaterial. It is purely secondary. All that is accomplished to God's ultimate satisfaction and of eternal worth, no matter what the means, is always the consequence of a return to first principles.

That is why, all down the history of the church, every spiritual awakening and every mighty movement of God has been the consequence of a return to the basic teachings of the Bible, and inevitably, in reverse, such a genuine spiritual awakening has always produced Bible-believing Christians.

This is one of the main lessons that we learn from the Book of Joshua. "Every place that the sole of your foot shall tread upon, that have I given unto you, as I said unto Moses" (Josh. 1:3).

Forty years had passed since God had brought the children of Israel out of Egypt, and Moses was dead; but God had not changed His mind. "Hath he said, and shall he not do it? or hath he spoken, and shall he not make it good?" (Num. 23:19b). The principle that God employed in bringing them out was the principle that God intended to employ in bringing them in, and God was simply waiting for the man who would return to this principle. "As I was with Moses [in bringing the children of Israel out of Egypt] so I will be with thee [in bringing them into Canaan]. . . . Have not I commanded thee?"—that is why! "Be strong and of a good courage; be not afraid, neither be thou dismayed; for the

LORD thy God is with thee withersoever thou goest"—that is
how! That is the *why* and the *how* of all spiritual activity,
and this is all you need to know.

Why? God told me to.

How? The God who told me to is with me.

This is the principle that the Lord Jesus Himself demonstrated. "For I do always those things which please Him." In
other words, in all that He did at any given moment, the
Lord Jesus could say, "He told me to." And because of this
fact, He could go on to say, "And he that sent me is with me:
the Father hath not left me alone." In other words, "The One
who told me to is with me" (John 8:29).

"Then Joshua commanded the officers of the people,
saying, Pass through the host, and command the people,
saying, Prepare you victuals; for within three days ye shall
pass over this Jordan, to go in to possess the land, which
the LORD your God giveth you to possess it" (Josh. 1:10–11).
Had he been alive to hear this message from Joshua to the
people, a lesser man than Moses might well have said, with
all the bitterness of sour grapes, "Is this swollen-headed
young upstart going to try to do in three days what I could
not do in forty years?" And the answer, of course, would
have been quite simple. Joshua was going to *try* to do
nothing—he had simply returned to the first principles!

Moses was the man who *tried*, and he gave them the law
without the land! Joshua was the man who *trusted*, and he
gave them the land in which to practice the law!

And on the third day, early in the morning, they were in!

Does this remind you of anything? What happened on the
third day early in the morning? Jesus Christ rose again
from the dead! And this is the land—to know Him in the
power of His resurrection.

We were buried therefore with Him by the baptism into death,
so that just as Christ was raised from the dead by the glorious
[power] of the Father, so we too might habitually live and

behave in newness of life. For if we have become one with Him by sharing a death like His, we shall also be [one with Him in sharing] His resurrection [by a new life lived for God]. (Rom. 6:4—5 AMPLIFIED NEW TESTAMENT)

If then you have been raised with Christ [to a new life, thus sharing His resurrection from the dead], aim at and seek the [rich, eternal treasures] that are above, where Christ is, seated at the right hand of God. For [as far as this world is concerned] you have died, and your [new, real] life is hid with Christ in God. (Col. 3:1, 3 AMPLIFIED NEW TESTAMENT)

[For my determined purpose is] that I may know Him. . . . And that I may in that same way come to know the power outflowing from His resurrection [which it exerts over believers]. . . . That if possible I may attain to the [spiritual and moral] resurrection [that lifts me] out from among the dead [even while in the body]. (Phil. 3:10—11 AMPLIFIED NEW TESTAMENT)

Yes, as we have seen again and again, the land of Canaan is nothing less than the believer's enjoyment, on earth, of the resurrection life of Jesus Christ.

Remembering that of the twelve spies sent by Moses, ten were duds who served only to discourage the heart of the people (Deut. 1:28a), Joshua streamlined his battle plans and sent only two men to spy secretly, saying, "Go view the land, even Jericho" (Josh. 2:1b).

Information reached the ears of the king of Jericho, whose intelligence service appears to have been commendably efficient, and but for the timely action of the harlot Rahab, the spies might have come to an untimely end. She hid them on the roof beneath the stalks of the flax and sent their pursuers on a false trail.

It was from this woman the spies made their amazing discovery:

And she said unto the men, I know that the LORD hath given you the land, and that your terror is fallen upon us, and that all the inhabitants of the land faint because of you. For we have heard how the LORD dried up the water of the Red Sea for you, when ye came out of Egypt; and what ye did unto the two kings of the Amorites, that were on the other side of Jordan, Sihon and Og, whom ye utterly destroyed. And as soon as we had heard these things, our hearts did melt, neither did there remain any more courage in any man, because of you: for the LORD your God, he is God in heaven above, and in earth beneath. (Josh. 2:9-11)

The spies made the startling discovery that already for forty years the inhabitants of Canaan had been a defeated foe! They had conceded victory to Israel from the day that they had heard how the Lord dried up the water of the Red Sea for them, when they came out of Egypt. Their hearts had melted and there was no more courage in any of them. They had become convinced that the God of Israel was God in heaven above and in earth beneath—that He was as competent to get His people in as He was competent to get His people out. The only thing that had amazed them was that Israel had taken so long to *take* what God had given!

The spies discovered that for forty years in the wilderness, Israel had been fighting a battle already lost, instead of enjoying in Canaan a victory already won!

This is the discovery that you too will make when by faith you obey first principles, the discovery that you have been defrauding yourself—maybe for ten, twenty, thirty, forty, or fifty years—of a victory that Christ won over nineteen hundred years ago, when He rose again from the dead that He might live His life in you.

So the two spies hurried back to Joshua to tell him the exciting news: "Truly the Lord hath delivered into our hands all the land; for even all the inhabitants of the country do faint because of us. . . . And the LORD said unto Joshua, This day will I begin to magnify thee in the sight of all Israel, that they may know that, as I was with Moses, so I will be with thee" (Josh. 2:24; 3:7).

So Joshua gathered all the people to him. He wanted them to know that a new chapter was being opened in the history of Israel, that life for them could never be the same again.

His language was the language of victory, and his faith became infectious. He said, "Hereby ye shall know that the living God is among you, and that he will without fail drive out from before you the Canaanites. . . . Behold the ark of the covenant of the LORD of all the earth passeth over before you into Jordan" (Josh. 3:10–11).

In so many words, Joshua said, "You have been living for forty years in the wilderness as though your God were dead, but you are going to live from now on knowing that your God is alive."

Ignoring what they say, and what they sing, and what they pray, countless Christians *live* as though God were dead—and the church of Jesus Christ needs above everything else to re-discover the fact that God is alive, and to act as though He were!

Suppose that God were to die tonight! Would it really make any difference to the way you live your Christian life tomorrow? For all you *really* count upon Him as you go about your daily business or even do your Christian work, would you notice any difference? Would it make the slightest difference next Sunday in the services in your place of worship, if God were to die tonight? Or would it be business as usual? Would anybody know if nobody told them? Or would the whole machine grind on, with the people in the pew, the parson in the pulpit, and the special offering for the building fund! Nobody ever told them that God was dead!

If we dare to face the hard, cold-blooded truth, we would have to admit today that there is so little in the life of our churches, so little in the activity of so many of our missionary societies and Christian organizations that cannot be explained in terms of man's ab....y and promotional activity, that few would cease to function if God were dead.

We see the evidence of this all around us, in so many enterprises that years ago came into being under the inspiration of Spirit-filled men of God, but which organizationally have slowly outgrown their spiritual content, until nothing of spiritual life remains, and God is no longer consulted in their counsels—but they do not cease to function! They continue to exist, but they do not live. Of these, as of the church in Sardis, God would say, "I know your record and what you are doing; you are supposed to be alive, but [in reality] you are dead" (Rev. 3:1b AMPLIFIED NEW TESTAMENT).

This, however, under Joshua was no longer to be the experience of the children of Israel. They were to know and to enjoy the fact that the living God was among them.

"When ye see the ark of the covenant of the Lord your God, and the priests the Levites bearing it, then ye shall remove from your place, and go after it. Yet there shall be a space between you and it, about two thousand cubits by measure: come not near unto it, that ye may know the way by which ye must go: for ye have not passed this way heretofore" (Josh. 3:3—4). Without enlarging upon the fact, we should note that the ark represented God's covenant with His people, and what was in it represented the spiritual content of their faith and God's purpose for their lives. And the ark was to go before them, with a space between it and them.

What a valuable lesson there is for us to learn in this. They were to keep well back from the ark, that they might know the way, and follow it wherever it went. Had they surrounded the ark, nobody would have known the way. There would have been nothing but confusion, with about fifty sub-committees all deliberating the issue!

They were to give God room to maneuver in time and space; they were not to crowd in on the situation, but to keep well back. The Bible records for us so many tragic blunders committed by good, earnest, sincere, well-meaning men in a hurry, who acted precipitately under the pressure of circumstance.

Learn to give God room to maneuver. Learn to be still and to know that He is God. You do not have the right to panic! If you are solidly convinced that God is the arbiter of your affairs, you will never be anxious. "Commit thy way unto the LORD, trust also in Him, and he will bring it to pass [act]. . . . Rest in the LORD, and wait patiently for Him" (Ps. 37:5, 7a).

God knows the way! Remember what God said to Joshua, "Every place that the sole of your foot shall tread upon, that have I given unto you." It was to be one step at a time. "There shall not any man be able to stand before thee all the days of thy life." It was to be one day at a time. One step at a time and one day at a time. This is the daily walk of the man of God. Hurry at your own peril, "for ye have not passed this way heretofore."

This could hardly have been said of the children of Israel in their wanderings in the wilderness, for they had traveled round and round in circles. There was hardly a grain of sand they did not know by name, nor a cactus bush upon which they had not sat! But this was to be a new experience. It was to be the daily exploration of the *land*, with new discoveries to be made and new areas to be possessed with every step they took.

Some wilderness Christians get very angry when you tell them about the indwelling life of the risen Lord Jesus Christ in all His sovereignty, and they are most indignant when you suggest that they have never been this way before.

"Do you mean to tell me," they will say, "that after forty years I still don't know how to live the Christian life?"—and they will shoot off all hot round the collar, to make another accelerated circuit round the course, and try to make up in speed what they lack in direction! If you insist on going round in circles, you will always get back to where you started, and the faster you go, the quicker you will get there!

"And the people passed over right against Jericho. And the priests that bare the ark of the covenant of the LORD stood firm on dry ground in the midst of Jordan, and all the Israelites passed over on dry ground, until all the people were passed clean over Jordan" (Josh. 3:16c–17)—they were out and they were in!

Joshua commanded twelve men, one out of every tribe, each to bring a stone from out of the midst of Jordan, from the place where the priests' feet had stood firm, and these he pitched in Gilgal, where Israel camped on their first day in the land. "And he spake unto the children of Israel, saying, When your children shall ask their fathers in time to come, saying, What mean these stones? Then ye shall let your children know, saying, Israel came over this Jordan on dry land" (Josh. 4:21–22).

These stones were to remind the children of Israel of the principle to which they had returned, for as God had dried up the waters of the Red Sea, so God had dried up the waters of Jordan. "That all the people of the earth might know the hand of the LORD, that it is mighty" (Josh. 4:24a).

How did they get through the Red Sea? They put their feet in the water and stood still. Why? God had told them to! What happened? God divided the waters and they passed through on dry ground. Why? God said they would!

How did they get through Jordan? They put their feet in the waters of Jordan and stood still. Why? God told them to! What happened? God divided the waters and they went through on dry land. Why? God said they would!

How much more difficult then was it to get in than to get out? No more difficult! It was as easy to get in as it was to get out. And how long did it take them to discover this? Forty years!

"As you have therefore received Christ Jesus the Lord, so

walk ye in him" (Col. 2:6). How are you to walk in Jesus Christ? As you received Him. How did you receive Him? By faith. Was that very difficult?

How then are you to walk in Him? By faith! Will that be any more difficult?

As you have learned to thank Him for His death, so you thank Him for His life, humbly assuming that He lives in you, as you have already humbly assumed that He died for you. Is that not simple? And how long has it taken you to find this out?

Remember, He does not give you strength—He *is* your strength! He does not give you victory—He *is* your victory! He cannot be your *life* without being *all you need*, for "in him dwelleth all the fulness of the Godhead bodily. And ye are complete in him" (Col. 2:9—10a).

Then count upon the fact—and stop asking for what you have!

"And the children of Israel encamped in Gilgal, and kept the passover on the fourteenth day of the month at even in the plains of Jericho. And they did eat of the old corn of the land on the morrow after the passover, unleavened cakes, and parched corn in the selfsame day" (Josh. 5:10—11). And so for the first time in forty years, they had legitimate grounds to celebrate the "day to be remembered in a land to be possessed," for that day, God had "rolled away the reproach of Egypt from off them."

For the first time the people began to enjoy that for which they had been redeemed, and their salvation made sense.

"And it came to pass, when Joshua was by Jericho, that he lifted up his eyes and looked, and, behold, there stood a man over against him with his sword drawn in his hand: and Joshua went unto him, and said unto him, Art thou for us, or for our adversaries?" (Josh. 5:13).

Joshua went out to make a reconnaissance of the walled city of Jericho and to draw up plans for tackling the first major task that confronted him, but as he did so he became strangely aware of the presence of a Man—a Man with His sword drawn in His hand—and in so many words, he said to Him, "Whose side are you on? Are you on our side or are you on their side?"

"And He said, Nay; but as captain of the host of the LORD am I now come" (Josh. 5:14a). The Man with the sword in His hand said, in effect, "I am neither on your side nor am I on their side. I have come as Captain of the host of the Lord. I have not come to take sides—I have come to take over!"

In the land, you do not make your plans, hoping that God will be on your side! Jericho is no longer *your* problem! It is God's problem, and you come under the supreme jurisdiction of the Man with the sword in His hand.

"And Joshua fell on his face to the earth, and did worship, and said unto him, What saith my lord unto his servant? And the captain of the LORD'S host said unto Joshua, Loose thy shoe from off thy foot; for the place whereon thou standest is holy. And Joshua did so" (Josh. 5:14b–15). He knew that he was in the presence of God, the God of the burning bush. There had been no change of principle, for God does not change. It was simply that Joshua had to re-learn what Moses forgot.

God does not take sides—He only takes over!
Including your Jericho!
Are you prepared for this?

Chapter XII

Victory and Vocation

Jesus Christ Himself is the final exegesis of all truth. He is all that we need to know about God, and He is all that we need to know about man. If "to live in the land" is to enjoy that quality of life which is made possible only by virtue of allowing Him to live His life in us, we could not do better than to conclude our studies in this book by turning our eyes again upon Him, whose perfect humanity is matched only by His perfect deity.

> Jesus knowing that the Father had given all things into his hands, and that he was come from God, and went to God; he riseth from supper, and laid aside his garments; and took a towel, and girded himself. After that he poureth water into a basin, and began to wash the disciples' feet, and to wipe them with the towel wherewith he was girded. (John 13:3–5)

The Lord Jesus knew that the Father had given all things into His hands—that as a man, all the illimitable resources of deity had been vested in His person. That is the first thing I would like you to notice, for although He was in the beginning with God, and was God, and *is* God—and although as the creative Word, all things were made by Him—when He came to this earth, in the very fullest sense of the term, He became man; but He became man as God intended man to be, and behaved as God intended man to behave, walking day by day in that relationship to the Father which God had always intended should exist between man and Himself.

> Who, although being essentially one with God and in the form of God [possessing the fullness of the attributes which make God God], did not think this equality with God was a thing to be eagerly grasped or retained; but stripped Himself [of all privileges and rightful dignity] so as to assume the guise of a servant (slave), in that He became like men and was born a human being. And after He had appeared in human form He abased and humbled Himself [still further] and carried His obedience to the extreme of death, even the death of [the] cross! (Phil. 2:6–8 AMPLIFIED NEW TESTAMENT)

We shall enlarge upon this as we proceed, but I mention it in particular now, that we may recognize the fact that in all His activities, in all His reactions, in every step He took and in every word He said, in every decision He made, He did so *as man*, even though He was God. He knew that in His perfection *as man*, the Father had vested in Him all that God intended to vest in man—all things! In other words, man in perfection has an unlimited call upon the inexhaustible supplies of deity.

To put it another way, all the inexhaustible supplies of God are *available* to the man who is *available* to all the inexhaustible supplies of God; and Jesus Christ was that Man! He was Man in perfection—totally, unrelentingly, unquestioningly available—and that is why there was available to Him all that to which He was available—all things! Now that is a principle to which we shall need to return on many occasions.

A second thing is this: He knew that He was come from God—that is to say, His divine origin; and He knew that He went to God—that is to say, His divine destination. He came from God and He was going to God. This is reiterated in

John 16:27–28: "The Father himself loveth you, because you have loved me, and have believed that I came out from God. I came forth from the Father, and am come into the world: again, I leave the world, and go to the Father." *From* the Father *to* the Father, and in between, thirty-three years on earth *in* the world; a parenthesis in time, as it were, with eternity on one side and eternity on the other, and a short, limited time space—thirty-three years—on earth. He was in the beginning with God in the past—*of* the Father. He was to be eternally with God in the future—*to* the Father. But in the meantime for thirty-three years He must play the role of Man in perfection, and as such He knew that the Father had given all things into His hands—that He had come from God and was going to God!

One might imagine that at this stage we are poised upon the threshold of some sensational event or some sensational utterance; but instead it comes almost as an anti-climax to read that He rose from supper, laid aside His garments, took a towel, girded Himself, poured water into a basin, and washed His disciples' feet. With all the illimitable resources of deity—of divine origin and divine destination—He washed His disciples' feet, something that was too lowly even for His own disciples, who felt themselves above such condescension.

Did He need all the illimitable resources of deity to wash His disciples' feet? *God* on His knees!

The Lord Jesus Christ was demonstrating a principle, that it is not the *nature* of what you are doing that determines its spirituality, but the *origin* of what you are doing. Not its nature, but its origin!

There was never a moment in the life of the Lord Jesus that was without divine significance, because there was never anything He did, never anything He said, never any step He took, that did not spring from a divine origin—nothing that was not the activity of the Father in and through the Son. Thirty-three years of availability to the

Father, that the Father in and through Him might implement the program that had been established and agreed on between the Father and the Son before ever the world was.

Why did the Father give all things into His hands? Because Jesus Christ was completely Man. And He was completely Man because He was completely available! For the first time since Adam fell into sin, there was on earth a Man as God intended man to be!

Which of His activities were the more spiritual, the Sermon on the Mount, the raising of Lazarus from the dead, or the washing of His disciples' feet? The answer, of course, is that no one activity was more spiritual than another, for *all* had their origin in the Father, who acted through the Son. "I do always those things that please Him" (John 8:29b). Spirituality in man is his availability to God for His divine action, and the *form* of this activity is irrelevant. If it pleases you, always and only, to do what pleases God—you can do as you please!

Let us us consider two passages in the epistle to the Hebrews, which at first sight appear a little strange. "But we see Jesus, who was made a little lower than the angels for the suffering of death, crowned with glory and honour; that he by the grace of God should taste death for every man. For it became him, for whom *are* all things, and by whom *are* all things, in bringing many sons unto glory, to make the captain of their salvation perfect through sufferings" (Heb. 2:9—10). It was necessary for God the Father to make Him, God the Son, perfect through suffering.

Bearing that in mind, we now turn to Hebrews 5:8—9, where it says, "Though he were a Son, yet learned he obedience by the things which he suffered; and being made perfect, he became the author of eternal salvation unto all them that obey him." In the second chapter it says that it was necessary for the Father to make Him perfect; in the fifth chapter it says that "being made perfect" He "became the author of eternal salvation." In other words, His "becoming" the author of our eternal salvation appears to have been dependent upon the successful conclusion of a process whereby He was "made" perfect.

He was "made perfect" in order to "become." Does that strike you as being a little bit strange? Was the Lord Jesus *not* perfect, that He needed to be made perfect? Was there, after all, in the Lord Jesus some blemish that needed to be rectified, some imperfection that had to be remedied, that He might "become the author of eternal salvation unto all them that obey Him"?

Here another principle is involved. The perfection of the Lord Jesus Christ was twofold. The Bible leaves us in absolutely no doubt about the absolute perfection of His person. We are told that God "made him to be sin for us, who knew no sin; that we might be made the righteousness of God in him" (2 Cor. 5:21). We are told that when the Father looked down from heaven before the beginning of Christ's public ministry, in reviewing as it were the first thirty years that Christ had lived as Man on earth—as a little child, as a son, as an apprentice, as a craftsman, as a neighbor, as a citizen—the Father said, "This is my beloved Son, in whom [in all these areas of human relationship] I am well pleased" (Matt. 3:17b).

Perfect! Perfect in person; but although He was perfect in person, He had to be made perfect in *vocation*—by the process of obedience through time, because as Man, perfect in person, He could only be perfect in vocation by the fulfillment of that purpose for which He had been incarnate, in an attitude of total dependence *upon* the Father, expressed in total obedience *to* the Father. Being perfect in His person, he was "made perfect" in His vocation.

Was He perfect in vocation—in that purpose for which He was incarnate and came into this world—as a baby at Bethlehem? Had He been able to speak as a baby, could He then have said, "It is finished!"? As a boy of twelve when His mother found Him in the Temple, and He said to her, "Wist ye not that I must be about my Father's business?" (Luke 2:49b)—was He perfect in vocation? When He preached the Sermon on the Mount or when He raised Lazarus from the dead or even when He washed His disciples' feet—was He perfect in vocation? When He was in the Garden of Gethsemane, sweating as it were great drops of blood—was He perfect in vocation?

It was no idle boast when He spoke to Peter in the presence of Judas and of those who arrested Him, and said, "Thinkest thou that I cannot now pray to my Father, and he shall presently give me more than twelve legions of angels?" (Matt. 26:53)—but had He spoken that word, and had the Father sent twelve legions of angels, and had He bypassed the Cross—would He have been perfect in the vocation for which He was incarnate? No indeed, and you and I would today be of all men most miserable, for there would not have been established any ground for redemption that could have satisfied the eternal, unrelenting, and absolute demands of God's holiness—but we are told that He set His face like a flint, He turned neither to the right hand nor to the left—He was "obedient unto death, even the death of the cross" (Phil. 2:8).

He was completely submissive to that purpose to which the Father was committed in Him, and as He hung upon the cross, the heavens were darkened as though in anguish for the Son of God for the space of three hours, and just before He bowed His head and died, He was able to cry (and know that it was true) with a voice that reverberated in victory across the city of Jerusalem—"It is finished!" In that moment of time He was "made perfect" in His *vocation* as He had always been perfect in His *person*, and He "became the author of eternal salvation to them that obey him." That was the nature of *His* victory, and that is the nature of *all* Christian victory! The positive fulfillment of the divine end through a man, *wholly* available to God!

The Lord Jesus did not live a victorious life just because

He did not commit sin in the negative sense, just because He did not tell lies, just because He was not dishonest, just because He never committed adultery or was never envious—that was not the nature of His victory. If that had been the nature of His victory and that the criterion of His righteousness, He could have stayed in heaven and been all that! The nature of His victory was that as Man, He positively implemented that purpose for which He was incarnate; that apart from not doing the things that were *wrong*, He positively *accomplished* all that was *right;* that His absolute availability to the Father for every moment of thirty-three years enabled the Father in His deity to do in and through the Son in His humanity all that had been agreed on between the Father and the Son before ever the world was.

A sense of vocation declares, "The things concerning me have an end!" (Luke 22:37c), and the language of victory cries, "It is finished!" (John 19:30).

I want you to notice *how* Jesus Christ made Himself available to the Father. Hebrews 10:5–7 in the *Amplified New Testament* reads, "Hence, when He (Christ) entered into the world, He said, Sacrifices and offerings You have not desired, but instead You have made ready a body for Me [to offer]; in burnt offerings and sin offerings You have taken no delight. Then I said, Lo, here I am, come to do Your will, O God: [to fulfill] what is written of Me in the volume of the Book." Even as the whole redemptive purpose had been foreshadowed by the prophets to the fathers and recorded under the inspiration of the Holy Spirit "in the volume of the Book"—the written word of the Old Testament Scriptures—so now the Lord Jesus as the Living Word says in effect to the Father, "The body that You have prepared for Me, I now present to You, that all that has been written of Me in the volume of the Book may now find its complete consummation in My person."

By the offering of His body we must understand that this

involved the offering of His total being as Man—body, soul, and spirit—in unreserved yielding of His human personality to the Father.

By what means, however, did the Lord Jesus Christ present His body to the Father, that during those thirty-three years the Father in and through the Son might implement all that had been written in the volume of the Book?

The answer to this question is found in Hebrews 9:14: "How much more shall the blood of Christ, who through the eternal Spirit offered himself without spot to God, purge your conscience from dead works to serve the living God?" The Son, as Man, gave Himself to the Father, as God, through the eternal Spirit; and the Father, as God, gave Himself to the Son, as Man, through the eternal Spirit—and through the eternal Spirit He walked, He moved, and had His being. Every step He took, every word He spoke, everything He did, all that He was, was an expression of the Father as God, in the Son as Man, through the eternal Spirit.

To complete the picture, the Lord Jesus summarized this in John 14:10: "Believest thou not that I am in the Father, and the Father in me? The words that I speak unto you I speak not of myself: but the Father that dwelleth in me, he doeth the works." In other words, "I have presented My body to the Father who indwells Me, that He may do His works in my body; and My Father does His works through His Spirit by whom He indwells Me, and through whom I have offered Myself without spot, faultlessly, to my Father." So we understand that the whole activity of the Lord Jesus on earth as man was the Father's activity in the Son, through the eternal Spirit through whom His body was presented to the Father.

Of the Father—through the Father—to the Father! That was the life of Jesus Christ on earth, from Bethlehem to the Mount of Olives. As *man* it was the office of the Son to *be;* as

God it was the office of the Father to *do!* Of His relationship to the Father the Son would say, "I am—He does! What I do, My Father does! What I say, My Father says! What I am, My Father is!" As Jesus said to Philip, "Have I been so long time with you, and yet hast thou not known me, Philip? He that hath seen me hath seen the Father; and how sayest thou then, Show us the Father?" (John 14:9).

Now what does the Bible say regarding your relationship to the Lord Jesus? The Bible declares again and again from the lips of the Lord Jesus that your relationship to Him now must be what His relationship to the Father was then; that *as* the Father sent Him, *so* He sends you. "Just as the living Father sent Me, and I live by (through, because of) the Father, even so whoever continues to feed on Me—who takes Me for his food and is nourished by Me—shall [in his turn] live through and because of Me" (John 6:57 AMPLIFIED NEW TESTAMENT). So whatever you may discover to be the basis of the life of Christ, in His relationship to the Father, inevitably this must be the basis of your life in relationship to Him. That should not surprise you, indeed, if it is not so, it should shock you!

Next let us consider Romans 11:36: "For of him, and through him, and to him, are all things: to whom be glory for ever. Amen." Of Him, through Him, and to Him! But that is precisely the relationship that existed between the Son as man and the Father as God—of the Father, through the Father, and to the Father!

May I ask you a question? Do you have eternal life? You say, "Yes, thank God, I do!" Well, that is fine—but what *is* eternal life? Did you ever give yourself a satisfactory answer to that question?

What is eternal life? Is it a place that you are going to when you are dead? Is it a peculiar feeling inside? If you were to ask a normal congregation or any sort of Bible class or Sunday school in an evangelical church to define eternal life, you would be amazed at the strange answers you would get!

What is eternal life? When does it begin? I noticed just the other day, in a hospital chapel where I was speaking, a tablet on the wall in memory of one of the previous chaplains, and in giving the date of his death it said, "He entered into eternal life." Is that true if he was a Christian? Is it right to imply, as did that tablet on the wall, that eternal life begins when a man is physically dead? No, indeed! "And this is the record, that God hath given to us eternal life, and this life is in his Son. He that hath the Son hath life; and he that hath not the Son of God hath not life" (1 John 5:11–12).

Jesus Christ and eternal life are synonymous terms, and eternal life is none other than Jesus Christ Himself, of whom it is written in John 1:4: "In him was life; and this life was the light of men." If you have eternal life at all, it simply means that you have the Son, Jesus Christ—now! Jesus said, "I *am* the way, I *am* the truth, I *am* the life" (John 14:6, emphasis added).

Eternal life is not a peculiar feeling inside! It is not your ultimate destination, to which you will go when you are dead. If you are born again, eternal life is that quality of life that you possess right now, at this very moment, in your own physical body, with your own two feet on the ground, and in the world *today!* And where does this life come from? Of Him! He *is* that life!

When was your Bethlehem? In the day that Jesus Christ was formed in you! (Gal. 4:19). When He came to take up residence and inhabit your redeemed humanity as God by His gracious presence, through the eternal Spirit, so that your body became "the temple of the living God," you were added to that body corporate called the church, which Paul writing to the Ephesians describes as "a habitation of God through the Spirit" (Eph. 2:22b). So if you have eternal life, it means that you have *Somebody*, Jesus Christ, and the life that you possess is *of* Him.

Where is that life going to? If you were to die physically tonight, what would happen? The Bible says that you would be "absent from the body" and "present with the Lord" (2 Cor. 5:8). You would go *to* Him, whose resurrection life you now enjoy, imparted to you by His indwelling Holy Spirit.

If the Lord Jesus were to come again today, as well He may, you would not "precede them which are asleep" in Jesus but you would be "caught up together with them in the clouds to meet the Lord in the air" (1 Thess. 4:17). And in this case also, you would go "to Him," whose resurrection life you now enjoy. So whether you sleep in Jesus or are alive and remain at His coming, that eternal life which you now have is both of Him and to Him.

What is there in between? Between *your* Bethlehem and *your* Mount of Olives? Thirty-three years? It could be! Or three years or fifty or six weeks. However, for whatever period of time you remain physically alive on earth, indwelt by Jesus Christ through His eternal Spirit—for many years or few—this is *your vocation!* That purpose for which as *man* you live on earth—that Christ might have His inheritance now, in you, on the way to heaven. Your humanity as unreservedly available to Him, as His humanity was once unreservedly available to the Father.

Romans 12:1 draws the logical conclusion from the argument of the last verse of chapter 11: "I beseech you therefore, brethren, by the mercies of God, that ye present your bodies a living sacrifice [just as He did to the Father, you do now to the Son] holy, acceptable unto God, which is your reasonable service. And be not conformed to this world [do not ape its methods, its techniques, its ways, or its spirit]: but be ye transformed by the renewing of your mind, that ye may prove what is that good, and acceptable, and perfect, will of God." As the "good, acceptable, and perfect will of God" was implemented by the Son through dependence on the Father, so that "good, acceptable, and perfect will of God" may be implemented by you through dependence on the Son.

This divine vocation into which you have been redeemed, as "his workmanship, created in Christ Jesus unto good works which God hath before ordained that you should walk in them" (Eph. 2:10) can only be fulfilled in the energy and power of the One who indwells you now by His Spirit, as He walked once only in the energy and power of the Father who indwelt Him through the Spirit. Of Himself He said, "I can of mine own self do nothing" (John 5:19), and of you He says, in John 15:5, "Without me *you* can do nothing" (emphasis added).

How much can you do without Him? Nothing! So what is everything you do without Him? Nothing!

It is amazing how busy you can be doing nothing! Did you ever find that out? "The flesh [everything that you do apart from Him] profiteth nothing" (John 6:63b), and there is always the awful possibility, if you do not discover this principle, that you may spend a lifetime in the service of Jesus Christ *doing nothing!* You would not be the first, and you would not be the last—but that, above everything else, we must seek to avoid!

So you discover that the life which you possess as a born-again Christian is *of* Him, and it is *to* Him, and every moment that you are here on earth it must be *through* Him—of Him, through Him, to Him, *all* things! "I beseech you therefore, brethren, by the mercies of God, that ye present your bodies a living sacrifice" (Rom. 12:1).

The Lord Jesus Christ claims the use of *your* body, *your* whole being, *your* complete personality, so that as you give yourself to Him through the eternal Spirit, He may give Himself to you through the eternal Spirit, that all your activity as a human being on earth may be His activity in and through you; that every step *you* take, every word *you* speak, everything *you* do, everything *you* are, may be an expression of Christ, in you as man.

If it is *of Him* and *through Him* and *to Him,* where do *you* come in? You do not! That is just where you go out! That is what Paul meant when he said, "For me to live is *Christ*" (Phil. 1:21a, emphasis added). The only Person whom God credits with the right to live in you is Jesus Christ; so reckon yourself to be dead to all that you are *apart* from what He is, and alive unto God only in all that you are *because* of what He is (Rom. 6:11).

When the world looked at Jesus Christ, they saw God! They heard Him speak and they saw Him act. And Jesus said, "As my Father hath sent me, even so send I you" (John 20:21b). The world again will hear God speak and see God act!

It is for you to *be*—it is for Him to *do!* Restfully available to the Saving Life of Christ, enjoying "the richest measure of the divine Presence, a body wholly filled and flooded with God Himself," instantly obedient to the heavenly impulse—this is your vocation, and this is your victory!

"I assure you, most solemnly I tell you, if anyone steadfastly believes in Me, he will himself be able to do the things that I do; and he will do even greater things than these, because I go to the Father. And I will do—I Myself will grant—whatever you may ask in My name [presenting all I AM] so that the Father may be glorified and extolled in [through] the Son" (John 14:12–13 AMPLIFIED NEW TESTAMENT).

The Mystery
of Godliness

Chapter I

The Quality of True Commitment

> *But Jesus did not commit himself unto them, because he knew all men. (John 2:24)*

All that glitters is not gold, and in the light of all that we are about to consider, it may well be profitable for us to make a sober re-evaluation of those standards of commitment that are prevalent today and that pass muster for Christian dedication.

All too often quantity takes precedence over quality, and in this highly competitive age those outward appearances of "success" that are calculated to enhance the reputation of the professional preacher or the prestige of those who have promoted him are of greater importance than the abiding consequences of his ministry.

In an unholy ambition to get "results," the end too often justifies the means, with the result that the *means* are certainly not always beyond suspicion, and the "results," to say the least, extremely dubious!

In this unhappy situation both the pulpit and the pew carry their share of the blame, though I suspect that it started in the pulpit! There are those who have insisted that to be valid, every spiritual transaction between the believer and his Lord must be matched by some outward physical act, and that apart from the accompanying act, no worth can be attached to the inward spiritual transaction.

Inevitably on the basis of this unfounded supposition, the work of the Holy Spirit in any given meeting through the ministry of the preacher, will be directly represented by the physical response of the congregation to some form of public appeal, "invitation" or so-called "altar-call"—a term that is singularly inappropriate in view of the fact that the Lord Jesus Christ has "offered one sacrifice for sins for ever" (Heb. 10:12), and there is no place today for another sacrifice or for another altar in the church of the redeemed—the *altar* has given place to a *throne* for the exalted Lamb!

The terrible dangers inherent in such a fallacy, however, are patently obvious!

The ambitious preacher, eager to climb the ladder of evangelical fame, and not altogether unmoved by the plight of the lost and the needs of the saints, will be subject to a temptation so strong, that for more than one it has proved to be irresistible—that of being heavily preoccupied with devising ways and means of ensuring that a large enough public "response" on the part of the congregation will adequately demonstrate the effectiveness of his preaching, vindicate his reputation, sufficiently reward the confidence of his sponsors, and suitably impress the crowd.

The preacher, of course, will not allow himself to be aware of the underlying motives which prompt the use of his clever techniques, being careful to persuade himself that they stem only from what he would describe as a genuine "passion for souls." But the sorry spectacle is exposed for what it is by the apparent indifference on the part of the preacher to the tragic aftermath of his endeavors, once "the show is over"!

It is little wonder that the pulpit, having drilled the pew into submission, now finds itself the victim of its own ill-conceived imposition, for the community which has been taught to accept outward, physical response to some public "invitation" as the criterion of spiritual success on the part of the preacher, invariably demands this tangible evidence of success on every occasion in which he engages in his ministry.

Thus the pastor of a small church, trapped in the grip of this vicious circle, may succeed over a period of time in bringing the whole of his congregation "out to the front"— to stand at the communion rail in response to his many appeals—but having had all his people out once, it will be incumbent upon him to get them out all over again and again and yet *again* if his fervor and his zeal are not to be called into question by his church officers, and his pastorate, perhaps, become vacant!

The pastor has no option under such circumstances but to whittle down the commitment he demands until its whole value and meaning has been lost, for it can never be final, otherwise he would preach himself out of business! Instead of being faced with complete capitulation to the Lord Jesus Christ, and final, irrevocable abandonment to all His will, the believer is presented again and again with "baby" issues, all of which should be comprehended in the greater, basic issue of true discipleship!

It is much easier to confront a person with his *sins* than it is to confront him with his "sin," for as will be fully demonstrated in later chapters of this book, "sin" is an attitude which affects a man's fundamental relationship to God; it has to do with what a man *is*; whereas "sins" have to do with what a man *does*, and we all have a happy knack of being able to detach what we *do* from what we *are!* We are all highly skilled in the art of self-justification and are able to produce innumerable reasons as to why what we did was excusable—even if it was wrong! We can even feel heroic, almost virtuous, in accepting the blame for that which so obviously (to us!) was only the *natural*, almost inevitable reaction to enticing, compelling or provocative circumstances or people! For this reason a man can admit and be sorry for what he has done, without admitting that what he has done is a result of what he is.

On this basis a person may be called upon a hundred times to face the lesser issues of what he has done, without once being confronted with the greater issue of what he is— indeed the "comfort" to be found in confession, bringing freedom from fear, and relief to a bad conscience will eliminate for him the need for any basic change in his fundamental relationship to God. This kind of confession falls hopelessly short of real repentance and remains unmatched by any change of purpose; Moses reduced his people to tears again and again—but it left them in the wilderness! They still had no heart for Canaan! There was no lack of response to Moses' preaching, but they would not do business with God! "And they said unto Moses, Speak thou with us, and we will hear: but let not God speak with us, lest we die" (Exod. 20:19).

They wanted secondhand religion! They wanted neither godlessness nor godliness—they did not know how to live, and they were afraid to die! Commitment to them was on the installment system, and Moses was their broker!

Secondhand religion may keep a preacher in business and make him indispensable to his congregation, but it cannot produce discipleship; there will be no spontaneity of action nor any other evidence of that divine initiative in man which springs only from man's total availability to God.

True commitment to the Lord Jesus Christ gives Him "right of way," and releases His life through you in all the freshness and power of divine action, so that according to His gracious promise, out of your innermost being "springs and rivers of living water shall flow (continuously)" (John

7:38b, AMPLIFIED NEW TESTAMENT)—and you do not have to push a river! It cuts its own channel and cleanses as it flows!

In drawing attention to those glaring abuses that have done so much to discredit modern evangelism and conventional ministry, I do not suggest for one moment that there is not a legitimate place for the public confession of faith in Christ, nor would I insist that true commitment to Christ may never be accompanied by an outward witness to the fact. That would be to throw away the baby with the bathwater, for without a doubt, there are many who have been greatly helped in their decision *for* Christ or in their commitment *to* Christ by a wise, gracious invitation to *act*, rather than to delay further in yielding obedience to the Truth.

My plea is simply for *reality*—on God's terms of reference! It is for this reason also, that no matter how intensely I may dislike the shallowness and showmanship of men, in their abuse of the holy art of preaching by the use of doubtful "response techniques," I cannot on the other hand, endorse in any way the empty accusation made by the champions of hollow, ritualistic formalism, that all activity outside the established "practice of religion" within the "respectable church systems" is of necessity all "mere ignorant emotionalism." That is sheer nonsense!

If there remains much to be desired in the quality of commitment prevalent today in evangelical circles and in the worldwide evangelistic outreach of that great body of born-again believers, which is the true church of Jesus Christ in all denominations, even more to be deplored are those wholesale opportunities for practicing hypocrisy provided by those formal, public acts of commitment to Christ common to so many of the denominations, which in the vast majority of cases are totally devoid of any spiritual content and which serve only to satisfy the traditional "niceties" of religious observance in an otherwise godless society!

Whether it be by baptism as an infant or as an adult, by "sprinkling" or by "immersion"; whether it be by confirmation in the early "teens" or by any other public act of dedication and acceptance into full church membership, there must be very few in the "Christianized" countries of Western Europe who have not in one way or another, "committed themselves to Christ"—yet by what strange twist of the mind or willful stretch of the imagination, any ecclesiastical hierarchy of any given church system can credit this performance with any real spiritual validity, when over ninety percent of the populations of these countries never darken a church door to worship God, is beyond all intelligent explanation!

The Lord Jesus Christ is neither accepted as Saviour nor honored and obeyed as Lord, yet the rubberstamp of church approval has been granted and is considered by the overwhelming majority to be an altogether adequate discharge of their responsibility toward God and a formidable defense against the unwelcome attentions of those who would insist upon a reality of spiritual experience, which has neither been demanded nor expected by their "church!"

If church attendance in the United States, representing something like sixty percent of the population, far and away exceeds that of any other Protestant country at this time, it should be a matter for genuine thankfulness to God. Yet there are few countries in the world where there are so many crimes of violence, so much juvenile delinquency, so much drug addiction, so many alcoholics, and where there is such widespread graft and corruption in government and commerce. Are only *those* responsible for this sorry record who have never conformed to the requirements of the church in some outward, formal act of dedication?

Why should international world communism with its

fanatical convictions, its thorough indoctrination, and utter dedication be afraid of this flabby monster called "the church," with its countless millions of nominal adherents who know neither conviction nor concern—who are colorless, spiritual nonentities, knowing neither what they believe nor believing what they know! Why should communism fear a church that is utterly without any sense of mission, that is governed by and large by men who are themselves riddled through and through with infidelity, boastful of their own wanton repudiation of all the essential ingredients of the faith they profess to proclaim! Why should communism fear a Christendom whose worst enemies are within its own ranks!

The Word of God to the Jews in Paul's day might well be the Word of God to Christendom today:

> For, as it is written, The name of God is maligned and blasphemed among the Gentiles because of you!—The words to this effect are from [your own] Scriptures. . . . For he is not a [real] Jew who is only one outwardly and publicly, nor is [true] circumcision something external and physical. But he is a Jew who is one inwardly, and [true] circumcision is of the heart, a spiritual and not a literal [matter]. His praise is not from men but from God. (Rom. 2:24, 28–29 AMPLIFIED NEW TESTAMENT)

It was into just such a situation that the Lord Jesus Christ entered, as at the Feast of the Passover He received such a tumultuous welcome in Jerusalem. "Hosanna to the son of David!" they cried. "Blessed is he that cometh in the name of the Lord; Hosanna in the highest" (Matt. 21:9).

No doubt the disciples were flushed with excitement and highly delighted that their Master should receive such a tremendous ovation—yet maybe there were some among them who had their misgivings! If only He could be prevailed upon not to say the wrong thing! If only they could persuade Him *just this once*, not to do anything that would spoil it all!

But He did it again!

What a heartbreak Christ would be today to some well-meaning "promotional committee" or to some "business manager"! It seemed that He always *did* the wrong thing or *said* the wrong thing, just as He was on the crest of the wave and at the height of His popularity! He never seemed to understand what was in His own best interests!

Amidst all this popular acclaim, the Lord Jesus Christ went straight to the temple and found "those that sold oxen and sheep and doves, and the changers of money sitting: And when he had made a scourge of small cords, he drove them all out of the temple, and the sheep, and the oxen; and poured out the changers' money, and overthrew the tables; And said unto them that sold doves, Take these things hence; make not my Father's house an house of merchandise" (John 2:14—16).

Had He been prepared to accept "religion" as He found it and to recognize the "status quo," no doubt the Lord Jesus Christ might well have found acceptance, even among the Pharisees; but He was a troublemaker! He dared to cleanse the temple!

Christ did not come to be "accepted," nor was He looking for a job in contemporary religion! He came to cleanse the temple—and to do a bigger job than just to cleanse the temple in Jerusalem; He had come to cleanse the temples of men's hearts, that they might be fit again to be "a habitation of God through the Spirit" (Eph. 2:22b).

Challenged to declare by what authority He presumed to disapprove and by what authority He was prepared to translate His disapproval into action, the Lord Jesus Christ gave this answer: "Destroy this temple, and in three days I will raise it up—But he spake of the temple of his body" (John 2:19b, 21).

Christ's death and resurrection were to be His mandate. Commitment to Christ for anything less than to be cleansed from sin and inhabited by God, misses the whole point of the Cross! He will accept nothing less!

"Now when he was in Jerusalem at the passover, in the feast day, many believed in his name, when they saw the miracles which he did. But Jesus did not commit himself unto them, because he knew all men, and needed not that any should testify of man: for he knew what was in man" (John 2:23–25). Although the crowd appeared to have committed themselves to Christ, the quality of their commitment was such that He was not prepared to commit Himself to them!

What is the quality of *your* commitment to Christ?

You may be accepted into membership by the "church," approved by your friends and entrusted with responsible office, but of what possible value can these things be if your commitment to Christ is such that He is not willing to commit Himself to you? The value of *your* commitment to Christ will only be the measure of *His* commitment to you!

The Lord Jesus Christ is the Truth, and as in all other things "that pertain unto life and godliness" (2 Peter 1:3b), He is the Truth about true commitment. He was committed to the Father for all that to which the Father was committed in the Son, and He was supremely confident that the Father who dwelt in Him was gloriously adequate for all that to which He was committed. We know also that the Saviour's commitment to His Father was such that the Father was completely committed to His Son!

The Lord Jesus Christ refused to be committed to the parochial needs of His own day and generation; He was not committed to the political situation in Palestine or to the emancipation of the Jewish nation from the Roman yoke! He was not committed to the pressing social problems of His time or to one faction as opposed to another, any more than today He is committed to the West against the East or to the Republicans against the Democrats (as though either were less wicked than the other!). Christ was not even committed to the needs of a perishing world; He was neither unmindful nor unmoved by all these other issues. But as perfect man He was committed to His Father, and for that only to which His Father was committed in Him—exclusively! "Then said Jesus unto them, When ye have lifted up the Son of man, then shall ye know that I am he, and that I do nothing of myself; but as my Father hath taught me, I speak these things. And he that sent me is with me: The Father hath not left me alone; for I do always those things that please him" (John 8:28—29).

The Lord Jesus Christ was fully aware from the beginning of that to which the Father was committed in Him, for He was "the Lamb slain from the foundation of the world" (Rev. 13:8c). Breaking the bread which pictured His body so soon to be broken and taking the wine as the symbol of His blood so soon to be shed, He could still look up into His Father's face and say, "Thank You!" He was completely committed, and there were no other issues then for Him to face!

The Lord Jesus Christ knew that before ever men like Wilberforce, Robert Moffat, and David Livingstone could be committed to Him for that to which He was to be committed in them—the abolition of slavery and the restoration of human dignity in the equality of all men under God; before ever men like Lord Shaftesbury, Dr. Barnardo, and George Mueller could be committed to Him for that for which He was to be committed in them—to gather the ragged, half-starved orphans off the streets of Britain and to restore hope to the unwanted; before He could attack the social evils and unschooled ignorance of a wanton nation through the persons of John Wesley and George Whitefield during the great evangelical awakening of their century or before He could use Elizabeth Fry to bring about a reformation within an unpitying penal system that left a community of despair to languish, unloved and unmourned, in the vermin-ridden prisons of her land—He the Son of God had first to commit Himself to the Father for that to which the Father was committed in Him!

The basis of His commitment to the Father is the basis upon which the Lord Jesus Christ claims your commitment to Him; you are committed to Him for all that to which He is committed in you—*exclusively!*

You are not committed to a church or to a denomination or to an organization; as a missionary you are not committed to a mission board, not even to a "field," and least of all are you committed to a "need"! You are committed to *Christ*, and for all that to which *Christ is committed in You*, and again I say—*exclusively!*

Thousands of earnest young Christians are challenged with the outworn slogan, "The need is the call!" and are then immediately presented with a dozen different needs, all representing a "call"! When the "invitation" is given, hundreds stand in their confusion, swept to their feet on a wave of sentiment, yet it has been determined on a strictly statistical basis that out of every hundred who stand, not more than five will ever reach the mission field, and of those who do, almost fifty percent will return home to stay at home by the end of their first term overseas!

Moses mistook the need for the "call," and moved with compassion, he went out to murder an Egyptian in defense of his brethren and became useless to God and man for forty years in the backside of the desert, herding a handful of sheep!

Abraham committed himself to the *will* of God, instead of to *God*, whose will it was, and in his misguided zeal tried to do God's work man's way! He felt that it was up to him and to Sarah to help God out of His predicament, for Sarah was old and had never borne, for she was barren. So they had a committee meeting! After all, God had said that Abraham was to have a son, and if this was God's will, and he was committed to God's will—a son he must have, at any price!

It was a heavy price that Abraham paid as Hagar, Sarah's maid, was summoned, and ill-begotten Ishmael was born to become the father of the Arabs! The Jews in Palestine today, surrounded by hostile Arab nations, reap the bitter harvest still of what was sown in Abraham's self-effort, those many centuries before. Ishmael was the by-product of a false commitment; conceived in sincerity, he was the Devil's *reasonable alternative to faith!*

When Isaac was born in God's perfect timing, fifteen years later, Ishmael mocked him—and he has been mocking him ever since! "As then he that was born after the flesh persecuted him that was born after the Spirit, even so it is now" (Gal. 4:29); "O that Ishmael might live before thee!" (Gen. 17:18b) is still the cry of those who in our own day and generation have yet to learn that "the son of the bond woman shall not be heir with the son of the free woman" (Gal. 4:30b)—that there is *absolutely no substitute* so far as God is concerned, for God's work done God's way!

When God tested Abraham and told him to offer up Isaac for a burnt offering, He said, "Take now thy son, thine only son Isaac, whom thou lovest, and get thee into the land of Moriah" (Gen. 22:2a). Abraham might have argued with God and said, "But I have *two* sons! What about Ishmael? Isaac is not my *only* son!" Then God would have replied, "So far as I am concerned, only Isaac is your son. I do not recognize Ishmael—he should never have been born!"

The church of Jesus Christ today is plagued with Ishmaels clamoring to be recognized—but God will only honor Isaac, and Isaac's Greater Son! Nothing infuriates the "flesh" more than failure to be recognized—and preaching that exposes it for the wicked counterfeit it is must inevitably be the object of its venom and its wrath! "Too subjective! Unrealistic! Otherworldly! Oversimplified! Mere passivity! Pantheistic mysticism!"—these are some of the epithets with which Ishmael still mocks Isaac, with which the "flesh" resists the Spirit!

At God's command, Abraham took Isaac, bound him, laid him on the altar he had built, and took his knife to slay him. With actions far more eloquent than words, said to God by what he did, "You promised me Isaac! I did not see how You could do it, and in my unbelief and in my folly I produced my Ishmael; I committed myself to Your *will*, and thought I was more competent than God. Now You tell me to slay him, my *only* son Isaac in whom You have promised that all the families of the earth shall be blessed! O God, if I slay him, I do not see *how* You can do it—but now I am committed to *You—exclusively* and to all that for which you are committed in me! If slay him I *must*, then slay him I *will*—even if You have to raise him from the dead!" (Heb. 11:17–19).

In so many words God said to Abraham, "Thank you, Abraham! That is all I wanted to know—now you can throw your knife away!" "Lay not thine hand upon the lad, neither do thou anything unto him: for now I know that thou fearest God. . . . By myself have I sworn, saith the LORD, for because thou hast done this thing, and hast not withheld thy son, thine only son: That in blessing I will bless thee, and in multiplying I will multiply thy seed as the stars of heaven, and as the sand which is upon the sea shore; and thy seed shall possess the gate of his enemies. . . . because thou hast obeyed my voice." (Gen. 22:12, 16–18)

Abraham had learned the secret of true commitment and became "the Friend of God" (James 2:23)! This is *reality*— and this is discipleship!

It is "godliness in action"! Presenting all that you are— *nothing*, to all that He is—*everything*, you are committed to the Lord Jesus Christ *exclusively*, for all that to which He is committed in you; and you may be supremely confident that

He who dwells in *you* as the Father dwelt in *Him*, is gloriously adequate for all that to which He is committed!

Are you prepared for this to be the quality of your commitment to Christ? If so, then every lesser issue has been comprehended in the greater. It is now no longer necessary for me to ask you whether you are prepared to go to the mission field! It is now no longer necessary for me to ask you whether you are prepared to put your bank account at Christ's disposal or your time or your home or face you with any other issue I could think of! You would say to me at once, "These issues now have all been settled—finally, once and for all! If Christ is committed in me to go to the mission field, I am already committed to Him for this! If He is committed in me to use the very last dollar I possess and every other dollar I shall ever earn, I am already committed to Him for this, and for everything and anything else to which He may be committed in me! There are no more issues for me to face—*only His instructions to obey!* I know too, that *for all His will,* I have *all that He is!* And this is *all* I need to know!"

Indeed it is! For you cannot have *more!*

And you need never have *less!*

Chapter II

How to Do the Impossible

He answered and said unto them, Give ye them to eat. (Mark 6:37a)

"It is not difficult for man to live the Christian life," somebody once said. *"It is a sheer impossibility!"*

A sheer impossibility, that is, without Christ—but for *all that He says,* you have *all that He is,* and that is *all that it takes!*

As we have already seen, this was the lesson that Abraham learned: "Being fully persuaded that, what he had promised, he was able also to perform" (Rom. 4:21). Mary, too, as we shall see later learned this lesson: "For with God nothing shall be impossible. And Mary said, Behold the handmaid of the Lord; be it unto me according to thy word" (Luke 1:37–38).

It was this same lesson which the Lord Jesus Christ wished to teach His disciples, but they were very slow to learn—and so are we! "And Jesus, when he came out, saw much people, and was moved with compassion toward them, because they were as sheep not having a shepherd: and he began to teach them many things" (Mark 6:34).

Luther's translation of this last sentence has always been a source of great comfort to me—"He preached a long sermon"! And it *was* a long sermon! It lasted right on into the evening, and so much so that the disciples began to get quite worried as to what they were going to do with this great crowd of people! "This is a desert place," they said to the Master, "send them away . . . for they have nothing to eat" (Mark 6:35–36).

To the disciples this seemed to be the only reasonable, sensible thing to do in the face of a situation that threatened to become increasingly embarrassing. There were five thousand men, Matthew records, "beside women and children" (Matt. 14:21), and if meetings in those days were anything like meetings in these days, five thousand men *plus* the women and children was a big meeting! The crowd was tired, hot, and hungry, and with no prospect of feeding them, there appeared to the disciples to be no alternative but to remind the Lord Jesus Christ of the lateness of the hour, and to say to Him in so many words, "Master, we simply *must* get these people off our hands!"

There is always a *reasonable* alternative to faith!

The Lord Jesus Christ answered them and said, "Give ye them to eat," in other words, "You don't send hungry people away; you feed them!"

"Shall we go and buy two hundred pennyworth of bread, and give them to eat?" (Mark 6:37b), asked the bewildered disciples, "Master, that's a sheer impossibility!"

"Exactly! To you it is a sheer impossibility," the Lord Jesus might well have replied, "and that is why we are going to do it; I am going to show you how to do the impossible!"

The Christian life can be explained only in terms of Jesus Christ, and if your life as a Christian can still be explained in terms of *you*—*your* personality, *your* willpower, *your* gift, *your* talent, *your* money, *your* courage, *your* scholarship, *your* dedication, *your* sacrifice, or *your* anything—then although you may *have* the Christian life, you are not yet living it!

If the way you live your life as a Christian can be explained in terms of *you*, what have you to offer to the man who lives next door? The way he lives his life can be explained in terms of *him*, and so far as he is concerned, you happen to be "religious"—but he is not! "Christianity" may be *your* hobby, but it is not *his*, and there is nothing about the way you practice it which strikes him as at all remarkable! There is nothing about you which leaves him guessing, and nothing commendable of which he does not feel himself equally capable without the inconvenience of becoming a Christian!

It is only when your quality of life *baffles* the neighbors that you are likely to *impress* them! It has got to become patently obvious to others that the kind of life you are living is not only *highly commendable*, but that it is beyond all *human explanation!* That it is beyond the consequences of man's capacity to *imitate*, and however little they may understand this, it is clearly the consequence only of God's capacity to *reproduce Himself* in you!

In a nutshell, this means that your fellowmen must become convinced that the Lord Jesus Christ of whom you speak, is essentially Himself the ingredient of the life you live!

How did Christ feed the five thousand? To discover this, we need to turn to the record found in the sixth chapter of John's gospel, for here it is as though the apostle takes a magnifying glass and allows us to examine the story in greater detail. "When Jesus then lifted up his eyes, and saw a great company come unto him, he saith unto Philip, Whence shall we buy bread, that these may eat? And this he said to prove him: for he himself knew what he would do" (John 6:5–6).

Was Christ seeking advice when He asked Philip this question? Was He at a loss to know what to do? Most certainly not, for "He Himself knew what He would do." He knew *exactly* what He would do! He always does, no matter with what situation He may be confronted, at any time, and anywhere! Nothing ever takes Him by surprise, and nothing shocks Him; He is *never* baffled—*never* bewildered! He is the God who declares "the end from the beginning," and upon whose head no emergency can ever break! As I once heard a noted Christian psychologist, Dr. Cramer, remark, "The Lord Jesus Christ was completely 'panic-proof' "—and He still is!

Are you?

This will be singularly characteristic of you, if you are really enjoying the life of the Lord Jesus Christ; you, too, will be "panic-proof"! Yours will be the "peace of God, which passeth all understanding" (Phil. 4:7)—that is to say, peace, which in the light of all the circumstances, is beyond all human explanation!

Christ was not seeking advice when He asked Philip this question, nor was He trying to discover anything *about* Philip, for again and again occasions are recorded in the Gospels, where the Lord Jesus Christ replied to a person's *thoughts*. He knew everything there was to know about Philip's heart, and a whole lot more than Philip knew himself, as He knows everything there is to know about your heart and mine! "And not a creature exists that is concealed from His sight, but all things are open and exposed, naked and defenseless to the eyes of Him with Whom we have to do" (Heb. 4:13 AMPLIFIED NEW TESTAMENT).

Then why did Christ ask this question?

He asked this question because He wanted Philip to discover something about himself! He wanted him to discover the utter poverty of his experience of Christ—how very far short he fell of living miraculously! Nor was it for Philip alone to make this discovery, but for all of His disciples. "Philip answered him, Two hundred pennyworth of bread is not sufficient for them, that everyone of them may take a little" (John 6:7).

With what then was Philip reckoning? Was it with the presence and power of the Lord Jesus Christ? No! Just with the money in the bag! Beyond that for him, in this situation, there was no further horizon; so far as Philip was concerned, for all the difference that the presence of Christ made to the problem, He might just as well have been dead!

Had a materialistically minded atheist been consulted in the face of this dilemma, the first question he would have asked would have been, "How much money do you have?" What then would have been the difference between Philip's outlook and that of an unbelieving atheist? There would have been *no* difference!

Philip had not learned to *reckon* with Christ! Because to him their financial resources were all important, Jesus Christ was unimportant! There was nothing about the kind of life he was living as an apostle which could not have been given its "dollar equivalent"!

What are *you* reckoning with? Are you *really* reckoning with Christ? Upon what basis have you evaluated the many different situations that have arisen within the last twenty-four hours, before taking this book in your hand and reading these pages? Did you take the Lord Jesus Christ into account—or did you consider Him to be irrelevant?

Remember that it is precisely in those areas of your life in which you have not considered Christ to be relevant, in which, as yet, you have not repented. In these areas you are still trying to be adequate without Him—trying to be the "cause" of your own "effect"; and if *you* are the cause, there will certainly be nothing miraculous about the effect!

In your disillusionment, you may well try, as the disciples did, to get the situation "off your hands," convinced that you are as inadequate with Christ as without Him! Then you *will* be miserable! Better not visit the neighbors *that* day!

The Lord Jesus Christ said, "How many loaves have ye? Go and see" (Mark 6:38a), and when they went, they found Andrew arguing with a small boy! I can imagine that the conversation ran something like this:

"It's kind of you, laddie, and I will tell the Master that you offered, but I don't think we should disturb Him now; you see, He's busy—and in any case, five loaves and two fishes just aren't enough to go around! That's just about your size—*you* could wrap yourself round that! But thanks again, lad—thanks a lot! I'll tell the Master. I promise!"

Indignantly the boy replied, "I don't care whether I've got *five* loaves or *fifty* loaves or *five hundred* loaves or *five thousand* loaves—*that* does not matter! *Please take me to that man!* That is *all* that matters!"

At that moment the others arrived on the scene, and maybe if the Master had not sent them, Andrew never would have brought that boy to the Lord Jesus; even when he did, it was only to apologize! "One of his disciples, Andrew, Simon Peter's brother, saith unto him, There is a lad here, which hath five barley loaves, and two small fishes: but what are they among so many?" (John 6:8-9).

Andrew, I am sure, was not unkind to the boy! I believe from the record that we have of him in the Gospels that Andrew was of a particularly kindly disposition, and maybe that was why the lad felt at liberty to speak to him; perhaps a friendly smile had given him the invitation! Andrew, I believe, had a face like a doormat—one that has "Welcome" woven into it! Some folk wonder why it is that no one ever comes to them for counsel—they have faces like a notice on the gate, "Beware of the Dog"!

Be that as it may, and kind as he may have been, what was Andrew reckoning with? Was he reckoning with the presence and the power of Christ? *No!* Just with five barley loaves and two small fishes, and because these to him were all-important, Jesus Christ was unimportant!

On the other hand, because to this small boy the Lord Jesus Christ was *all-important*, the vastness of the need and the poverty of supply were totally *unimportant!* He had already learned the secret of living miraculously, for the lad had learned in his own way to *reckon with Christ!*

This is always a precious story to me, for the Lord Jesus Himself "knew what He would do" long before Andrew spoke to that small boy or ever anyone else had recognized the potential in him. Christ knew his heart and had already chosen him!

In *every* crowd there is always *one* at least whose heart He knows, and whom He has already chosen! To *discern* that one and to bring that one—without apology—is the holy art of soul-winning; "And he that winneth souls is wise" (Prov. 11:30b).

It will not always be the most prominent nor even the most promising—maybe just a lad with a lunch bag and a twinkle in his eye! "And Jesus took the loaves; and when he had given thanks, he distributed to the disciples, and the disciples to them that were set down; and likewise of the fishes as much as they would" (John 6:11).

Whatever second thoughts some "learned theologians" may have had about the memorable events that took place on that exciting day, those who were present and were witnesses were obviously in no doubt at all, as to what had really happened, for "those men, when they had seen the miracle which Jesus did, said, This is of a truth that prophet that should come into the world" (John 6:14). They recognized the fact at once, as they watched the Lord Jesus Christ at work, that here was a man for whose activities there could be absolutely no explanation at all, apart from God!

There are those of course, who would have you accept "the

little paper-bag" theory! They would seek to persuade you that when the crowd saw the unselfishness of the little boy, taking out his lunch pack and being willing to share his five loaves and two small fishes with the multitude, they were so touched and ashamed that suddenly about five thousand "little paper bags" appeared—and everyone began to share with everyone else what till then they had been hiding underneath their shirts!

Isn't that sweet?

Some folks call this "scholarship" and grant "doctorates" on the strength of it! The twelve baskets might have been better used to gather up the litter than to gather up the fragments that remained!

If you have only a "little paper-bag god," then you must content yourself with "little paper-bag miracles"—but with *our God*, "nothing shall be impossible" (Luke 1:37)!

> When they were filled, he said unto his disciples, Gather up the fragments that remain, that nothing be lost. Therefore they gathered them together, and filled twelve baskets *with the fragments of the five barley loaves*, which remained over and above unto them that had eaten. (John 6:12–13, emphasis added)

There was a secret to the miracle that the Lord Jesus Christ performed; a secret which He wanted to share with His disciples and which He wants to share with you, too! To miss this, is to miss the object of the exercise, the lesson to be learned! It is at the very heart of the mystery of godliness! It is written that "Jesus took the loaves; and *when he had given thanks*, he distributed to the disciples" (emphasis added). Whom did Christ thank? Did He thank Himself? God as God certainly has no one to thank but Himself, and Jesus Christ was God! It is quite obvious that the Lord Jesus Christ as the Son, gave thanks to His Father as God, and in His perfect role as perfect man, relentlessly refused to be the "cause of His own effect"!

As the Creator God, there is absolutely no doubt but that Christ could Himself have fed the five thousand, or for that matter, five hundred times five thousand—but then He would not have been behaving as man, He would have been behaving as God; and as we shall discover later, had He both *been* and *behaved* as God, no one would have seen Him! No one has seen God at any time!

As the "only begotten Son," Christ "declared" the Father (John 1:18) in all that He said, in all that He did, and in all that He was; and as I shall remind you yet again, the Lord Jesus said, "The Father that dwelleth in me, He doeth the works" (John 14:10b).

So who fed the five thousand? The Father through the Son!

In spite of His eternal equality with the Father and with the Holy Spirit in the Trinity of the Deity, the Lord Jesus Christ for our sakes made Himself *nothing* (Phil. 2:7 NEB), that the Father might be *everything*, and be glorified in Him! In an attitude of total dependence, He exercised toward the Father as God, that perfect "faith-love" relationship for which man by Christ Himself had been created!

Confronted by this hungry multitude of people, Christ deliberately subjected Himself to the limitations that He as the creative Word had imposed upon man as His own creation—He exposed the situation to His Father, and in humble dependence upon His adequacy said quite simply, "Thank You"—and then He reckoned with the Father as He divided the loaves and the fishes!

That is how to do the impossible!

When the Lord Jesus Christ raised Lazarus from the dead, how did He do it?

"Jesus said, Take ye away the stone. Martha, the sister of him that was dead, saith unto Him, Lord, by this time he stinketh: for he hath been dead four days" (John 11:39). Clearly, by any natural standards, the situation was impossible; yet Christ said to Martha, "Said I not unto thee, that, if thou wouldest believe, thou shouldest see the glory of God?" (John 11:40). Once more the Father was to be glorified in and through the Son! "Then they took away the stone from the place where the dead was laid" (John 11:41a).

Christ on this occasion was confronted by a man four days dead, and with all the indisputable evidences of decay, He stood before the open cave; was this to be His problem? Was His the right to challenge the awful finality of death? The *power* indeed He had, for He was God, but not the *right*, for He was man! "For even Christ pleased not himself" (Rom. 15:3a).

How then did Christ do the impossible and raise this man from the dead?

Christ raised Lazarus from the dead just as He had fed the five thousand! He exposed the situation to His Father, and in humble dependence upon His adequacy, He said quite simply, "Thank You"—and then reckoned with the Father as He cried with a loud voice, "Lazarus, come forth. And he that was dead came forth" (John 11:43b—44a).

It was just as simple as that! "And Jesus lifted up his eyes, and said, Father, I thank thee that thou hast heard me. And I knew that thou hearest me always: but because of the people which stand by I said it, that they may believe that thou hast sent me" (John 11:41b—42).

Christ sought then, as He had sought by the feeding of the five thousand, to demonstrate the principle by which He lived His supernatural life as man on earth; that you with all men might believe that He was the "sent one," and His Father the "sender," and that you might know and believe that as the *Father* sent *Him*, so *He* sends *you*—to live miraculously! "Verily, verily, I say unto you, He that believeth on me, the works that I do shall he do also; and greater works than these shall he do; because I go unto my Father" (John 14:12).

The Lord Jesus Christ wants to be to you now, all that the Father was to Him then—*God;* if only you will be to Him now, all that He was to the Father then—*man!*

Have you learned to expose *every* situation to the Lord Jesus Christ in humble dependence upon His adequacy, and simply to say, "Thank You," and then to reckon with Him as you act to meet that situation?

By the feeding of the five thousand in humble dependence on the Father, the Lord Jesus Christ showed His disciples how to do the impossible and how to live miraculously!

How much did His disciples learn?

Nothing!

Chapter III

I Am—Thou Art!

For they considered not the miracle of the loaves: for their heart was hardened. (Mark 6:52)

"*Get them off our hands!* Send them away, for they have nothing to eat!" That was the pitiful cry of the disciples as they came in panic to the Lord Jesus Christ; but instead, He *fed* the hungry multitude, *and got His disciples off His hands!*

It is one of the hardest lessons for us to learn, that none of us are ever indispensable to God, but God is *always* indispensable to us! "And they that did eat of the loaves were about five thousand men. And straightway he constrained his disciples to get into the ship, and to go to the other side before unto Bethsaida, while he sent away the people" (Mark 6:44–45).

Why did He send His disciples away? He sent them away because they had learned *nothing*—absolutely *nothing!* "For they failed to consider *or* understand [the teaching and meaning of the miracle of] the loaves; [in fact] their hearts had grown callous—had become dull and had lost the power of understanding" (Mark 6:52 AMPLIFIED NEW TESTAMENT)— "their heart was hardened"!

Called to be apostles and the closest companions of the

Saviour during His earthly ministry, they lived and worked and walked and talked with Him; they shared His platform, basked in His limelight, and had a name to be His most devoted followers! Yes, they were *big names*—but they were *big names* with *hard hearts!*

To hold office does not in itself make a man spiritual! Unfortunately, too often it is the *unspiritual* who fight and edge their way into office, where the flesh can indulge its insatiable appetite for position and power; for the flesh loves to be recognized, consulted, honored, admired, and obeyed!

You may be a bishop, a pastor, the church secretary, an elder or deacon; you may be the president, principal, or dean of a college; you may be chairman of some mission board or the field director as the senior missionary on the field; you may hold any office of any kind, however distinguished it may be—*and still have a hard heart!* Where this is the case and where there is *real* business to be done, you must not be surprised if Christ gets *you* off His hands too—unless and until you repent!

> God is not impressed with the positions that men hold *and* He is not partial *and* recognizes no external distinctions. (Gal. 2:6b AMPLIFIED NEW TESTAMENT)

> Because thou sayest, I am rich, and increased with goods, and have need of nothing; and knowest not that thou art wretched, and miserable, and poor, and blind, and naked: . . . As many as I love, I rebuke and chasten: be zealous therefore, and repent. (Rev. 3:17, 19)

Do not allow the poverty of self-sufficiency to rob you of the miraculous! It is a particularly subtle form of conceit which denies to God the possibility of doing what you consider to be beyond the bounds of your own carnal self-esteem!

How patient Christ was with His disciples! Having learned nothing, they were given the same lesson all over again, but in another setting. A setting, indeed, which was little to the liking of the disciples themselves, for having been sent away, they found themselves "in the midst of the sea, tossed with waves: for the wind was contrary" (Matt. 14:24).

With their backs bent to the oars, perspiration pouring down their faces, and every muscle aching, they battled against the storm! Darkness had already fallen, and the shoreline had long been lost to sight. As the mountainous waves beat into the little boat, threatening to swamp it and send it to the bottom, the disciples began to wonder whether they would ever reach their destination! "And in the fourth watch of the night Jesus went unto them"—doing what?

Doing the impossible—"walking on the sea" (Matt. 14:25)!

How did the Lord Jesus Christ do the impossible? How did He walk on the water? He did this as He had fed the five thousand and as He had raised Lazarus from the dead! He *reckoned* with His Father—just one step at a time—and for every step He took, He said, "Thank You, Father."

Christ demonstrated to His disciples that everything that threatened to be *over their heads*, His Father had already put *under His feet!*

What is it that is threatening *you?* What makes you afraid? What is it from which you are running away? Is there something that seems about to swamp *your* little boat—something that baffles, beats, and bewilders you? Here is *good news* for you! There is nothing that could ever threaten to be over your head that He does not already have under His feet—and He is waiting for you to share His victory! "And when the disciples saw Him walking on the sea, they were terrified, and said, It is a ghost! And they screamed out with fright. But instantly He spoke to them, saying, Take courage! I AM; stop being afraid!" (Matt. 14:26–27 AMPLIFIED NEW TESTAMENT).

They thought they had seen a ghost! A man walking on

the water—that is impossible! But the Lord Jesus said, "I AM ; stop being afraid!" In so many words, Christ said to His disciples. "I AM—all that you could *ever* need, at *any* time, in *any* storm; and all that I AM, you HAVE! Stop being frightened!" "And Peter answered him and said, Lord, if it be thou, bid me come unto thee on the water" (Matt. 14:28).

"Master," Peter might have said, "if it be *Thou*, then please put under *my* feet what is already under *Thy* feet!" You can almost imagine the smile there must have been on the face of the Master! "Why, Peter! That is all I have been waiting for! I have simply been waiting for *you* to reckon with Me, as *I* reckon with My Father! Come on! Come!"

At the command of the Lord Jesus Christ, Peter stepped over the side, "And when Peter was come down out of the ship," what do you think he did? He did the *impossible!* "He walked on the water, to go to Jesus" (Matt. 14:29b).

One step at a time, and for every step he took, you could almost have heard Peter crying in his excitement, "This is wonderful, Lord! Thank You! Thank You, Lord!—This is tremendous; this is an entirely new experience for me. I have never walked on water before! Thank You, Lord! Thank You!"

As Peter kept his eyes upon the Saviour and related his situation to Christ for every step he took, he shared the victory of his Lord! The impossible became possible!

Suddenly an unkind wave slapped Peter on the face from one side, and yet another hit him from the other side, and he almost lost his balance! His attention was distracted from Christ, and once more he became aware of the howling of the wind and the swelling of the waters; he stopped relating the situation *to the Lord* and began again to relate the situation *to himself.* He began immediately to think, *I can't do this! A man can't walk on water—that's impossible!* And he was quite right! Peter began to go down for a dunking, and he "cried, saying, Lord, save me" (Matt. 14:30b).

The Lord Jesus Christ immediately stretched forth His hand and caught him; He recaptured Peter's attention and once more He put the threatening waters beneath his feet, and they walked *together* until they were come into the ship, and "the wind ceased" (Matt. 14:32). The exercise was over!

What do you think Christ said to Peter? Perhaps you think He should have congratulated him! "Peter, I just want you to know how immensely I appreciated your *tremendous* faith! The way you got out of that boat and walked toward Me was a masterpiece! I *must* congratulate you; I haven't seen such great faith in a long time!" Is that what Christ said? Oh no! Far from it! Instead He said to him, "O thou of little faith, wherefore didst thou doubt?" (Matt. 14:31b). In so many words He said, "It is not *difficult*, Peter, to do the impossible! It is *inevitable* so long as you reckon with *Me!* Why did you stop reckoning? I can't *congratulate* you, Peter. I'm just sorry that your faith was so small!"

The lesson, however, was not in vain! "Then they that were in the ship came and worshiped him, saying, Of a truth thou art the Son of God" (Matt. 14:33).

In the midst of the storm, when everything was against them, the Lord Jesus Christ appeared and said, "I AM; stop being afraid," and now at last they had learned to say, "Of a truth *thou art* the Son of God!" (emphasis added). If there is nothing else that you remember of all that has been written in this book, this in itself would comprehend the whole relationship of God to man, and man to God: "for he that cometh to God must believe that he is ["Thou art"] and that he is a rewarder of them that diligently seek him ["I AM"]" (Heb. 11:6b). All that you could ever need at any time, in *any* storm; "and all that I AM," He said, "You *have!*"

It may be that your need is still that of a sinner seeking forgiveness; you need to be redeemed and you are still trying to find your way back to God and godliness. Christ is saying to you now, as He said to His disciples of old in the Upper Room, after He was risen from the dead, "Behold my hands and my feet, that it is I myself" (Luke 24:39a); in other words, "I AM—all that a guilty sinner needs! The wounds in My hands and My feet are the hallmarks of My Saviourhood; put your trust in Me, and I will save you!"

All you need to say to Him is this, "Lord Jesus—*Thou art!* For *me*—just what I need! *My* Saviour and *my* Redeemer— for ever!"

> Behold Him there, the risen Lamb!
> My perfect, spotless righteousness,
> The great unchangeable I am,
> The King of glory and of grace.

You will be redeemed, and He will give you *life*; by the gift of His indwelling Holy Spirit, Jesus Christ will give you *His* Life, and this is what it means to "*live* in the Spirit." But "If we live in the Spirit, let us also walk in the Spirit" (Gal. 5:25), and *this* is what it means to "*walk* in the Spirit"—to take *one* step at a time, and for every new situation into which every new step takes you, no matter what it may be, to hear Christ saying to your heart, "I AM!"—and then to look up into His face by faith and say, "*Thou art!* That is all I need to know Lord, and I thank Thee; for Thou art never *less* than adequate!"

Thus to walk is to experience with Paul the apostle:

I know how to be abased and live humbly in straitened circumstances, and I know also how to enjoy plenty *and* live in abundance. I have learned in any and all circumstances, the secret of facing every situation, whether well-fed or going hungry, having a sufficiency *and* to spare or going without *and* being in want. I have strength for all things in Christ Who empowers me—I am ready for anything and equal to anything through Him Who infuses inner strength into me, [that is, I am self-sufficient in Christ's sufficiency]. (Phil. 4:12–13 AMPLIFIED NEW TESTAMENT)

Without this kind of faith it is impossible to please God, for without this kind of faith, it is impossible for God to reproduce His character in you—and that is godliness!

True godliness leaves the world convinced beyond a shadow of a doubt that the only explanation for *you*, is *Jesus Christ*—to whose eternally unchanging and altogether adequate "I AM!" your heart has learned to say with shatterproof faith, *"Thou art!"*

That is really all you need to know!

"And all of us, as with unveiled face, [because we] continued to behold and to reflect like mirrors the glory of the Lord, are constantly being transformed into [His very own] image in ever increasing splendor and from one degree of glory to another; [for this comes] from the Lord [Who is the] Spirit" (2 Cor. 3:18 AMPLIFIED NEW TESTAMENT).

Chapter IV

The Nature of the Mystery

Without controversy great is the mystery of godliness: God was manifest in the flesh. (1 Tim. 3:16)

Godliness is a mystery! Fail to grasp this fact and you will never understand the nature of godliness.

God did not create you to have just an ape-like capacity to imitate God. There would be no mystery in that, nor would this lift you morally much above the status of a monkey or a parrot! The capacity to imitate is vested in the one who imitates and does not derive from nor necessarily share the motives of the person being imitated, who remains passive and impersonal to the act of imitation.

The kindness and sheer generosity of a certain individual may be an act of pure benevolence, a genuine, selfless expression of the love of God. You may be tempted to imitate this person's act, to reproduce it in kind, or even to outmatch it, but *your motives may be entirely evil*, though the act identical!

Pride may persuade you "not to be outdone!" Jealousy may compel you to prove that the other party "is not the only pebble on the beach!" You may resent the gratitude or affection or respect that the other person, however unintentionally, has justly earned and deserved, or you may feel that the regard in which the other is now held may lessen your own influence over the future course of events!

In this case, you may deceive the undiscerning with your generosity and achieve your ends, but your "generosity" will not be godliness—your "generosity" will be *sin!*

In direct contrast to this, godliness—or Godlikeness—is the direct and exclusive consequence of *God's* activity in man. Not the consequence of your capacity to imitate God, but the consequence of God's capacity to *reproduce Himself* in you! This is the nature of the mystery!

Remove the mystery or try to explain it away, and the result inevitably must be disastrous, for you will no longer be anchored to anything absolute; you will be at liberty to choose your own God—the object of your own imitation; and your "godliness" will be the measure of your conformity to the object of your choice.

This, in point of fact, is what has been happening all through human history since Adam repudiated the basic principles of his own humanity and decided to go it alone—without God! Man may hide from God—as Adam did—but still the voice of God pursues him, echoing within the spiritual vacuum of his homesick, godless soul with all the relentless persistency of a love that never fails, crying, "Son of Adam, where *art* thou? Where *art* thou? Where *art* thou?"

This is what makes even the most degenerate individual incurably religious, even though his "religion" may be most horrible in character and assume the most hideous of forms—sometimes even disguising itself as a political creed, as in the national socialism of Adolf Hitler or as in the atheistic communism of Karl Marx, which for all their political flavor and advertised contempt for religion, *are nonetheless religions in themselves.*

It is one of Satan's subtleties that causes men to flee from God and seek to silence His voice *in the very practice of religion.*

So it is that man, to suit his own convenience, has reduced God to a theological formula, an ethical code or political program, a theatrical performance in a religious setting, the hero worship of some vivid personality of noble—or doubtful—reputation, or some dreamed-up image of his own better self; everything from a white cow to the wind in the trees or a "Christless Christianity" has been and still remains the object of man's idolatry!

The moment you come to realize that only *God* can make a man godly, you are left with no option but to *find* God, and to *know* God, and to let God *be* God in you and through you, whoever He may be—and this will leave you with no margin for picking and choosing—for there is only *one* God, and He is absolute, and He made you expressly for *Himself!*

Beware lest even as a Christian, you fall into Satan's trap! You may have *found* and come to *know* God in the Lord Jesus Christ, receiving Him sincerely as your Redeemer, yet if you do not enter into the mystery of godliness and allow God to *be* in you the origin of His own image, you will seek to be godly by submitting yourself to external rules and regulations and by conforming to behavior patterns imposed upon you by the particular Christian society that you have chosen and in which you hope to be found "acceptable." You will in this way perpetuate the pagan habit of practicing religion in the energy of the flesh, and in the very pursuit of righteousness commit idolatry in honoring "Christianity" more than Christ!

If then you have died with Christ to material ways of looking at things *and* have escaped from the world's crude *and* elemental notions *and* teachings of externalism, why do you live as if you still belong to the world?—Why do you submit to rules and regulations? [such as], Do not handle [this], Do not taste [that], Do not even touch [them], referring to things all of which perish with being used. To do this is to follow human precepts and doctrines. Such [practices] have indeed the outward appearance [that popularly passes] for wisdom, in promoting self-imposed rigor of devotion and delight in self-humiliation *and* severity of discipline of the body, but they are of no value in checking the indulgence of the flesh—the lower nature. [Instead, they do not honor God] but serve only to indulge the flesh. (Col. 2:20–23, AMPLIFIED NEW TESTAMENT)

God Cannot Be Seen

"And God said, let us make man in our image, after our likeness: . . . so God created man in his own image, in the image of God created he him" (Gen. 1:26–27a). This does not mean that man was created physically in the shape of God, nor that God looks like a man. We do not know what God looks like, for "no man hath seen God at any time" (John 1:18a). The Bible declares expressly that God is *invisible*: "Now unto the King eternal, immortal, invisible, the only wise God, be honor and glory for ever and ever. Amen . . . Who only hath immortality, dwelling in the light which no man can approach unto; whom no man hath seen, nor can see: to whom be honor and power everlasting. Amen" (1 Tim. 1:17; 6:16).

The Bible is equally emphatic concerning the absolute deity of the Son and His equality with the Father, which the Lord Jesus Christ never once repudiated; yet no man has seen God at any time—did no one ever see Jesus Christ? This is part of the mystery! "God was manifest in the flesh" (1 Tim. 3:16b), and further, "the only begotten Son, which is in the bosom of the Father, he hath declared him" (John 1:18b).

Philip said: "Lord, show us the Father, and it sufficeth us." And the Lord Jesus replied, "Have I been so long time with you and yet hast thou not known me, Philip? He that hath seen me hath seen the Father; and how sayest thou then, show us the Father?" (John 14:8–9). To reconcile this statement of the Lord Jesus and the fact of His own deity, with the fact that no man has seen God at any time, would seem at first to present an insuperable problem, for we are presented with the baffling conclusion that in spite of His total equality within the Trinity of Deity, it was possible, nineteen hundred years ago, for men on earth to look into the face of the Son, see the Father, and yet not see God!

The solution to this mystery, as I trust you will discover, is really remarkably simple—for in Jesus Christ Himself it has become an open secret and one which He invites *you* to share with Him!

It is of paramount importance, from the very outset, that we recognize the fact that when the Lord Jesus Christ was here on earth, He could *be* God and *be* man at one and the same time, but He could not *behave* as God and *behave* as man at one and the same time.

Allow me to explain a little, for to understand this is calculated to bring you untold comfort and encouragement and to give you an entirely new understanding of the Christian life, and a richer, fuller experience of Christ Himself.

Man was created in such a way that he could bear the *image* of God without God Himself becoming *visible*, so that not his *physical form* but his *capacity to behave* was designed to be the means through which God intended to express His nature and His character. As we have already seen, however, this godliness or Godlikeness was not to have been an imitation of God *by* man, but the direct result of the activity of God *in* man. In other words—God Himself behaving in and through *you!*

Man's behavior as the *effect*, was to have been the result of God's behavior as the *cause*. The former was to have been the "brightness" or the "out-shining" of the latter's glory, the "express *image*" of His Person! (Heb. 1:3). The image was to have been *visible*, while the Person still remained *invisible!*

Had the Lord Jesus Christ been the source of His own godliness, as He could have been, He would have been *behaving* as God only—both *cause* and *effect*—but the result would not have been visible! He had the *right* to behave as God only—for He *was* and *is* God, but He could not then have behaved as man: He would not in point of fact have been godly, or "Godlike," He would just simply have been God; but "no man hath seen God at any time," so that had He in this world both *been* and *behaved* as God, no one would have seen Him! In order to be seen, He had to be made "in the likeness of men" and be found "in fashion as a man" (Phil. 2:7–8) and *behave* as man.

To perform in perfection on earth the role for which Christ as God had created man, He had of His own free volition to accept the limitations imposed upon His own creature and to allow the Father *as God*, to be the origin of all His own behavior *as man*, so that His godliness as man was derived directly and exclusively from the activity of the Father in and through the Son.

In His sinless and perfect humanity Christ became "the sole expression of the glory of God—the Light-being, the out-raying of the divine—and He is the perfect imprint *and* very image of [God's] nature" (Heb. 1:3a AMPLIFIED NEW TESTAMENT). Or as Paul declares: "He is the exact likeness of the unseen God—the visible representation of the invisible" (Col. 1:15a AMPLIFIED NEW TESTAMENT).

This will help us to understand more fully what the Bible means when it says, "He humbled himself, and became obedient" (Phil. 2:8b). Not simply that He accepted the physical limitations of the human body but that He adopted an attitude of total dependence upon the Father and denied Himself the right to exercise all those prerogatives of deity that were undoubtedly His by virtue of the fact that He *was* both God and man, at one and the same time. He deliberately made Himself of "no reputation" and consistently refused to be the "cause" of His own "effect," declaring emphatically: "I can of mine own self do nothing" (John 5:30).

To use a simple illustration, no man has seen electricity at any time, yet an electric light bulb is so designed that whenever it receives the invisible electric current, *expression* is given to the *invisible* in terms of *light*.

It would not be true to say that the *bulb* is giving light, for it has no power to do so apart from the current which it receives: its behavior as a "light-giver" is the direct and exclusive consequence of the activity of the electricity in it and through it. The current is the *cause*; light is the *effect*. And though you can see the effect, you still cannot see the cause, though both represent the same source of energy!

You can enjoy the light, but you still cannot say that you have seen electricity! You can only say that you have seen a pure expression of it. In the same way, your behavior was intended by God to be a pure expression of His divine nature, though He remains unseen, and you can no more produce this effect *of yourself*, than a bulb can produce light *of itself!* Try, and you will soon be exhausted, and at best you will only produce a shabby imitation of the real thing. It may impress *you*, but it certainly will not impress anyone else!

It is only the Spirit of God acting within you, who can ever enable you to behave as God intended you to behave! "According as His divine power hath given unto us all things that pertain unto life and godliness through the knowledge of Him that hath called us to glory and virtue" (2 Peter 1:3). His divine power is all that it takes to be godly—*but it takes nothing less!*

In other words, it takes *God* to be a *man!* Man, that is, as God intended man to be! God created man to be inhabited *by* God *for* God! "In Him was life, and the life was the light of men" (John 1:4). The light depended on the life! Once the life was removed, the light went out, for the one was the consequence of the other, and man was plunged into the abysmal darkness of his own spiritual bankruptcy!

What of the "image"? Without a *cause* there was no *effect*, and the attributes of godliness gave way to the anarchy of godlessness! "God looked down from heaven upon the children of men, to see if there were any that did understand, that did seek God. Every one of them is gone back: they are altogether become filthy; there is none that doeth good, no, not one" (Ps. 53:2–3).

That is why a spiritual regeneration or new birth— "renewing of the Holy Spirit" (Titus 3:5c)—is absolutely imperative if man is to "put on the new nature (the regenerate self) created in God's image, (Godlike) in true righteousness and holiness" (Eph. 4:24 AMPLIFIED NEW TESTAMENT).

God Cannot Be Tempted

"Let no man say when he is tempted, I am tempted of God: for God cannot be tempted with evil, neither tempteth he any man" (James 1:13). If God cannot be tempted with evil, and Jesus Christ was God, how could He be tempted? "For we have not a high priest which cannot be touched with the feeling of our infirmities; but was in all points tempted like as we are, yet without sin" (Heb. 4:15).

It is no explanation to suggest that though He was *tempted*, the Lord Jesus Christ was not tempted with *evil*, but only in the sense that He was tested—for the statement, "yet without sin," clearly indicates that the nature of the temptation was such that it would have led to sin had it not been resisted. Indeed, we may safely assume that the temptations were as sinister and wicked and painful as anything that the Devil could devise, and for this very reason "in that he himself hath suffered being tempted, he is able to succor those that are tempted" (Heb. 2:18).

This then is also part of the mystery, that inherent in His

willingness to be made man, was the willingness of the Lord Jesus Christ to be made subject to temptation, for strange as it may seem, inherent in man's capacity to be godly is man's very capacity to sin! This may not at first be obvious, but we shall return to it at the appropriate time.

In the meantime, we are left with no alternative but to recognize the fact that it was not as *God* that Christ was tempted, but as *man*; that the limitations inherent in His ability to be tempted, were the same limitations that He had so willingly accepted as being inherent in His ability, though Creator, to play the role of man as His creature and thereby to become the visible representation of the invisible.

It has been shown that the primary limitation imposed upon you as man, in order that you may be in the likeness of your Maker and bear the image of the invisible, is that of total dependence upon God—in that your behavior, to be godly, must derive directly and exclusively from God's activity in you and through you. Any activity, therefore, in which you may engage, no matter how nobly conceived, which does not stem from this humble attitude of dependence upon God, violates the basic principles of your true humanity and the role for which you were created. By independence (or the absence of faith), you eliminate *God*, and substitute *yourself*, to become both cause and effect— the source of your own "godliness." But only God has the right to be the source of His own godliness, so that however unwittingly, you are acting as your own god!

You will still believe or pretend that you are worshiping God; but as the object of your imitation, even Christ Himself may only be an excuse for worshiping your own ability to imitate—an ability vested in yourself. And this is the basis of all self-righteousness!

It is startling to discover that even God may be used as an excuse for worshiping yourself, demonstrating again the satanic genius for distorting truth and deceiving man—for it was to this temptation that Adam and Eve fell in the Garden!

Satan said, "For God doth know that in the day ye eat thereof, then your eyes shall be opened, and ye shall be as gods, knowing good and evil" (Gen. 3:5). Satan succeeded in introducing into human experience an attitude toward God which he himself had already adopted, one of arrogant self-sufficiency, at once hostile to God, repudiating both the indispensability of the Creator to the creature and the moral responsibility of the creature to the Creator.

In so many words, Satan persuaded man that he could be Godlike without being God-conscious; that he had an adequate capacity in himself for being *good*, without the necessity of having *God;* that he could be righteous in his own right, *morally adult* without the need of being *spiritually alive!* In short, that man could be independent—both cause and effect!

Revelation 4:11 declares, "Thou art worthy, O Lord, to receive glory and honour and power: for thou hast created all things, and for thy pleasure they are and were created." If then, man is to be true to the purpose of his creation, his primary responsibility will be to please God; but the Bible declares emphatically that "without faith it is impossible to please him" (Heb. 11:6a). So that the first requirement in man, if he is to please God, is *faith.*

Faith involves something more than an academic nod! It involves that total dependence upon God that produces divine action in man.

Perhaps you may say, "Very well, I understand that faith is essential for those preoccupied with pleasing God, but I am *not* preoccupied with pleasing God! I do not wish to *displease* God, nor do I wish militantly to *oppose* Him. Frankly, I am disinterested! In my particular way of life, to me and to the circle in which I live and to the ambitions which I cherish, He is simply irrelevant. So far as God is concerned, I intend to maintain a passive neutrality!"

This, of course, is a sheer impossibility!

Created for a specific purpose, you cannot adopt an attitude of neutrality toward the God who made you, without being morally irresponsible. God is not optional, God is an imperative! For this reason, *faith* is not optional—faith is also an imperative! You either implement the purpose of your creation, by dependence upon God, or prostitute your humanity! "For whatsoever is not of faith is sin" (Rom. 14:23b).

The facts of the case are transparently clear: you were created to please God! Without faith it is impossible for you to please Him, so that without faith, whatever you do, no matter what it may be, is sin! The *only* alternative to faith is *sin!* That is why Satan will always present you with a reasonable alternative to faith, for he knows that if only he can get you to act in other than dependence upon God, you are defying your Creator, no matter how lofty your motives or otherwise commendable your actions.

Of the One who came to be perfect man, we read, "For even Christ pleased not himself" (Rom. 15:3a). As *God*, the Lord Jesus Christ had the right to please Himself, but as *man* He did not have that right. Whom then did He please? He pleased the Father! "For I do always those things that please him" (John 8:29b).

So that at the end of thirty years, before Christ's baptism by John and again during His public ministry, the Father could look down from heaven and say, "This is my beloved Son, in whom I am well pleased" (Matt. 3:17; 17:5). To have acted other than in dependence upon the Father would have violated the perfection of His own humanity. That is why Satan's attacks upon the Son were designed to trick Him, somehow, into acting on His own initiative; but though tempted again and again, and *in all points* like as we are, He was without sin. He never once acted in other than dependence on the Father.

God Cannot Be Taught

God is answerable to no one but to Himself, for He is the omnipotent Creator. "O man, who art thou that repliest against God? Shall the thing formed say to him that formed it, Why hast thou made me thus?" (Rom. 9:20). God's authority is final, and He obeys no one, for to obey would be less than an act of God. "Before me there was no God formed, neither shall there be after me. I, even I, am the LORD; and beside me there is no saviour" (Isa. 43:10c–11).

Yet herein is the "foolishness" and the "weakness" of God (1 Cor. 1:25), that the Word, who was in the beginning with God and was God, and by whom all things were made (John 1:1–2), and "in whom are hid all the treasures of wisdom and knowledge . . . the head of all principality and power" (Col. 2:3, 10b), should come into this world for your sake and mine, and do what as God He had never done! He learned to obey! He entered the school of obedience, for "though he were a Son, yet learned he obedience by the things which he suffered" (Heb. 5:8).

Was it possible for God to be in the school of obedience?

Only if as God He was prepared to behave as man! Had the Lord Jesus Christ on earth not only *been* God, but also *behaved* as God, not only would no one have seen Him and not only would it have been impossible for Him to be tempted, but it would have been impossible for Him to obey. But because He was willing to *be God* and *behave as man* at one and the same time, He was able to say, "For I have not spoken of myself; but the Father which sent me, he gave me a commandment, what I should say, and what I should speak" (John 12:49). As the "sent one," the Son placed Himself at the disposal of and submitted Himself in total obedience to the "sender," His Father, and "carried his obedience to the extreme of death, even the death of [the] cross!" (Phil. 2:8 AMPLIFIED NEW TESTAMENT). He was willing to "taste death for every man" (Heb. 2:9c) and suffer as Man for men what as God *behaving* as God, it would otherwise have been impossible for Him to do—for *God can never die.*

God, "the King eternal," is not only *invisible,* He is *immortal* (1 Tim. 1:17)—"in the sense of exemption from every kind of death" (1 Tim. 6:16a AMPLIFIED NEW TESTAMENT). But of the Lord Jesus Christ, the Son, it is written, "For both He Who sanctifies—making men holy—and those who are sanctified all have one [Father]. For this reason He is not ashamed to call them brethren, . . . Since, therefore, [these His] children share in flesh and blood—that is, in the physical nature of human beings—He [Himself] in a similar manner partook of the same [nature], that by [going through] death He might bring to nought *and* make of no effect him who had the power of death, that is, the devil" (Heb. 2:11, 14 AMPLIFIED NEW TESTAMENT).

In this amazing way our wonderful Redeemer, though never less than our Creator God, by His miraculous incarnation "made himself of no reputation, . . . and being found in fashion as a man, he humbled himself, and became obedient unto death" (Phil. 2:7–8b), and says to you and to me now, "As my Father hath sent me, even so send I you" (John 20:21b)—to learn to obey in the school of obedience and to enter into all the unspeakable privileges and blessings inherent in the *mystery of godliness.*

Chapter V

The Nature of Man

> And the very God of peace sanctify you wholly; and I pray
> God your whole spirit and soul and body be preserved
> blameless unto the coming of our Lord Jesus Christ.
> (1 Thess. 5:23)

It takes God to be a man, and godliness is the consequence of God's capacity to reproduce Himself in you!

In the light of these facts, it is necessary for us to examine the nature of man, discover how he has been made, and with what equipment he has been endowed which makes it *possible* for God to reproduce Himself in him. I am going to ask you to do a little "donkey-work" with me in exposing some of the basic facts of man's humanity.

If we are to place ourselves at God's disposal so that we may be used intelligently for the purpose for which we have been created, then we need to know something about ourselves. Sanctification is not a tight-lipped expression of piety dressed in black lace and a bonnet, so heavenly that it is of no earthly use. To be sanctified means that God is able to put us completely to our correct use, and only when this is the case are we truly sanctified.

For the sake of simplicity we are going to base our considerations upon the threefold description given to us by the Holy Spirit through the apostle Paul in 1 Thessalonians 5:23, "And the very God of peace sanctify you wholly; and I pray God your whole spirit and soul and body be preserved blameless unto the coming of our Lord Jesus Christ."

Quite obviously, this description presents man as a trinity—"spirit and soul and body"—and this is called a "trichotomy." I am fully aware that there are many earnest folk who prefer to think of man as consisting only of two parts: a tangible part, the body, and an intangible part, the soul and the spirit lumped together as an individual entity. This is called a "dichotomy."

It will not be my purpose to engage in any kind of theological controversy, for in this, as in so many other similar matters, there is truth in both suppositions, as there is truth to both sides of a coin. No matter how it falls, a nickel is worth a nickel, and you do not need to fight over which side is up—unless your game depends upon the toss!

To the fact that the body is tangible and that both soul and spirit are intangible, I readily agree, and in this sense I am a dichotomist; but that the Bible deliberately discerns between soul and spirit is to me equally indisputable, and in this sense I am a trichotomist!

> For the Word that God speaks is alive and full of power— making it active, operative, energizing and effective; it is sharper than any two-edged sword, penetrating to the dividing line of the breath of life (soul) and [the immortal] spirit, and of joints and marrow [that is, of the deepest parts of our nature] exposing *and* sifting *and* analyzing and judging the very thoughts and purposes of the heart. (Heb. 4:12 AMPLIFIED NEW TESTAMENT)

The Bible declares that "the life of the flesh is in the blood" (Lev. 17:11; see also Gen. 9:4 and Deut. 12:23). It is a physiological fact that the blood is manufactured in the marrow, and this "source of life," being of such paramount importance to the body as a whole, is buried and protected deep within the joints and the bones. The "joints" provide a unique "behavior mechanism," but it is ultimately from the "marrow" that there flows the life that *motivates the mechanism*, and this in turn gives *expression* to the life that does the motivating!

This is a beautiful illustration given to us by the Holy Spirit! The joints and the marrow are interdependent if they are both to function properly, and the one is buried deep within the other. Together they form one entity, yet each remains distinct; they may not safely part company, but the one must not be mistaken for the other. The final paradox is this: that the marrow itself lives only as there flows *through* it the very life that stems from it—the blood. "For the blood [not the marrow!] is the life" (Deut. 12:23).

This is why the blood is sacred in the Bible. It represents the *very life of God Himself*—the Spirit of God *within* the human spirit, as the blood flowing through and from the marrow, imparting the very life of God *to* the human spirit, from whence this life must flow to activate the "joints" within the human soul and produce that pattern of behavior which enables man to bear the image of the invisible and give expression to the indwelling, quickening, motivating life of God.

It takes *God* to be a *man!*

I believe that you will find it of immense value and a source of great enlightenment to consider man as Paul describes him, "spirit and soul and body"—a complete trinity. Much that is otherwise confusing will become refreshingly clear, and large tracts of the Bible will become infinitely more meaningful.

The most important part of man is his spirit; that is why it comes first in Paul's description. The next important part of man is his soul, and the least, though not *unimportant* part of him, is his body.

In that the body is the most tangible part of our being, and that with which we are best acquainted (having spent many hours admiring it in the mirror), it will be simplest for us to begin with this, the least important part of our humanity.

The Body

The body given by God to man is described in 2 Corinthians 5:1: "For we know that if our earthly house of this tabernacle were dissolved, we have a building of God, a house not made with hands, eternal in the heavens." This is your "earthly house," your temporary dwelling place, and you do not know how long you are going to be "at home." One atom bomb, and a whole lot of people are going to find themselves "homeless"—without a body—and you do not need to wait for a bomb if you would like to walk in front of a bus!

All forms of created life, however, have a "house to live in," vegetable, animal, or man. Look out of the window, and you will see many forms of created life, all of which have bodies, and you recognize them individually and specifically by the particular *shapes* of their bodies.

In your mind you say to yourself, "That's a tree—it lives in a tree-house; and there's a boy—he lives in a boy-house; but that's a dog—it lives in a dog-house!" You know a cow is not a carrot, and I would know *you* from a cat! We recognize each other individually as men by our own peculiar shapes—some more peculiar than others!

In common with all other forms of living creatures, we also possess that *physical* quality of life that enables us to grow and to reproduce. The tree in the garden was not always that size—nor were you! Some of us feel that our capacity to grow in certain directions is a privilege which we might acceptably be spared!

Our bodies, too, present us with a convenient means of inter-communication. The flowers invite their insect guests with exotic colors, scent, and form, and a little nectar puts the final touch to their seductive art! No one could say that a nightingale fails to communicate, or for that matter—a flea!

My busy fingers commit to paper what before too long your eyes will read, and should good fortune so dictate, maybe our paths one day will cross, and by the exercise of my thoracic and abdominal muscles, I will cause the thoracic cavity of my chest to operate like a bellows, causing a draught of air to pass swiftly through my larynx and cause my vocal cords, all suitably controlled, to produce a series of vibrations in a multiplicity of wavelengths to be conveyed in their own turn through the atmosphere; these will be caught by a cup-shaped appendage on the side of your head, called the ear, directed toward the outer eardrum and conveyed by an intricate mechanism to the inner ear, there to stimulate the waiting nerve ends, which will dutifully communicate an impulse to a certain section of your brain, and you will know that I have said, "Good morning!"

I will have communicated!

Maybe we will shake hands on the strength of it, and add physical communication to verbal communication, but in any case our bodies will have come in quite handy as a means of expression!

There is, however, a marked difference between the animal and the vegetable kingdoms. A tree does not get aggravated by a lot of little weeds in the garden or frightened by a bull! That is one of the advantages of being a vegetable! At the same time, a tree does not fall in love with the young bush over the wall or laugh when a fat man falls through his deck chair! That is one of the *disadvantages* of being a vegetable!

In other words a vegetable does not *behave!* It has a body but no behavior mechanism that enables it to calculate, react, or decide; this ability is peculiar to the animal kingdom and constitutes essentially the difference between an animal and a vegetable. The seat of all animal behavior is the soul, and it is with this part of our humanity we must now concern ourselves.

The Soul

That man is an animal goes without saying! We eat and drink the animal way; we breathe and breed and bleed—and die—the animal way! That man is not *only* animal will I trust become equally clear, but *animal* he is! Furthermore, as "fallen man," he is perfectly capable of behaving though *spiritually destitute* and completely "alienated from the life of God" (Eph. 4:18). His spiritual condition determines not *whether* he can behave, but only *how* he will behave.

Do animals, then, have souls? The answer to this question is found simply in the first chapters of Genesis.

"And to every beast of the earth, and to every fowl of the air, and to every thing that creepeth upon the earth, wherein there is life, I have given every green herb for meat" (Gen. 1:30). "And the LORD God formed man of the dust of the ground, and breathed into his nostrils the breath of life; and man became a living soul" (Gen. 2:7).

The expression used in the first verse quoted above, "wherein there is life," as relating to "every beast of the earth, and to every fowl of the air, and to everything that creepeth upon the earth"—the animal kingdom—in contrast to "every green herb"—the vegetable kingdom—is an expression which corresponds precisely to that found in the second verse quoted from Genesis 2:7 and referring to man, "and man became a living soul." Exactly the same Hebrew word is used in both cases, though differently translated in the King James Version and translated differently again as "creature" in Genesis 1:20, 21, 24; Genesis 2:19; and Genesis 9:10, 12, 15–16. In every case it is the same Hebrew word, and it means "soul" as applied to man or animal throughout the whole Bible.

The soul broadly speaking, is also a trinity—mind, emotion, and will—and enables all forms of animal life to react mentally, emotionally, and volitionally within the "capacity limits" with which each has been endowed by the Creator. A worm, for instance, is rather less intelligent than the average schoolboy, and certainly less affectionate, but it can still find its way around!

You *behave* by the exercise of your will under the influence of your mind and your emotions, and this process does not in itself require any visible activity on the part of the body. Your body is required only when you wish to give *outward* expression to your *inward* behavior—in other words, when you wish to communicate with your external circumstances, and the way in which you ultimately communicate by physical activity may far from represent your true *internal* behavior! "The words of his mouth were smoother than butter [external behavior], but war was in his heart [internal behavior]: his words were softer than oil, yet were they drawn swords" (Ps. 55:21).

Do you get the point? You said to him, "You're welcome"—but in your heart you could have strangled him!

When last did *you* sit in church with the body neatly propped against the back of the seat, and with the gaze politely set in the preacher's direction, while all the time you were visiting with someone *fifty miles away*? How many heated verbal exchanges have *you* had with some absent foe whilst standing at the kitchen sink—and you never uttered a word!

What exciting moments you have had, and what frightening adventures—lying fast asleep upon your bed! Some of the best sermons I ever preached, I preached in bed! A pity only that on those rare occasions of unusual eloquence, it was the preacher himself who slept—and not the congregation!

Psychiatrists declare that far more damage can be done and far deeper impressions be made upon the character by this "unseen behavior" of the soul, unmatched by physical action, than by the actual deeds themselves. The fascination of the cinema, in watching television, soaking in a novel, or in scanning the many crime reports that fill the daily newspapers is that the unsuspecting victim of this process "lives" the part of the chosen character in the innermost recesses of the mind and emotions, thereby satisfying some inward urge to be a "hero," attracting attention to himself, wreaking some awful vengeance upon unkind society, indulging some illicit lust, or fulfilling such ignoble ambitions in the secret of the soul, as might otherwise be incompatible, *if performed*, with the impression he would like to give to others of himself!

"The thoughts of the wicked are an abomination to the LORD" (Prov. 15:26a).

"For as he thinketh in his heart, so is he" (Prov. 23:7a).

"Whosoever hateth his brother is a murderer" (1 John 3:15a).

"Whosoever looketh on a woman to lust after her hath committed adultery with her already in his heart" (Matt. 5:28).

Fortunately, this activity within the soul can be as beneficial as it can be damaging, nourishing nobility of character and making such indelible impressions as may shape our future ends. Lofty deeds first cradled in the soul and later clothed with action in the light of day! It was with this in mind that Paul wrote to the Philippian church: "Finally, brethren, whatsoever things are true, whatsoever things are honest, whatsoever things are just, whatsoever things are pure, whatsoever things are lovely, whatsoever things are of good report; if there be any virtue, and if there be any praise, think on these things" (Phil. 4:8).

Paul knew that to *"think on these things"* would inevitably provide the "dress rehearsal" for their ultimate performance, profoundly affecting the behavior from within and from without.

The behavior process of the soul may be protracted and leisurely. On the other hand it can take place with amazing rapidity and be matched almost instantly with the appropriate physical action, as a driver in an emergency applies his brakes and swerves to a grinding halt, a fielder leaps to catch a ball and win the game, or some bodyguard throws himself in a splitsecond between his master and the deadly missile of his murderous assassin!

Supposing you became very angry with me, and highly excited—your *emotions* thus disturbed might well say to your *will* "Hit him!"—and if your emotions dominated your will, what would you do? You would hit me! Probably, however, in the meantime, your *mind*—acting on information received through the eyes—would say to your will, "Don't do that! He's bigger than you are. And he will hit you back!" This is how you function thousands of times a day. You look at your watch, and the *mind* says to the *will*, "It's time to go!" and the *will* says to the *legs*, "Quick march!" and off you go!

Perhaps, however, your watch is slow! No matter, then, how sincere your mind may be in the conclusions drawn from the false information provided by the watch—you will be *sincerely wrong!* The train has gone!

Having believed what you heard about a certain person, your emotional reactions toward that individual may be adversely affected—and what you heard may well have been a wicked lie! Quite obviously, if your mental conclusions and your emotional attitudes are to be not only quite *sincere*, but *right*, they must derive from *truth!* Your morality may be determined by the degree to which your *will* responds to *right* mental conclusions and to *right* emotional reactions, and translates these influences into positive action. The basis therefore, of all true morality is *Truth!*

The Bible makes it abundantly clear that Truth is expressed through the Word. "In many separate revelations—each of which set forth a portion of the Truth—and in different ways God spoke of old to [our] forefathers in and by the prophets. [But] in the last of these days He has spoken to us in [the person of a] Son" (Heb. 1:1–2a AMPLIFIED NEW TESTAMENT).

Words are essentially a means of communicating information, and the information conveyed will affect the behavior of the recipient to the degree in which he acts upon it. When you *act* in strict obedience to the *Truth* revealed through the *Word*, the Truth *behaves*, and the end effect is *righteousness!*

As the absolute source of Truth revealed through the Word, God is the absolute source of righteousness. Satan, on the other hand, as the absolute source of all that is *false*, is the absolute source of all *unrighteousness!* The first word he ever spoke to man was a lie, and he has been deceiving him ever since! He "masquerades as an angel of light" (2 Cor. 11:14 AMPLIFIED NEW TESTAMENT), and propagates his malicious lies through those of his dupes who "by good words and fair speeches deceive the hearts of the simple" (Rom. 16:18b).

It is interesting to note that within the animal kingdom only man is capable of producing words and of recognizing them to any great extent in order to convey and to receive exact items of information; to hear, utter—or to distort—the Truth! Maybe his capacity for speech plays a far bigger part than we had thought in man's capacity to behave as a moral being. It lays him open to the Word!

Monkeys chatter in the trees and dogs may bark at cats, but though it may be very meaningful to them, what they have to say is somewhat ungrammatical! Even if the parrot *can* say "Pretty Poll" or "Kiss me, darling," it has only learned to copy certain sounds—no *message* is conveyed! What added complications would result for all mankind if once our poor, dumb friends could get together and discuss the stupidity and wickedness of men! What *lies* our Tabby Cat might tell the cat next door about the way we live at home! Let this then be our consolation—if these lesser creatures cannot *know* the Truth, neither can they very well distort it!

Notwithstanding this, neither animal nor man needs any particular relationship to God just simply to "behave." If you own a dog, when you get home does he not recognize you as his master, wag his tail, and run to meet you, indicating with his muddy paws all down your front how pleased he is to see you? The dog does not object when you enter the house through the front door; he knows you have the right, because you live there; but what if someone climbs through the bathroom window at three o'clock in the morning? The dog would think to himself, "My master doesn't *usually* come in through the bathroom window at three in the morning—not often!" Then after suitable investigation, sufficient to satisfy himself that the shape of the body does not correspond with that of any friend of the family, as previously recorded in his memory, the faithful dog would discharge his responsibilities by indicating his distinct displeasure with the other, sharper end of his anatomy, probably to the detriment of the intruder's pants!

Take the dog for a walk, and when he strays too far, you call him; then, standing in the distance, head to one side with one ear up and the other ear down, and with a mischievous grin on his face, the dog will hesitate! "What shall I do? Shall I obey—or chase the cat? That would be far more interesting!" Then you shout a little louder, and with some impatience in your voice, and the dog remembers what happened last time that he disobeyed you—and it hurt! So he comes to heel, tail half between his legs, and just far enough away from you to be safe!

All this behavior has in the first instance taken place within the soul of the dog, and the muddy paw marks on your trousers indicate that on your arrival home, the dog has "functioned"; communicating to you his mental recognition and his emotional delight by translating them into volitional action, using his body to run through the dirtiest puddle he can find, and then jumping up to greet you!

I was staying on the east coast of New England some years ago, and my hostess explained the great dilemma in which she had found herself, in her desire to feed both birds and squirrels at one and the same time. She discovered that the squirrels had the unhappy knack of getting all that she provided for the birds, and she had used all her ingenuity to discover a means whereby she could segregate their appetites!

Then she hit on the master plan! From the second story of her home there was a laundry line which ran out over a pulley to a distant tree, over a lawn; and so, taking about two yards of fine thread and the lid of a tin to act as a small tray, she placed the peanut butter on the lid and suspended it from the clothesline with the thread and pulled it out half-way between the house and the tree. That was for the birds, and no squirrel could get at that!

My hostess went on to explain that only a matter of minutes later, as she looked out of the window, she saw a squirrel run up the trunk of the tree, climb upside-down along the laundry line, hang by its hind legs over the tray, pull it up by the thread with its front paws, and eat the peanut butter! Then, dropping the tin lid, the squirrel returned by the same route to the tree with a big, satisfied grin on its face. That was not just *instinct*—as far as my hostess was concerned, it was not even *funny!* It was cold calculation, brilliantly executed. And still outwitted by the squirrels, this good lady has given up trying to feed the birds!

We may understand, therefore, that if all that we consist of is body and soul, then man is nothing more than a clever animal, and the natural man, in his "unregenerate" condition, behaves as if this were so. He busies himself primarily with "servicing" the body, and to this end goes out to work to earn his daily bread and such other luxuries as will add to the comfort or pleasurable use of his body; he is only vaguely aware that he has a soul, but somehow recognizes that he must "keep body and soul together," otherwise his kindly relatives will come and bury the body!

This is not irrelevant to the times in which we live, for although we may not discuss the matter within the compass of this book, the hypothesis that man is nothing more than the highest form of animal life as yet developed on this particular planet, lies at the very heart of Christless, godless, and God-hating communism. This is the very basis upon which the theory of atheistic dialectic materialism is founded—a philosophy admirably suited to clothe that satanic attitude of arrogant self-sufficiency, which we saw in chapter 4 to be the very essence of the attitude introduced by the Devil into human experience at the Fall, repudiating both the indispensability of the Creator to the creature and the moral responsibility of the creature to the Creator.

According to this supposition, not only does man cease to be morally responsible, but he has no eternal destiny; when he dies, he dies like a dog, forfeiting thereby only animal existence. Little wonder, therefore, that life on the other side of the Iron Curtain is held so cheap! We are threatened today on every side, from within and from without, by this wicked philosophy of human existence, and we need to know why it is that we consider ourselves to be *men* as *distinct* from mere animals and not just *animals* that happen to be called men.

The Human Spirit

What is the essential difference between man as God intended and the rest of the animal kingdom?

God has given to man what He has *not* given to any other form of created life—the human spirit; this though intrinsically indivisible *from* the human soul must not be mistaken *for* the human soul. As the marrow within the joints, so is the human spirit buried deep within the human soul, remaining essentially distinct, yet *together* forming that complete *immaterial entity* capable of endless survival after physical death, as opposed to the purely "animal soul" common to the rest of the animal kingdom, which possesses no such capacity either to survive or to be held morally responsible beyond the grave.

This capacity for endless survival beyond physical death must not be confused with "immortality," which is a characteristic, strictly speaking, of God alone.

> I give thee charge in the sight of God, who quickeneth all things ["preserves alive all living things," AMPLIFIED NEW TESTAMENT] and before Christ Jesus, who before Pontius Pilate witnessed a good confession; . . . which in his times he shall show, who is the blessed and only Potentate, the King of kings, and Lord of lords; who only hath immortality; ["In the sense of exemption from every form of death." AMPLIFIED NEW TESTAMENT] (1 Tim. 6:13, 15–16a)

In God and God alone is life eternally inherent—eternally *pre*-existent and self-*perpetuating*—and this characteristic of deity is shared equally by the Son, the Lord Jesus Christ, with the Father, and with the "Eternal Spirit" (Heb. 9:14)— "For even as the Father has life in Himself *and* is self-existent, so He has given to the Son to have life in Himself *and* be self-existent" (John 5:26 AMPLIFIED NEW TESTAMENT).

It is for this reason that God is absolute, self-sufficient, and completely *independent*. All other forms of life—vegetable, animal, spiritual or angelic—are essentially "created" and not "self-existent," and remain *dependent* upon the Creator as the one who is the only source and sustainer of all life.

> God that made the world and all things therein, seeing that he is Lord of heaven and earth, dwelleth not in temples made with hands; neither is worshiped with men's hands, as though he needed any thing, seeing he giveth to all life, and

breath, and all things: . . . For in him we live, and move, and have our being. (Acts 17:24–25, 28a)

In whose hand is the soul of every living thing, and the breath of all mankind. (Job 12:10)

And the God in whose hand thy breath is, and whose are all thy ways, hast thou not glorified. (Dan. 5:23c)

To quote the late Archdeacon T. C. Hammond, M.A., onetime principal of Moore Theological College, Sydney, Australia (*In Understanding Be Men*): "Immortality does not merely mean endless 'survival,' but 'eternal life.' It is its *quality* which is important. Whilst the souls of the unregenerate will survive the disintegration of the body, only the regenerate can experience the life, which is of the same quality as the Divine Life—which has been 'brought to light' through the gospel" (see 2 Tim. 1:10).

The human spirit is this unique capacity which God has given to man, which enables him both to receive and be motivated by the very life of God Himself. To return to my illustration of chapter 4, the human spirit is the lamp, incapable itself of producing light, but capable of receiving that which working in and through it produces light, and upon which it must be constantly dependent if it is to fulfill the purpose for which, as a lamp, it was created. "The spirit of man is the candle of the LORD" (Prov. 20:27a).

As translated in Proverbs 20:20, the word "candle" means lamp, and what the electricity is to an electric lamp and what oil is to an oil lamp, the Holy Spirit is to the human spirit. With relentless consistency throughout the Scriptures, oil represents the person and office of the Holy Spirit, in whose person God is able to inhabit man's humanity and make him a partaker of His own divine nature, whereby man may be not only physically alive, as an animal, but spiritually alive, like God.

For thus saith the high and lofty One that inhabiteth eternity, whose name is Holy; I dwell in the high and holy place, with him also that is of a contrite and humble spirit, to revive the spirit of the humble, and to revive the heart of the contrite ones. (Isa. 57:15)

Whereby are given unto us exceeding great and precious promises: that by these ye might be partakers of the divine nature. (2 Peter 1:4a)

It is your capacity to receive God, to enjoy God, and to be enjoyed *by* God which makes you man as opposed to mere animal, and it is only God in you that enables you to function as He intended you as man to function.

Lose God, and lose everything that truly makes you man and enables you to behave as God intended man to behave! The anarchy of godlessness begins! The human spirit destitute of the Holy Spirit leaves the soul abandoned as a ship without a rudder on a storm-tossed sea, spiritually bankrupt, dead—"alienated from the life of God" (Eph. 4:18)—an easy prey to every evil, malicious, and malevolent influence of which it may fall foul!

This has been the unhappy lot of man since Adam made his fateful choice! To rescue him, God sent His Son—to make man *man* again, man as God intended man to be!

"For I will not contend for ever, neither will I be angry always, for [were it not so] the spirit of *man* would faint *and* be consumed before Me, and *My purpose in* creating the souls of men would be frustrated" (Isa. 57:16 AMPLIFIED OLD TESTAMENT).

Chapter VI

The First Man—Adam

And so it is written, The first man Adam was made a living soul. (1 Cor. 15:45a)

Thank you for the "donkey-work" of the preceding chapter, and I trust that you are still with me! We have seen that when you act in strict obedience to the *Truth*, the Truth *behaves*, and the result is *righteousness*—"conformity to the divine will in thought, purpose and action" (Rom. 6:18b AMPLIFIED NEW TESTAMENT). We have seen also that the Truth is communicated through the Word, having its absolute source in God. "Every good gift and every perfect boon is from above, and comes down from the Father, who is the source of all Light. In Him there is no variation nor the shadow of change" (James 1:17 WEYMOUTH).

We have seen also, as we considered the nature of man, that the human spirit is that part of man created to be inhabited by the Holy Spirit, that man might exercise his will under the influence of a God-taught mind and of God-controlled emotions, to the exclusion of all other alien influences that would deflect him from conformity to the divine will in thought, purpose, or action.

GOD
(THE TRINITY OF DEITY)

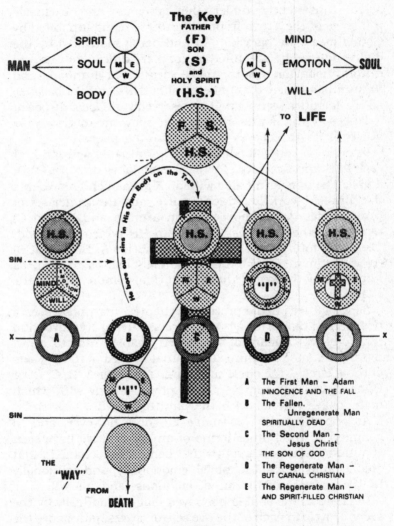

The Key
FATHER
(F)
SON
(S)
and
HOLY SPIRIT
(H.S.)

SPIRIT · SOUL · BODY → **MAN**

MIND · EMOTION · WILL → **SOUL**

TO **LIFE**

He bore our sins in His Own Body on the Tree

SIN

SIN

THE **"WAY"**

FROM **DEATH**

A The First Man – Adam
INNOCENCE AND THE FALL

B The Fallen, Unregenerate Man
SPIRITUALLY DEAD

C The Second Man – Jesus Christ
THE SON OF GOD

D The Regenerate Man – BUT CARNAL CHRISTIAN

E The Regenerate Man – AND SPIRIT-FILLED CHRISTIAN

Chart 1

Adam in His Innocency

In his innocency and before the Fall, the first man Adam acted consistently under the gracious and exclusive influence of the Truth from *within* him, being inhabited by God Himself. By partaking of and being motivated by the divine nature, he was lifted out of mere *animal* status and *animal* behavior into the noble vocation of *manhood* and *human* behavior—that of being altogether *godlike* because all his faculties were placed unreservedly at God's disposal.

To clarify the matter still further, allow me to draw your attention to the charts on the following pages.

In chart 1, you will notice a line terminated with an X at each end and five sets of circles, each labeled, A, B, C, D, and E. The line terminated with an X at each end represents the physical world in which we live, and the center set of three circles (superimposed upon a cross and labeled C) represents the Lord Jesus Christ in His perfect manhood. The other four sets of three circles (labeled A, B, D, and E) represent man in four different relationships to God, as indicated by the key at the bottom right-hand corner of the chart.

As explained in the preceding chapter, man possesses a body in common with all other forms of living creatures and that physical quality of life which enables him to grow, reproduce, and communicate, so that in each of the five sets of three circles, the circle containing the letter A, B, C, D, or E, as in chart 2, represents the physical body with which man makes contact with the physical world.

As opposed to the vegetable kingdom however, and in common with all other forms of animal life, we have seen that man possesses a soul—that behavior-mechanism that enables him to react mentally, emotionally, and volitionally by the exercise of his mind, emotions, and his will.

In chart 2, the soul is portrayed diagrammatically by the second circle in each of the five sets of circles, four above the line and one below the line. Basically each of these circles is divided into three sections, representing mind (M), emotion (E), and will (W) (see further description in the key at the top right-hand corner of chart 1).

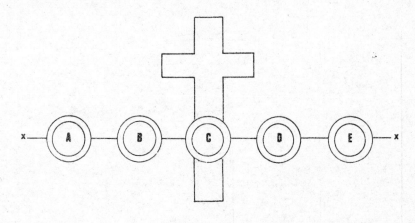

Chart 2

The presence of the capital I in the circles representing the soul in figures B and D and the presence of the cross in the circle representing the soul in figure E is explained more fully later in this and in succeeding chapters of the book.

In chapter 5 it has been clearly demonstrated that what distinguishes man from the animal kingdom is that he possesses a human spirit—the "candle [lamp] of the Lord" (Prov. 20:27)—this unique capacity that enables him both to receive and to be motivated by the very life of God Himself. Chart 4 adds a third circle to each of the five sets of circles, which represents the human spirit; this circle is the highest of the three circles in each case, except in that of figure B, where it is the lowest.

Thus by each set of three circles, extending either above

the line (as in figures A, C, D, and E) or below the line (as in figure B), the whole man is represented—spirit, soul, and body (as indicated in the key at the top left-hand corner of chart 1).

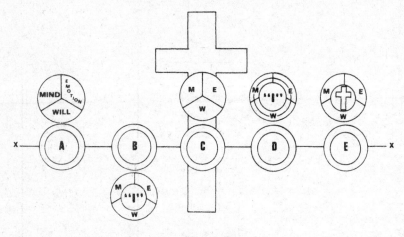

Chart 3

Furthermore, above figures A, B, C, D, and E in chart 1, God is represented in the Trinity of Deity by the large circle subdivided into three sections, representing the Father (F), the Son (S), and the Holy Spirit (H.S.), whose presence is also indicated in the top circles of figures A, C, D, and E.

Figure A represents the first man Adam before the Fall. I would like you to consider this with me for a moment, bearing in mind that to commit spiritual issues to paper in diagrammatic form must inevitably involve a certain amount of oversimplification.

You will notice in figure A (chart 1) that the human spirit of the first man Adam is shown with a smaller circle within it, marked H.S. and representing the Holy Spirit. And though this in itself may be the first oversimplification, I believe it to be legitimate, and I know of no better way of indicating the indisputable fact that God created man to be not only *physically* but also *spiritually* alive.

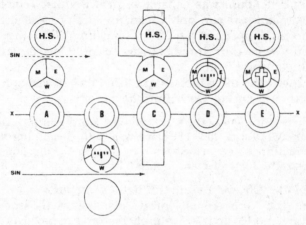

Chart 4

When God gave to Adam the solemn warning, "For in the day that thou eatest thereof thou shalt surely die" (Gen. 2:17b), it is quite obvious that He was not referring to physical death as the first consequence of sin, though this did become a *secondary* consequence. God was referring to spiritual death, and it is equally obvious that Adam was capable of *spiritual* death whilst remaining *physically* alive, a fact constantly asserted in the New Testament. To the redeemed Paul writes: "But yield yourselves unto God, as those that are alive from the dead" (Rom. 6:13) and "And you hath he quickened, who were dead in trespasses and sins" (Eph. 2:1).

For a Christian is literally a person who has been raised spiritually from the dead.

Apart from life however, death is meaningless! You can

say of a piece of wood, "It's dead!" But you cannot say the same of a lump of clay. Clay has no capacity for life, and therefore it cannot die—it cannot forfeit what it does not have; death is what is *left* when the life *that should be there* is absent! If Adam was capable of death whilst remaining physically alive, it can only mean that he possessed originally, in his innocency, a quality of life *other than physical,* which under certain circumstances he could forfeit, without forfeiting physical life.

What was the life which Adam forfeited? It was spiritual life—the very life of God Himself!

> In the beginning was the Word, and the Word was with God, and the Word was God. The same was in the beginning with God. All things were made by him . . . In him was life; and the life was the light of men. (John 1:1—4)

When the life went out, the light went out!

When the Lord Jesus Christ raised Lazarus from the dead, how did He do it? He simply restored to Lazarus' body the physical life which his body had forfeited, and without which his body could only rot. What happens when a sinner turns to Christ and his sins are forgiven? Paul says, "For as in Adam all die, even so in Christ shall all be made alive" (1 Cor. 15:22). Raised from the dead! "He made us alive together in fellowship *and* in union with Christ—He gave us the very life of Christ Himself, the same new life with which He quickened Him" (Eph. 2:5b AMPLIFIED NEW TESTAMENT). Raised from the dead!

As the raising of Lazarus from the dead involved the restoration to him of the quality of life which he had forfeited—*physical life*—so it is reasonable to suppose that being *spiritually* raised from the dead involves the restoration to man of *that* quality of life which he forfeited by the Fall—*spiritual life.* The life restored in resurrection must be that life which *being forfeited* left behind the state of death from which the dead are raised!

How then is spiritual life restored to those who are redeemed? We know that it is by the presence of the Holy Spirit.

> But when the goodness of God our Saviour and His love to man came to light, not in virtue of any righteous deeds which we had done, but in His own mercy, He saved us by means of the bath of regeneration and renewal by the Holy Spirit, which He poured out on us richly through Jesus Christ our Saviour. (Titus 3:4—6 WEYMOUTH)

> Strengthened with might by his Spirit in the inner man. (Eph. 3:16b)

> Know ye not that ye are the temple of God, and that the Spirit of God dwelleth in you? (1 Cor. 3:16)

If therefore spiritual life is restored by the presence of the Holy Spirit, it is a reasonable supposition that spiritual death took place by the *forfeiture* of the presence of the Holy Spirit. Furthermore, as already discussed in the first chapter, when here on earth, the Lord Jesus Christ did not play the part of *fallen* man, nor did He demonstrate only the role of *regenerate* man—He came simply to be *man* as He as Creator had created him, with all the privileges and with all the limitations involved, and as *man*, He lived constantly by the Father through the Holy Spirit. Is it not safe to assume, therefore, that the first man Adam in his innocency enjoyed the life of God through the Holy Spirit, even as the Lord Jesus as man enjoyed the life of the Father through the Holy Spirit, and as every redeemed sinner is *renewed* with the life of God through the Holy Spirit?

I have taken time to consider this matter with you at some length, because in the absence of chapter and verse, you have the right to know by what process of reasoning the first man Adam, as represented in my figure A, is shown as possessing the Holy Spirit within his human spirit. There may be others who would wish to explain the matter differently, and I will not quarrel with them so long as it is clearly recognized that Adam in his innocency was not only *physically* but also *spiritually* alive; that the spiritual life he possessed was the very life of God Himself, not *inherent* in Adam, but *derived* from God and God-imparted; and that by the forfeiture of this life, Adam was capable of suffering a spiritual death, which physically, both in the area of his soul and of his body, he could survive. This will be the sense in which I speak of Adam being indwelt by the Holy Spirit before he sinned.

Referring again to figure A, we see the human spirit of the first man Adam filled with the life of God through the presence of the Holy Spirit; imagine now that this life floods his soul—his "behavior mechanism"—so that his mind is totally, unreservedly placed at the disposal of the Holy Spirit, and his emotions are placed totally, unreservedly at the disposal of the Holy Spirit. Who now controls his will? The Holy Spirit—the Spirit of Truth! Everything he does and every attitude he adopts will be an expression of the God who made him, who lives within him, and expresses Himself through him. He becomes the "brightness of his glory" and the "express image of his Person" (Heb. 1:3); Godlike not by imitation, but by allowing God to behave through him.

Had we been given the opportunity at that time of watching Adam in action, we would have seen a perfect image of God, expressing *His* nature and *His* character, but God Himself would still have remained invisible. This image of God is represented in the diagram by the unshaded margin at the circumference of the circle representing the body, for as we have already seen, it is by physical activity that expression is given to the behavior processes of the soul, making visible to the world without what is invisible within.

As God made Adam in his innocency, Adam's external behavior *in the body* corresponded completely to his internal behavior *in the soul*, which in turn reflected *exactly* the gracious activity of the Holy Spirit. He was a lamp that was lit, fulfilling the purpose for which God made him.

It is quite obvious that if this process had been purely mechanical and if Adam had possessed no capacity to exercise his own choice, he would have been no more than a robot, an impersonal "device," completely incapable of responding to or of satisfying the love of God, for only love can satisfy love, and love cannot be compelled! To win a person's friendship you clasp his hand—you do not clench your fist! All genuine affection springs from free volition, and you cannot truly love without the power to choose.

A little girl will love her china doll, because her imagination is vivid enough to imagine every kind of response; it answers back, it laughs, and it cries—it can be spanked when it is naughty, and it can be kissed when it is good! But there comes a day when the old china doll lies neglected, staring glassy-eyed in the corner of the cupboard—jettisoned for the lifeless thing it is! Nothing now but the real thing—for all the calls a child may make upon her time and patience—can ever satisfy a mother's love. And the supreme prize? To be loved back! And God is love!

Man was made to love God back, to reciprocate God's love to man. And Adam in his innocency, knowing that he had been created to please God and to bear His image, and knowing that he could only do so by maintaining an attitude of total dependence upon Him, expressed his love *to* God by total dependence *on* God! This was a faith-love relationship, which could not help but express itself in total obedience, for obedience is the only logical consequence of faith.

If you give me your advice and I depend on it, then I do as you say! This is the characteristic of faith, as the word is used in the Bible; it involves an attitude toward God which always *does* what *He* says, and if you always *do* what He *says*, the world will see *Him* behaving through *you*—and that is godliness!

The picture then that we have of the first man Adam before the image was marred, is of one whose love for God was demonstrated by his dependence on God, resulting in obedience *to* God—*indwelt* by the life of God, *controlled* by the life of God, and *expressing* the life of God! Adam's spirit, soul, and body were wholly filled and flooded by God Himself.

> When I view *and* consider Your heavens, the work of Your fingers, the moon and the stars which You have ordained *and* established; What is man, that You are mindful of him, and the son of [earthborn] man, that You care for him? Yet You have made him but little lower than God *and* heavenly beings, and You have crowned him with glory and honor. You made him to have dominion over the works of Your hands; You have put all things under his feet. (Ps. 8:3—6 AMPLIFIED OLD TESTAMENT)

Made by God to have dominion over all the works of His hands, man's authority was vested in him only by virtue of this "faith-love" relationship to God which would keep him always conformed to the divine will, in "purpose, thought and action," he was to be the visible means of communication between an invisible God and His visible creation, whose sovereignty "over all the works of His hands" would be subject only to the sovereignty of God Himself.

This was the significance of the forbidden fruit! It was at this point that Adam was to recognize the limits of his own authority and to maintain his attitude of humble dependence upon his Maker, knowing that his own "dominion" derived from God alone. Given the moral capacity to choose, it was necessary for man to have a point at which choice could be exercised, and by humbly submitting to this divine prohibition at the tree in the Garden, Adam was able to affirm both his desire to please God and at the same time to acknowledge that his very life *depended* on Him. In this way his love toward God found tangible expression in the obedience of faith, and it qualified him to be the recipient of the divine life, as the agent of the divine Will.

Adam had nothing to do to be alive spiritually—he *was alive!* God made him that way!

The Conversion of Adam

Perhaps you did not know that Adam was converted! But he was, for conversion begins with a change of mind, and Adam changed his mind about God! He allowed the Devil to poison his understanding, and believing a lie, *he died by faith!*

God had made it abundantly clear that the moment Adam repudiated his faith-love relationship toward Him, he would surely die, forfeiting the life of God which makes man *man*—for it takes God to be a man! Satan, as we saw in chapter 4, succeeded in persuading Adam that he could lose God and lose nothing! That he could exercise dominion over all the works of God's hands without subjecting himself to the demands of God's will! He would now be his own free agent, enjoying liberty of action in the area of his mind, his emotion, and his will, without the restrictive influence of the Spirit of God. He was to trade dependence for independence! He was to throw out his own big chest, stick out his own big chin, stand on his own big feet, and demonstrate the adequacy of a man without God! He acted on what he believed from the lips of a liar—and died!

In chart 1, you will notice the introduction of the sin principle into human experience (the dotted arrow in figure A): "Wherefore, as by one man sin entered into the world, and death by sin; and so death passed upon all men, for that all have sinned" (Rom. 5:12).

What happened? God had said, "For in the day that thou eatest thereof thou shalt surely die" (Gen. 2:17). Did Adam die in the day that he ate thereof? Not physically! The next morning when he awoke, the sky was still blue, the sun was still shining, and the birds were still singing in the trees! He could think with his mind, react with his emotions, and decide with his will; body and soul, he still functioned! Physically alive and soulishly active, the animal part of him survived, but the very day that he repudiated his dependence *on* God, Adam forfeited the presence *of* God! He was dead! Only the shell remained, henceforth to be a monstrous parody of the real thing (chart 1, figure B).

God had thrown the master switch, and the Holy Spirit withdrew from the human spirit, and when the life went out, the light went out, and the soul of man was plunged into the abysmal darkness of a fallen humanity, uninhabited by God; and ever since Adam fell into sin, every child born into this world has been born in the pattern of fallen man: "By nature the children of wrath, even as others . . . Having the understanding darkened, being alienated from the life of God through the ignorance that is in them, because of the blindness of their heart" (Eph. 2:3b; 4:18).

Godlessness, lifelessness, and lightlessness were the inevitable consequences of Adam's conversion! Of his own free volition he stepped out of dependence into independence, out of life into death, and out of light into darkness! He was on his own! At least—he thought he was!

Figure B in chart 1 shows the human spirit of fallen man (the lowest circle) now destitute of the Holy Spirit; sin had come between him and God. This in itself would have been bad enough; for in the absence of the motivating life of God, in terms of his behavior, man would simply have been reduced to the status of a very clever animal, for remember, being spiritually alive does not determine *whether* a man can behave, but simply *how* he will behave—and even so, he might have been as harmless and as pleasant as a flock of sheep!

Something happened, however, even worse than the

forfeiture of the presence of God! You will notice in figure B (chart 1) that a small circle has been introduced into the center circle representing the soul, and in the center of the smaller circle, a capital I! From now on man is to be "ego-centric" instead of "Deo-centric!"—he has become an "I" specialist! And this principle of ego-centricity is called in the Bible "the flesh" (not to be confused with the human body) and has its origin and roots in the Devil himself (Rom. 7:18; 8:3). Another word used for this evil principle in the Bible is "sin," as opposed to "sins" (Rom. 7:14, 20; John 16:9) and yet again "the old man" (Rom. 6:6; Eph. 4:22; Col. 3:9), or "self" (2 Cor. 5:15).

In the absence of the Holy Spirit instructing and controlling Adam's mind and emotions and will with Truth, Satan, who is the father of lies (John 8:44), invaded the soul of man, usurped the sovereignty of God, and introduced this evil agency to pollute, corrupt, abuse, and misuse his soul and so to twist and bend his will that the behavior mechanism in man, designed by God to be the means whereby he should bear the divine image, was prostituted by the Devil to become the means whereby man would bear the satanic image, for "He that committeth sin is of the devil" (1 John 3:8a), or "takes his character from the evil one" (AMPLIFIED NEW TESTAMENT). His body became an instrument of *unrighteousness,* instead of being an instrument of righteousness. Thus man became infinitely worse than an animal, for emptied of his divine content and his soul invaded by the flesh, the animal part of him became the plaything and the workshop of the Devil himself. Yet in spite of this unpleasant fact, to which human behavior has given ample testimony all down the centuries, it is important to point out at this stage, that even in his unregenerate, fallen condition, man is still not just *mere animal,* for there is still within him—though empty of God and spiritually dead— his human spirit. This, added to his soul (as the marrow to the joints), not only enables man, though unredeemed, to survive physical death and remain morally responsible to God, but *before* physical death, makes it possible for a man to be spiritually regenerate by faith in Christ, no matter how degenerate he may have become.

To illustrate what I mean, supposing you were to hang potatoes from the ceiling of your sitting room in addition to the lamps already there! How much *less* light would you get from the potatoes than from your lamps, if you did not switch on the lamps! You would say, "No *less* light from the potatoes, for I would get no light from *any* of them, lamps or potatoes!" Exactly! Then why do you not use potatoes—if you get no less light from them; are they not cheaper than lamps? "Don't be so stupid!" you would say, "You can switch on a lamp, but you cannot switch on a potato!" Right again! A potato cannot *receive* what it *takes* to produce light!

That is the essential difference between "the animal man" ("L'Homme animal," 1 Cor. 2:14 FRENCH TRANSLATION) and mere animal. The unregenerate man "behaves" on the same principle on which an animal "behaves," and as we have seen because of the flesh, far worse than an animal, for he produces the "works of the flesh" (Gal. 5:19–21; Mark 7:20–23) but there remains within him the capacity to be "switched on again" by the "washing of regeneration and renewing of the Holy Spirit" (Titus 3:5), and so to be restored to his true humanity, if he will repent and receive Christ as his Saviour; "if any man be in Christ, he is a new creature: old things are passed away: behold all things are become new" (2 Cor. 5:17).

By his "conversion," therefore, the first man Adam not only lost the life of God and ceased to be in the image of God, but his whole personality became available to the Devil, to be exploited by him, producing a race of men whose ungodly behavior, represented by the solid margin at the circumference of figure B, is a demonstration of "the mystery of iniquity" (2 Thess. 2:7) or "that hidden principle of rebellion against constituted authority" (AMPLIFIED NEW TESTAMENT).

> For God's [holy] wrath *and* indignation are revealed from heaven against all ungodliness and unrighteousness of men, who in their wickedness repress *and* hinder the truth *and* make it inoperative. For that which is known about God is evident to them *and* made plain in their inner consciousness, because God [Himself] has shown it to them. For ever since the creation of the world His invisible nature *and* attributes, that is, His eternal power and divinity have been made intelligible *and* clearly discernible in *and* through the things that have been made—His handiworks. So [men] are without excuse— altogether without any defense or justification. Because when they knew *and* recognized Him as the God, they did not honor *and* glorify Him as God, or give Him thanks. But instead they became futile and godless in their thinking—with vain imaginings, foolish reasoning and stupid speculations—and their senseless minds were darkened. Claiming to be wise, they became fools—professing to be smart, they made simpletons of themselves. And by them the glory and majesty *and* excellence of the immortal God were exchanged for *and* represented by images, resembling mortal man and birds and beasts and reptiles. (Rom. 1:18—23 AMPLIFIED NEW TESTAMENT)

In other words, man was no longer anchored to anything absolute, and so was at liberty to choose his own gods as the objects of his own imitation, to suit his own convenience, to satisfy his own unholy lusts, and to feed his own incorrigible pride! "Because they exchanged the truth of God for a lie and worshiped and served the creature rather than the Creator, Who is blessed forever!" (Rom. 1:25 AMPLIFIED NEW TESTAMENT).

Chapter VII

The Mystery of Iniquity

*For the mystery of iniquity doth already work. (2 Thess.
2:7a)*

When the Lord Jesus Christ turned to Peter and said, "Get
thee behind me, Satan: thou art an offense to me" (Matt.
16:23a), He meant exactly what He said—He was talking to
the Devil!

It was Peter who had *spoken*, but the Lord Jesus Christ
knew perfectly well that it was Satan who was *behaving*,
borrowing Peter's humanity as a means of expressing his
malicious and subtle attempt to dissuade Christ from going
to the Cross. Peter's reasoning was sincere, and his emotional concern for his Master genuine, but the conclusions
which he drew and the attitude which he adopted were
false, for neither stemmed from Truth!

The Lord Jesus Christ had already begun to show His
disciples the Truth about His messianic mission, "how that
he must go unto Jerusalem, and suffer many things of the
elders and chief priests and scribes, and be killed, and be
raised again the third day" (Matt. 16:21), but Peter resisted
the Truth unwittingly under the evil influence of the flesh
(that sin-principle of satanic origin, always hostile to God
and always opposed to Truth), and what to Peter was a noble

sentiment, "God forbid, Lord! This must never happen to you!" (Matt. 16:22b AMPLIFIED NEW TESTAMENT), was recognized by Christ to be a wicked thrust from the Devil himself, seeking to thwart the redemptive purpose of God.

The Devil knew that Calvary would be not only the place of his own defeat, but also the place where man would be rescued from his clutches and restored to his true humanity!

Little wonder then, that the Lord Jesus continued, "You are in My way—an offense and a hindrance and a snare to Me; for you are minding what partakes not of the nature and quality of God, but of men" (Matt. 16:23 AMPLIFIED NEW TESTAMENT). Of men, that are, "sold under sin" (Rom. 7:14). "For the story and message of the cross is sheer absurdity and folly to those who are perishing and on their way to perdition. . . . And we are setting these truths forth in words not taught by human wisdom but taught by the (Holy) Spirit, combining and interpreting spiritual truths with spiritual language [to those who possess the (Holy) Spirit]" (1 Cor. 1:18a; 2:13 AMPLIFIED NEW TESTAMENT).

As godliness is the direct and exclusive consequence of God's activity, and God's capacity to reproduce *Himself* in you, so all ungodliness is the direct and exclusive consequence of Satan's activity, and of *his* capacity to reproduce *the Devil* in you!

This is the "mystery of iniquity"! For iniquity is no more the consequence of your capacity to imitate the Devil, than godliness is the consequence of your capacity to imitate God!

For I know that nothing good dwells within me, that is, in my flesh. I can will what is right, but I cannot perform it. —I have the intention and urge to do what is right, but no power to carry it out; For I fail to practice the good deeds I desire to do, but the evil deeds that I do not desire to do are what I am [ever] doing. Now if I do what I desire not to do, it is no longer I doing it—it is not myself that acts—but the sin [principle] which dwells within me [fixed and operating in my soul]. (Rom. 7:18–20 AMPLIFIED NEW TESTAMENT)

It is a frightening experience to discover what really happens when you commit sin! You cannot, however, begin to understand the mystery of godliness without beginning to understand the mystery of iniquity, because the principles involved are identical! When you act in obedience to the Truth, the Truth behaves, producing godliness; when you act in obedience to the lie, the lie behaves, producing iniquity!

The Lord Jesus Christ said, "I am . . . the truth" (John 14:6)—all that He was, all that He did, and all that He said was *God* speaking; He was the Word, and what He communicated was Truth—the Truth about God! To see Him was to see the Father. He was the image of the invisible because as man, He always obeyed the Spirit of truth, and the Father *behaved* by the Spirit *through* the Son!

If you listen to what God has to say through the Son, you, too, will know the Truth, for He said, "If you abide in My Word—hold fast to My teachings *and* live in accordance with them—you are truly My disciples. And you will know the truth, and the truth will set you free" (John 8:31–32 AMPLIFIED NEW TESTAMENT)—you will be godly! The Truth will behave, that is to say, the *Son* will behave by the Spirit *through you*, and "if the Son therefore shall make you free, ye shall be free indeed" (John 8:36)!

Consider now, however, what the Lord Jesus Christ had to say to the Pharisees: "Your father is the devil and you choose to carry out your father's desires. He was a murderer from the beginning, and is not rooted in the truth; there is no truth in him. When he tells a lie he is speaking his own language, for he is a liar and the father of lies. But I speak the truth and therefore you do not believe me" (John 8:44–45 NEB). In other words, as God is the author of Truth, so the

Devil is the author of deception; he is the *big lie!* Everything he is, everything he does, and everything he says is *deceit!*

Imagine for one moment that I steal the uniform of a policeman, step out into the middle of a busy street, and hold up my hand. What is the result? All the traffic stops! Although I am exercising a stolen authority, all the drivers obey me for the policeman they believe me to be. But what I am is a lie! They obey my signal—but what I *do* is a lie! All that I *am* and all that I *do* is *one big lie,* but the traffic still stops, and I control the behavior of every driver who does not know the truth! Everything I say as a bogus policeman will carry the weight of an authority I do not possess in them who are still in the dark about the truth, and who go on believing a lie!

This—precisely this—is the Devil's business; and men are his merchandise! "For the god of this world has blinded the unbelievers' minds (that they should not discern the truth), preventing them from seeing the illuminating light of the Gospel of the glory of Christ, the Messiah, Who is the image and likeness of God" (2 Cor. 4:4 AMPLIFIED NEW TESTAMENT), and although there is no truth in him, and all that he is and says and does is a lie, so long as men walk in darkness and reject the Truth as it has been "embodied and personified" in Jesus Christ (Eph. 4:21 AMPLIFIED NEW TESTAMENT), the Devil will go on deceiving them, controlling their behavior, and producing iniquity; they will continue to *do* what *he* says—and the big lie will continue to behave through them! "And the lusts of your father ye will do" (John 8:44b).

Iniquity is the inevitable consequence, no matter what you may be doing, if *what* you are doing is the result of acting in obedience to the big lie operating in the area of your soul, through the subtle agency of the flesh. Peter was sublimely ignorant of this wicked process, and what he said was quite sincere, but his sincerity did not make it any less iniquitous! He was the mouthpiece of the Devil, and what he said was loaded with mischief—and Christ rebuked the Devil in the man!

You must be careful not to fall into the same trap! It is pathetically possible to be engaged in all kinds of religious activity that is nothing less than Satan's subtle substitute for salvation; he will pose as "an angel of light" and he will appeal to your nobler sentiments, and his ministers also will "be transformed as the ministers of righteousness; whose end shall be according to their works. . . . For such are false apostles, deceitful workers, transforming themselves into the apostles of Christ" (2 Cor. 11:14–15, 13); by "good words and fair speeches" they will "deceive the hearts of the simple" (Rom. 16:18c) and "with feigned words" they will "make merchandise of you" (2 Peter 2:3).

If you are deceived in this way, the end result for you, as it was for the Jews, will be "a zeal of God, but not according to knowledge" (Rom. 10:2b), and that is to say—in ignorance!

What was the nature of their ignorance? They did not know the *Truth* about God's *righteousness!* They had never entered into the mystery of godliness! They did not know that godliness is the consequence of God's activity in man, so that "being ignorant of God's righteousness," they went about "to establish their own righteousness," and did not submit themselves "unto the righteousness of God" (Rom. 10:3).

Of course, when you go about to establish your own righteousness, all you produce is "self-righteousness"— your own generous estimate of the measure in which you have conformed, by your own ability, to the object of your own imitation;—any credit which is due, of course, is due to you, and to you alone! You are to be congratulated!

Is God impressed?

Not every one that saith unto me, Lord, Lord, shall enter into the kingdom of heaven; but he that doeth the will of my Father which is in heaven. Many will say to me in that day, Lord, Lord, have we not prophesied in thy name? and in thy name have cast out devils? and in thy name done many wonderful works? And then will I profess unto them, I never knew you: depart from me, ye that work iniquity. (Matt. 7:21–23)

In the very name of God and in the practice of religion, you can "work iniquity!" This is the mystery of iniquity! It is a perpetuation of the Adamic response to the wiles of the Devil. The Fall of man began with an *act of unbelief;* what Adam *did* when he disobeyed God in the Garden, was the result of what he *did not believe,* but what he *did not believe* was the result of what he *did believe!*

He did *not* believe the Truth because he *did* believe a lie, and the lie that he believed was that he could be independent of God with impunity.

God had said, "Lose Me, and lose everything—you will die!" and the Devil said, "Lose God and lose nothing—you will not die!" What God said was the Truth, and what the Devil said was a lie about the Truth; *every* lie is a lie about the Truth. The Truth is constant, it never changes; once you have told the truth, the whole truth, and nothing but the truth, you have said everything there is to say; there is nothing more to be said! There is absolutely no limit however, to the variety of lies that can be told about the Truth, but the Truth espouses every lie for the lie it is! There is no neutrality in *this* war! What is not *Truth* is a *lie* about the Truth and is the *enemy* of Truth!

Adam believed the Devil's lie about the Truth, and had no alternative but to *reject* the Truth and *behave* the lie! Because the *lie he believed* was that he could be independent of God, the *lie he behaved* was an *act of independence* of God—he ate of the forbidden fruit! This was his *act of unbelief* in relation to the Truth, perpetuated by an *attitude of unbelief* in relation to the Truth—*an attitude of independence!* This attitude is the very essence of "sin"—of what we have seen is called in the Bible "the flesh," and from it stem all the acts which we call "sins." *Sin* is the cause and *sins* are the effect; *sin* is the dirty well, *sins* are the dirty water!

> For from within, out of men's hearts, their evil purposes proceed—fornication, theft, murder, adultery, covetousness, wickedness, deceit, licentiousness, envy, slander, pride, reckless folly: all these wicked things come out from within and make a man unclean. (Mark 7:21–23 WEYMOUTH)

It is, however, possible to keep the dirty water inside the dirty well, but this does not make the well clean! Self-interest may produce a hundred-and-one good reasons for curbing the "acts" of the flesh without making one iota of difference to its "attitude"; it will remain as arrogant and proud and hostile to the Truth as ever before, whilst presenting a "virtuous front" to the world around, all "dandied up" with pious platitudes!

The flesh has an incredible capacity for self-deception, for it derives its nature from the "father of lies"; at one moment it will advertise its independence of God and hostility to the Truth by cursing and swearing, and the next moment will give a pious demonstration of its own self-righteousness by curbing this, its own wicked habit—like a man who stops beating his wife to show her how kind he is!

That is why God says that "The heart is deceitful above all things, and desperately wicked: who can know it?" (Jer. 17:9) and no matter how strenuously we may seek to be godly without letting God be the source of our godliness, "we are all as an unclean thing, and all our righteousnesses are as filthy rags; and we all do fade as a leaf; and our iniquities, like the wind, have taken us away" (Isa. 64:6).

Perhaps I can clarify the issues still further by the use of this simple illustration. Let the human spirit represent the Royal Residence, prepared by God for the Royal Resident, the Holy Spirit; imagine next that the soul represents the

Music Room, and in it there is the Grand Piano of human personality—mind, emotion, and will. The body, as the amplifier, will communicate the music from the Music Room to the world around!

Do you get the picture? When God created Adam in his innocency, the Holy Spirit—as the Royal Resident imparting the life of God—was at home in Adam's human spirit, the Royal Residence (see the top circle in figure A, chart 1, chapter 6). He had unchallenged and exclusive access to Adam's soul, the Music Room (see the center circle in figure A, chart 1), and He alone had the right to sit, as it were, at the keyboard of human personality, the Grand Piano.

Instructing the mind, controlling the emotions, and directing the will, the Spirit of Truth struck every chord in perfect harmony with the heart of God in heaven, and a matchless melody rang out in evidence that God was reigning in the heart of man on earth!

God, however, had given to man the key to the Music Room—that is to say to his soul or heart—and this key was man's right to choose out of a free will. He would not outstay His welcome! The presence of the Royal Resident in the Royal Residence was to be a matter for mutual consent, for there was to be a "faith-love" relationship between man and God. So long as the Music Room remained unlocked, offering to the Holy Spirit unchallenged and exclusive access to the keyboard of human personality, God promised that the Royal Resident would remain within the Royal Residence—the Spirit of God within the human spirit—and man would share the very life of God Himself and would declare Him to the world in which he lived.

At the same time, God made it very clear to man, that should the door be locked and access to the Music Room be denied to the Royal Resident, He would not remain within the Royal Residence, and the human spirit would become destitute of the Holy Spirit. In that day, man would cease to share the life of God; spiritually, he would die!

Man continued to enjoy unbroken fellowship with God, until one day the Deceiver came—the Arch-Enemy of God and Destroyer of Man-soul, whose name was Lucifer, son of the morning (Isa. 14:12). He had rebelled against The Truth, and had become The Lie, and the Father of Lies—for there was no more Truth in him! More commonly he is known as the Devil, or Satan, but cannot always be readily identified, for often he masquerades as an Angel of Light.

This deceiver persuaded the first man Adam that man could play the Grand Piano of human personality without God—and just as *well* as God! He pointed out the great advantages of being free from the restrictive presence of the Holy Spirit, whose absence, far from detracting from human experience, would undoubtedly enhance it, for man would then be able to pick and choose his own tunes; tunes that needed only to be in harmony with *himself* and certainly not in harmony with God! Far from *losing* life by losing God, man would *gain* life in an entirely new dimension—enjoying things which tasted even better than they looked, and which would make him wise—as wise as God! Indeed man would become his *own* god, and what could be better than that?

Suffice it to say that the first man Adam believed the lie and locked the door of the Music Room, and the Royal Resident left the Royal Residence, which became strangely cold and empty, and although he could not quite explain it, Adam had a new and queer sensation which he had never known before; for the want of a better name he called it fear, and it has never left man since, and it still has the same strange effect on him that it had on Adam then! It always makes man want to hide or run away! The funny thing is this—again and again he finds that what has made him run away from God has traveled with him! It is a *bad conscience!*

However, at least Adam was on his own now and could have a crack at that Grand Piano! What he did *not* know, however, was that while he was talking to the Lie (that Deceiver called Satan), one of the Lie's sons (for he is the Father of Lies) *had slipped into the Music Room!*

Later, when Adam looked into the Music Room, there he was, sitting at the keyboard thumping away at the notes, and producing the most excruciating noises, all out of harmony with each other and with everyone else! His name was The Flesh—and man has never been able to get him away from the Grand Piano since! At least, not on his own!

It was still the same Grand Piano, that is to say, the same human personality, but having once produced harmony, it now only produced discord! Adam started quarreling with Eve, and said it was all her fault; but she blamed the Devil— and she wasn't far wrong! Then it spread to the children, and Cain murdered Abel—and the whole miserable story has been going on ever since!

No! This is not an extract from *Alice in Wonderland*—I have been telling you the story of *your* heart and mine! The Holy Spirit at the keyboard is the source of all godliness; and the flesh at the keyboard is the source of all iniquity!

You do not need a new *piano!* You need a new *pianist!* That is what the gospel is all about—how to get the wrong man *out,* and the Right Man *in*—and to exchange The Lie for The Truth!

On your own you cannot do it! But I have good news for you!

You can't! . . . *But He can!*

Chapter VIII

The Second Man—
The Lord From Heaven

The last Adam was made a quickening spirit . . . the second man is the Lord from heaven. (1 Cor. 15:45b, 47b)

The first man was Adam, and he died. The Last Adam was Christ, who came to raise the dead! The first man was of the earth, earthy; and the Second Man is the Lord from heaven! The first was the one who made the mess—and the Second was the One who came to clean it up!

In the preceding chapters I trust that you have come more fully to understand what happened when Adam fell, and what the inevitable consequences were for him and for the whole race of fallen men. Deprived of the life of God, the "animal" part of man no longer bore the image of deity, for although "in the day that God created man, *in the likeness of God* made he him: . . . Adam lived a hundred and thirty years, and begat a son *in his own likeness*" (Gen. 5:1b, 3a, emphasis added). Children were born, but not in the likeness of God (God-like); they were born in the likeness of their fallen forebear, to carry the marred image of behavior patterns dominated by the flesh throughout all generations.

Each child born into the world since the first man Adam died spiritually and ceased to be true man—has been born "in Adam"; and the consequence of being born "in Adam" is threefold—if nothing happens to change it!

In Adam You Are Alienated from the Life of God
(Eph. 4:18)

There is no exception to this rule, and it is not something that *will* happen, it is something that has *already* happened! As one who himself had forfeited the life of God, it was utterly impossible for Adam by the physical process of reproduction to impart anything of the divine nature to his offspring; all born "in Adam," in all succeeding generations, have been born physically alive, soulishly active, but spiritually dead. "Dead in trespasses and sins . . . by nature the children of wrath" (Eph. 2:1b, 3c).

In Adam You Walk after the Flesh
(Rom. 8:1; Eph. 2:2–3)

There is no exception to this rule! "The LORD looked down from heaven upon the children of men, to see if there were any that did understand, and seek God. They are all gone aside, they are altogether become filthy: there is none that doeth good, no, not one" (Ps. 14:2–3; cited in Rom. 3:10–11). Men are sinners not because they commit sins; men commit sins because by nature they are sinners: "By one man's disobedience many were made sinners" (Rom. 5:19a), and you were born, as I was, with the *wrong* man at the "Grand Piano"! "Estranged from God; you were his enemies in heart and mind, and your deeds were evil" (Col. 1:21 NEB).

In Adam You Will Die in Your Sins
(John 8:24)

This is the third and final consequence of being "in Adam" at the time of physical death; it means that if nothing happens to change the situation between your physical birth and your physical death, you will *die* in the condition in which you were *born*, spiritually dead; but your soul will survive to be held morally responsible to God for a wasted life and to "pay the penalty *and* suffer the punishment of everlasting ruin (destruction and perdition) and [eternal exclusion and banishment] from the presence of the Lord and from the glory of His power" (2 Thess. 1:9, AMPLIFIED NEW TESTAMENT); and there is certainly no exception to this rule!

Had God not intervened, there never could have been a *Second Man* to walk this earth as God intended man to be; that is why the *Virgin Birth* of Jesus Christ is not a matter of secondary importance, it is *imperative!*

Had Jesus Christ been born as you and I were born, by natural conception, He too would have been "in Adam," spiritually dead, uninhabited by God, and dominated only by the flesh with its roots in the Devil—condemned already to die physically as He had been born physically, cut off from God! As a sinner by nature, He would have been a sinner in practice—a fallen member of the fallen race of fallen men!

The Virgin Birth of Jesus Christ Presupposes the Utter Depravity of Man!

You cannot reject the Virgin Birth of Jesus Christ without repudiating His deity and His sinlessness—unless you are prepared to repudiate the Fall of man! For fallen man does not have what it takes to be sinless. He is spiritually bankrupt and without God; and it takes God to make a man godly!

To insist that Jesus Christ came into this world by natural birth and lived a sinless life is to repudiate the Fall of man! It means that what was possible to Him as a *natural* man, must be possible to you and to me as *natural* men, so that if we are not what He *was*, it is only because we do not try *hard enough!* If this were true, the message of the gospel would simply be an exhortation to greater effort—an attempt to realize the inherent adequacy that is self-existent within every human being—including Christ! A message of spiritual regeneration would become patently superfluous and the Fall of man a myth, for by nature man would have what it takes!

This in fact would mean that man can master his own "Grand Piano" and emancipate himself, conquering his own soul! Pardon me, but if I am not mistaken, I think I just saw the Big Lie smiling round the corner! Someone has just made him a Doctor of Divinity!

A theological student came to me not long ago and said that he had just had his first lecture on Luke's gospel. The learned Professor had announced his subject as "The Virgin Birth of Jesus Christ—*neither true nor necessary!*" To be as ignorant as that of the basic essentials of the Truth would be tragic enough in the simple minded, but to *expose* such ignorance in the name of *scholarship* to a class of students is *criminal negligence* and a masterpiece of satanic genius of which only the Devil himself could be capable!

To *accept* the Fall of man and still insist upon the natural birth of Christ is to number Him at once with sinful men, for "all have sinned, and come short of the glory of God" (Rom. 3:23) and "the scripture hath concluded all under sin" (Gal. 3:22a). John is speaking of the whole race of man when he says in his epistle, "If we say that we have no sin, we deceive ourselves, and the truth is not in us. . . . If we say that we have not sinned, we make him [God] a liar, and his word is not in us" (1 John 1:8, 10), and Christ would have been no exception to the rule of those who "in Adam" walk after the flesh and inevitably sin.

Robbed of His deity and robbed of His sinlessness, what would be left of His work of redemption? His vicarious suffering on the Cross would be stripped of all validity, for He could only have suffered for His own sins, but never for the sins of others. His glorious act of atonement would be reduced to an empty, sentimental gesture—the tragic end of a noble idealist who drifted to disaster because He lived before His time. His resurrection would be totally unnecessary, and to avoid embarrassment must be explained away as the wishful thinking of some hysterical women or the ingenious invention of some of His over-enthusiastic disciples!

Deny the Virgin Birth of Jesus Christ, and you have laid the axe to all the essential doctrines of the Bible: the Fall and depravity of man, the deity and sinlessness of Christ, the atoning efficacy of His death and resurrection, the necessity for spiritual regeneration as the basis for holiness of life, and the truth of the Bible itself! Little wonder that those who deny the Virgin Birth of Christ have little love for the Word of God; for the Truth exposes every lie for the lie it is, and every lie is a lie about the Truth!

The miraculous birth of Jesus Christ not only presupposes the total depravity of man,

It Furnishes the First Requirement for Man's Redemption—a Sinless Sacrifice

As descendants of the first Adam, *we* were born *uninhabited* by God—heirs of His absence—and inhabited only by sin. The Lord Jesus Christ, miraculously conceived by the Holy Spirit in the womb of Mary, was born *uninhabited* by sin and wholly inhabited by God! He was the Last Adam— the *Second Man*, as sinless as He Himself had created man to be; He was able to turn to His disciples and say, "The prince of this world [the Devil] cometh, and hath nothing in me" (John 14:30b).

Look again at chart 1 in chapter 6 and consider figure C. This represents the Lord Jesus Christ as He was on earth; never *less* than *God*, but *always* completely *man!* Who, though tempted in all points like as we are, was without sin, and though of all *other* men the Father could only say,

"There is none righteous, no, not one" (Rom. 3:10), of *this*, the Second Man, the Father could say, "This is my beloved Son, in whom I am well pleased" (Matt. 17:5)—the first requirement for man's redemption—a sinless sacrifice and substitute.

> To wit, that God was in Christ, reconciling the world unto himself, not imputing their trespasses unto them; and hath committed unto us the word of reconciliation. . . . For he hath made him to be sin for us, who knew no sin; that we might be made the righteousness of God in him. (2 Cor. 5:19, 21)

How did the Lord Jesus Christ in His perfect manhood present Himself to the Father? Through the Holy Spirit—represented by the horizontal shading in the small circle at the top of figure C. "How much more shall the blood of Christ *who through the eternal Spirit* offered himself without spot to God, purge your conscience from dead works to serve the living God?" (Heb. 9:14, emphasis added).

So that the life of God, once clothed on earth with the humanity of the first man Adam in his innocency (figure A) and forfeited by the first man Adam in his depravity (figure B), is now clothed again on earth with the spotless humanity of the second man, Christ—the Lord from heaven (figure C), the Last Adam, the quickening Spirit—restoring the dead to life!

You will notice that in figure C there is no smaller circle placed within the center circle representing the soul (as in figures B, D, and E) of the Lord Jesus Christ, for as perfect man, He placed His total personality at the Father's disposal; the prince of this world, the Devil, had nothing in Him. The result was that for the first time since Adam fell into sin, there was the perfect image of the invisible God in bodily form on earth: ". . . the exact likeness of the unseen God. . . . For in Him the whole fullness of Deity (the Godhead), continues to dwell in bodily form—giving complete expression of the divine nature" (Col. 1:15; 2:9 AMPLI-FIED NEW TESTAMENT).

To indicate the unchanging deity of Christ, even in His humanity, the bottom circle in figure C, representing the body of Christ, is diagonally shaded, as are both the middle and top circles in figure C, representing His soul and spirit. The complete expression of the divine nature in all His human behavior is indicated by the unshaded margin at the circumference of figure C, as this once was true of the first man in his innocency, in figure A.

If God *withdrew* His life from man when sin came in, under what circumstances will God *restore* His life to man? Only when sin has been cleansed and forgiven. The Lord Jesus said, "I have come that men may have life, and may have it in all its fulness" (John 10:10 NEB)—He did not come that men might have *physical* life—they had that; He came that men might have *spiritual* life—restoring the dead to life!

As the first requirement for man's redemption—a sinless sacrifice—the Lord Jesus gave Himself upon the Cross and "suffered for sins, the just for the unjust, that he might bring us to God" (1 Peter 3:18a) and "the blood of Jesus Christ his Son cleanseth us from all sin" (1 John 1:7), but it is essential that you should realize that His Cross was the means *to* an end; for to confuse the means *for* the end is to rob the Lord Jesus of that for which He came.

He came that you might have *life! His* life—imparted to you by the renewing of the Holy Spirit on the grounds of redemption, to *re-inhabit* your spirit, to *re-conquer* your soul, so that you might be "transfigured into His *very own* image in ever increasing splendor *and* from one degree of glory to another; [for this comes] from the Lord [Who is] the Spirit" (2 Cor. 3:18b AMPLIFIED NEW TESTAMENT). He came to restore to you all that makes the mystery of godliness an open secret—the presence of the living God within a human soul!

This is the Way from Death to Life!

When the Holy Spirit convicts you of the fact that you are a sinner, spiritually dead—"in Adam" and at enmity with God—and you repent and turn to Christ, humbly accepting Him as your Saviour and welcoming Him back by His Holy Spirit to live within you and take control of you—this is your *conversion!*

In point of fact, it is a re-conversion; as the first man Adam was once converted—changing his mind about God at the place of first choice, the tree in the Garden—you, the heir by nature of his Adamic attitude of independence, change your mind *about his change of mind,* at the place of second choice, the tree on the hill—the Cross!

Adam was created knowing the Truth from *within,* through the Spirit, and he listened to the lie from *without,* through the word of Satan; and he exchanged the Truth of God for a lie. The Truth went out and the lie came in! He stepped out of dependence into independence—out of life into death! You were born blinded by the lie from *within* through the flesh, and you listen to the Truth from *without* through the Word of God. When you *repent,* you accept the Truth and obey it, stepping back out of independence into dependence—out of death into life! "Verily, verily, I say unto you, He that heareth my word, and believeth on him that sent me, hath everlasting life, and shall not come into condemnation; but is passed from death unto life" (John 5:24).

The moment you repent and obey the Truth in genuine conversion, God accepts you for Christ's sake as a forgiven sinner, for He bore "our sins in his own body on the tree" (1 Peter 2:24a). Judgment has already been executed on your sin vicariously, in the person of the sinless substitute, and you are acquitted, and this is called *redemption.*

Conversion is "man-to-Godward," and redemption is "God-to-manward." God took the initiative through His incarnation in the Virgin Birth of Christ, in *providing* at Calvary the place where sinners may be reconciled to Himself through the atoning sacrifice of His sinless Son; but man must take the initiative in *appropriating* by faith this salvation, which grace has provided. Grace provides, but faith appropriates, so that "it is by grace that you have been saved through faith; and that not of yourselves. It is God's gift, and is not on the ground of merit" (Eph. 2:8–9 WEYMOUTH).

God bears witness to the faith which appropriates redemption by the gift of the Holy Spirit, and this renewing of the Holy Spirit is called *regeneration* or *new birth*. "And God, who knows all hearts, gave His testimony in their favour by bestowing the Holy Spirit on them just as He did on us; and He made no difference between us and them, in that He cleansed their hearts by their faith" (Acts 15:8–9 WEYMOUTH).

The gift of the Holy Spirit to those who believe is the end toward which the Cross was but the *means;* redemption was never designed by God simply to make you fit for heaven—it was designed to clear the decks for spiritual regeneration, which would make you fit for *earth* on the way to heaven! You cannot be spiritually regenerate without first being redeemed, but you cannot be redeemed without becoming, in consequence, spiritually regenerate; it is the latter that adds validity to the former and that is the seal of your faith.

And in Him you also, after listening to the word of the truth, the Gospel of your salvation—having believed in Him—were sealed with the promised Holy Spirit; that Spirit being a pledge and foretaste of our inheritance, in anticipation of its full redemption. (Eph. 1:13 WEYMOUTH)

It had always been God's plan to abolish "death and bring immortality to light" by the "appearing of our Saviour Jesus Christ" (2 Tim. 1:10) and speaking to "that old serpent, called the Devil, and Satan, which deceiveth the whole world" (Rev. 12:9), God had said, "I will put enmity between thee and the woman, and between thy seed and her seed; it shall bruise thy head, and thou shalt bruise his heel" (Gen. 3:15). This "her Seed"—the seed of the woman (Mary)—was the seed promised by God to faithful Abraham, "And in thy seed shall all the nations of the earth be blessed" (Gen. 22:18a).

Miraculously conceived, and born at Bethlehem, the Second Man, the Lord from heaven—*Christ*—"hath redeemed us from the curse of the law, being made a curse for us: for it is written, Cursed is every one that hangeth on a tree: That the blessing of Abraham might come on the Gentiles through Jesus Christ; that we might receive the promise of the Spirit through faith" (Gal. 3:13–14).

Thus the "promise" inherent in God's word to Abraham was the renewing of the Holy Spirit—spiritual regeneration—the raising of the dead! Just as the Virgin Birth of Jesus Christ furnishes the first requirement for man's redemption, so also

The Virgin Birth of Jesus Christ Establishes a Precedent in Procedure for Spiritual Regeneration

What were the events that led up to the birth of Christ? How did it all begin, so far as Mary was concerned?

It began with the Word—a message of Truth faithfully delivered by the angel Gabriel, who "was sent from God" (Luke 1:26). The Truth the angel communicated was at once strange and startling, contrary to all human experience and beyond natural explanation: "thou hast found favour with God. And, behold, thou shalt conceive in thy womb, and bring forth a son, and shalt call his name JESUS. He shall be great, and shall be called the Son of the Highest: . . . of his kingdom there shall be no end" (Luke 1:30–33).

The natural reaction of the natural heart of this natural woman was one of astonishment! The obvious question to be asked and to be answered was "How?" And so Mary said to the angel, "How can this be, seeing that I have no husband?" (Luke 1:34 WEYMOUTH); she deliberately denied the prerequisite for natural birth, and Joseph, too, denied any responsibility for parenthood!

The circumstances of the birth of Christ were these. After his mother Mary was betrothed to Joseph, before they were united in marriage, she was found to be with child through the Holy Spirit. Now Joseph her husband, being a just man and unwilling publicly to disgrace her, determined to release her privately from the betrothal. (Matt. 1:18–19 WEYMOUTH)

The facts of the case are quite clear: Mary denied intimacy with any man, and Joseph repudiated responsibility for the birth of Christ so emphatically, that he was about to break his engagement with Mary for her infidelity! Those who would have you reject the Virgin Birth of Christ, therefore, would have you believe that He was the illegitimate child of a woman who was both unfaithful and a liar! Others would have you believe that a matter of such gravity is of no particular consequence! Remember that every lie is a lie about the Truth—and every lie comes from the same source, the big Lie, who is the father of lies!

But as he was thinking this over, behold, an angel of the Lord appeared to him in a dream, saying, Joseph, descendant of David, do not be afraid to take Mary [as] your wife, for that which is conceived in her is of (from, out of) the Holy Spirit. She will bear a Son, and you shall call His name Jesus [in Hebrew means Savior], for He will save His people from their sins [that is, prevent their failing and missing the true end and scope of life, which is God]. (Matt. 1:20–21 AMPLIFIED NEW TESTAMENT).

Joseph, too, received the Word of Truth, and believed it— a message from God in confirmation of the prophecy of Isaiah (49:1), "The LORD hath called me from the womb; from the bowels of my mother hath he made mention of my name." He was announced and named a boy, Jesus—*before He was born!* Maybe you have never thought of this—for we take so much for granted—but supposing Mary had had a baby girl!

"You ask how, Mary?" the angel might have said. "There is no human explanation! Yet I will *tell* you how—'The Holy Spirit will come upon you, and the power of the Most High will overshadow you (as a shining cloud); and so the holy (pure, sinless) Thing which shall be born of you, will be called the Son of God'" (Luke 1:35 AMPLIFIED NEW TESTAMENT).

How was it to be?

By the Word of God, *through* the Holy Spirit!

All the mighty *power* of God to implement the *Word* of God, to clothe the very *life* of God in view with the humanity of the *Son* of God, was made available through the Holy Spirit; but was this enough? No! One condition still needed to be met! Mary's availability to this gracious, life-begetting ministry of the Holy Spirit!

Maybe you tend to take for granted the fact that Mary should place herself at God's disposal! Is there any reason why you should? Have you placed *yourself* completely at God's disposal? Is there any reason why you should expect of her what you are not prepared to do yourself?

Mary might have said, "I do not want God to interfere in my life! I am engaged to be married, and I have my own plans! This is going to spoil everything!" Isn't this what *you* have often said or thought? In any case, who was going to believe her story?

Who *did* believe Mary's story? When the Pharisees said to

the Lord Jesus Christ, "We are not illegitimate children *and* born of fornication; we have one Father, even God" (John 8:41b AMPLIFIED NEW TESTAMENT), it was a sly, stinging, wicked reference to the birth of the Saviour, by which these "snakes" and "brood of vipers" (Matt. 23:33 NEB and WEYMOUTH) identified themselves with those godless theologians of all generations who have denied and still deny the Virgin Birth of Christ! Of these Christ would say today, as He said of the Pharisees then, "Ye are of your father, the devil" (John 8:44).

In the light of events and in retrospect it is easy for us to call her blessed, but for Mary *then* it was the *deliberate obedience of faith;* by it she died to all her own plans, to all her own reputation, and to all those hopes that had been fixed in the one whom she had loved most dearly! "And Mary said, Behold the handmaid of the Lord; be it unto me according to thy word" (Luke 1:38a). From that moment on the onus was on God to fulfill the promise He had made and to *do* what He had *said!*

By the Word of God, *through* the Holy Spirit *acting* on the obedience of faith! That is how the miracle took place, and Christ was born at Bethlehem—the Second Man, the Lord from heaven! Utter God and perfect man, by His Incarnation the Lord Jesus Christ had established a precedent in procedure for spiritual regeneration.

The words of the Lord Jesus Christ to Nicodemus were as startling and as strange as those of the angel Gabriel to Mary! "Verily, verily, I say unto thee, Except a man be born again, he cannot see the kingdom of God" (John 3:3b); and the natural reaction of the natural heart of this natural man to these unnatural words was one of utter incredulity! The obvious question to be asked and to be answered was "How?" And "Nicodemus saith unto him, How can a man be born when he is old? Can he enter the second time into his mother's womb, and be born?" (John 3:4).

"You want to know how, Nicodemus?" the Lord Jesus might have said. "There is no human explanation! Yet I will *tell* you how—'The wind bloweth where it listeth, and thou hearest the sound thereof, but canst not tell whence it cometh, and whither it goeth: so is every one that is born of the Spirit'" (John 3:8). That is how, Nicodemus—by the Holy Spirit!"

By the Word of God (from the lips of Christ Himself!) and *through* the Holy Spirit!

By his very question, though one of the noblest of the Pharisees, Nicodemus exposed the fact that he only knew of one quality of life—that which he had received by his natural, animal birth, from his natural, animal parents; but "God is a Spirit: and they that worship him must worship him in spirit and in truth" (John 4:24). So the Lord Jesus Christ had to explain to him, "That which is born of the flesh is flesh" (John 3:6) and "flesh and blood" no more inherit the kingdom of God than "doth corruption inherit incorruption" (1 Cor. 15:50c).

"That which is born of the Spirit is spirit" (John 3:6b), and if there is nothing "born of the Spirit" in that which is "born of the flesh," that which is "born of the flesh" is spiritually bankrupt! If you are still in this condition, you need to be born again, and all the mighty *power* of God to implement the *Word* of God and so to clothe the *life* of God with *you* has been made available through the Holy Spirit!

Is it enough, however, that the Holy Spirit is both able and willing to give to you "all things that pertain unto life and godliness" and to make you a partaker "of the divine nature"? (2 Peter 1:3–4). No! You, too, must yield the obedience of faith! Changing *your* mind about *Adam's* change of mind about God, you must get back to God by a deliberate *act of faith*, as Adam lost Him by a deliberate *act of unbelief!*

You must look up into God's face, and say, "Maybe I do not

247

fully understand how the death of Your dear Son and the precious blood He shed can cleanse my heart from sin and clear the record—but this is what you have said! Be it unto me according to Your Word! Maybe I do not fully understand how You can come by Your Holy Spirit to live in me, making me a partaker of the very life of Jesus Christ Himself, so that He through me can reveal the invisible God to a visible world, but this is what you have said! Be it unto me, O God!—be it unto me according to Your Word!"

Do that, and the onus is on God to keep the promise He has made and to *do* what He has *said!* You *can't*—but He *can!*

Finally,

The Virgin Birth of Jesus Christ Demonstrates the Principle of an Imparted Life

Joseph and Mary were accustomed each year to go to Jerusalem at the feast of the Passover, and on one of these occasions, when the Lord Jesus Christ was just twelve years old, they were returning home, and "supposing him to have been in the company, went a day's journey" (Luke 2:44a), and having missed Him, they went back to Jerusalem, to find Him three days later in the temple "sitting in the midst of the doctors, both hearing them and asking them questions" (Luke 2:46b).

When Joseph and Mary saw the little Lord Jesus, "they were amazed, and His mother said to Him, 'Child, why have You treated us like this? Here Your father and I have been anxiously looking for you—distressed and tormented'" (Luke 2:48 AMPLIFIED NEW TESTAMENT), and He asked them a very pointed question, "How is it that you had to look for Me?" (v. 49). In other words, "Why did you *suppose* that I was in the company? Don't you know that I am wholly, exclusively available to My Father; that My whole humanity is at *His* disposal, and I must always be about *His* business and

248

doing the things that please Him? Why should you *suppose* that where *you* want to go is where *I* want to go? It all depends whether where *you* want to go is in My Father's interests."

By the miraculous birth of the Lord Jesus Christ, conceived of the Holy Spirit, the Father clothed Himself with the sinless humanity of the Son, in that body which He had "prepared" for Him in the womb of Mary (Heb. 10:5), and the Son presented Himself without spot to the Father, so that He could say, "The Father that dwelleth in me, He doeth the works" (John 14:10b).

Through His obedience as the Second Man and the Last Adam, the Lord Jesus became a life-giving Spirit (1 Cor. 15:45 AMPLIFIED NEW TESTAMENT), able to cleanse you from sin through His atoning death, and to restore you to life by His indwelling Spirit, that He might live *in* and *through you*, as the Father lived *in* and *through* Him, why then do you "*suppose*" that He is "in the company"—that where *you* want to go and what *you* want to do is always where *He* wants to go and what *He* wants to do! Don't you know that the Lord Jesus Christ lives in you *to be about His Father's business?* "And he went down with them, and came to Nazareth, and was subject unto them" (Luke 2:51a).

Having established the principle quite clearly at this early age of twelve, both to Joseph and to Mary, that He was irrevocably committed to His Father, the amazing thing is that He then "was subject unto them." In other words, He would go where they went and do what they did, but "His mother carefully treasured up all these incidents in her heart" (Luke 2:51b WEYMOUTH), and she knew from then on, that wherever she asked Him to go and whatever she asked Him to do, she first had to ask her own heart, "Am *I* committed to *Him* for all that to which *He* is committed to His Father?"

Are you committed to Christ without question and

without complaint, for all that to which He in you is committed to the Father?

This is the principle of His imparted life!

It involves complete, deliberate abandonment to Christ in everything.

"Do you not know that your body is the temple—the very sanctuary—of the Holy Spirit Who lives within you, Whom you have received [as a Gift] from God? You are not your own. You were bought for a price—purchased with a preciousness and paid for, made His own. So then, honor God *and* bring glory to Him in your body" (1 Cor. 6:19–20 AMPLIFIED NEW TESTAMENT).

There came a day, at the marriage feast in Cana of Galilee, when Mary learned to say, "Whatsoever he saith unto you, do it" (John 2:5b); she had learned that *He* was not subject to *her*, but that *she* was subject to *Him*, and that was at the beginning of His public ministry!

When you have learned that *He* is not subject to *you* but that *you* are subject to *Him*, that will be the beginning of His public ministry in you; you will "be constantly renewed in the spirit of your mind—having a fresh mental and spiritual attitude"; and you will "put on the new nature (the regenerate self) created in God's image, (Godlike) in true righteousness and holiness" (Eph. 4:23–24 AMPLIFIED NEW TESTAMENT), and the Second Man, the Lord from heaven, will reveal Himself again to a needy world through you!

The wrong man will be *out*—and the right man will be *in!*

Chapter IX

The Law of the Spirit of Life

For the law of the Spirit of life in Christ Jesus hath made me free from the law of sin and death. (Rom. 8:2)

The Spirit and life are as inseparable as sin and death, and there can be no more compromise between the Spirit and sin than there is between life and death; each is diametrically opposed to the other—that is why to be "in Christ" instead of "in Adam" involves a radical change of government! It introduces a new law!

It was to bring about this change of government and to introduce this new law, that the Second Man was born at Bethlehem, lived, died, and rose again from the dead; "For as by one man's disobedience many were made sinners, so by the obedience of one shall many be made righteous" (Rom. 5:19). The total availability of the Lord Jesus Christ to the Father—to be "about His business"—was such that "after He had appeared in human form, He abased *and* humbled Himself [still further] and carried His obedience to the extreme of death, even the death of [the] cross" (Phil. 2:8 AMPLIFIED NEW TESTAMENT), and as we have already seen obedience is the criterion of faith!

As the Last Adam, the Lord Jesus Christ was the antithesis of the first Adam; *he* died by faith, because he obeyed the lie; Christ *lived* by faith because He obeyed the Truth. That is to say, He was so subject to the "law of the Spirit of life" that His total personality "declared" the Father.

No man has ever seen God at any time; the only unique Son, the only-begotten God, Who is in the bosom [that is, in the intimate presence] of the Father, He has declared Him—He has revealed Him, brought Him out where He can be seen; He has interpreted Him, and He has made Him known. (John 1:18 AMPLIFIED NEW TESTAMENT)

It is this law, however, operating "in Christ Jesus," which, the apostle Paul writes, "hath made me free from the law of sin and death" (Rom. 8:2). How can a law which operated in *Him*, liberate *you* and *me?* This is the question I want to explore with you in this chapter!

What the Law Could Not Do (Rom. 8:3)

Do not confuse the Law with the law of the Spirit of life, nor with the law of sin and death. This is the Old Testament Law, and contained within it, of course, the Ten Commandments. It is the Law of righteousness; what then could this Law *not* do?

The Law "made nothing perfect" (Heb. 7:19a)—and the reason for this is now self-evident, for although the demands of the Law are strong and uncompromising, it is "weakened by the flesh [that is, the entire nature of man without the Holy Spirit]" (Rom. 8:3b AMPLIFIED NEW TESTAMENT). As one born uninhabited by God and inhabited only by the "flesh," you discover that "the mind of the flesh—with its carnal thoughts and purposes—is hostile to God; for it does not submit itself to God's Law, indeed it cannot" (Rom. 8:7 AMPLIFIED NEW TESTAMENT).

God, as it were, wrote the score, but the "wrong man at the Grand Piano" (chapter 7) refuses to play the tune! He prefers the liberty of improvisation to the discipline of following the music, and the thrill of self-willed syncopation to the steady rhythm of a life in tune with God! Every departure from the score is a transgression of the Law, and the transgression of the Law is sin! (1 John 3:4). Has this not been your experience?

Written with the "finger of God" (Exod. 31:18), the Law represents the minimum demands of God's righteousness, and godliness will no more derive from your attempts to fulfill the Law than from your attempts to imitate God—you can do neither! For the law of sin and death within you is hostile both to God and to His Law of righteousness, and so the Law "made nothing perfect"!

It is a source of untold relief to discover that God has never expected anything of *you* but unremitting failure! Nothing that ever shocks you about yourself shocks Him; it *grieves* Him, but never shocks Him. You cannot be shocked by what you *expect!* If you are still shocked at your own capacity for wickedness, it is because you have never fully repented; you still do not believe what God says about you, that you are "unspiritual, sold to sin"; and that in you, that is in your "lower self, nothing good has its home" (Rom. 7:14, 18 WEYMOUTH).

You are still believing the Devil's lie about the Truth and rejecting God's Truth about the Devil's lie. You are still committing the sin of Saul, who presumed to spare "the best" and "all that was good" in what God had totally condemned (1 Sam. 15:9), and the folly of Jehoshaphat, who had false hopes of an unholy covenant, helped the "ungodly" and loved "them that hate the Lord" (2 Chron. 18:3; 19:2).

You may be "in Christ," but you are behaving as though you were "in Adam," perpetuating the Adamic creed of self-sufficiency, shocked when you *can't* only because you insist on believing that you *can!* You adopt the attitude of the defeated tennis player, who says there must be something wrong with his tennis racket!

I do not mean that God *excuses* your sin or expects you to go on sinning; I simply mean that He has absolutely no delusions whatever about *you*, for what you are, apart from what He is! Why go on having delusions about yourself?

Repentance does not simply go on apologizing to God for the things you have done wrong, as though you were surprised at yourself; in that way you only advertise your own conceit, as though you were waiting for God to say, "I know you did not *mean* it, and it is not what I would normally *expect* of you," when it is exactly what you *did* mean and exactly what God *always* expects of you! Why not call your own bluff (and the Devil's!) and recognize the "nature of the beast," for true repentance humbly admits not only that what you have done is wrong, but that what you have *done* is the inevitable consequence of what you *are*, unless what you *are* is replaced through the Holy Spirit, by what *He is!*

It is the Holy Spirit who is diametrically opposed to sin, and only His presence introduces the liberating law of Life. The flesh *loves* sin—and in all its most subtle forms, including "our righteousnesses," the "filthy rags" of pseudo-piety and self-advertisement (Isa. 64:6). Stop being deceived into thinking that the flesh will ever change its nature; its roots are *always* in the Devil! The late Captain Reginald Wallis used to say, "Far too many people have shares in the Old Adam Improvement Society. . . ." It has been a bankrupt concern ever since the company was floated, and when the Lord comes, it will go into final liquidation!

The Law can no more make you godly than a railway guide can make a train run on time—and by nature you are always behind schedule! There is good news however, good news for you, no matter how discouraged you may be, for

"God has done what the Law could not do" (Rom. 8:3a
AMPLIFIED NEW TESTAMENT, emphasis added).

How did He do it? He did it by "sending his own Son in a form like that of our own sinful nature, and as a sacrifice for sin, he has passed judgment against sin within that very nature, so that the commandment of the law may find fulfilment in us, whose conduct, no longer under the control of our lower nature, is directed by the Spirit" (Rom. 8:3 NEB).

God passed judgment upon sin in your very nature in a twofold way: *morally* and *vicariously*.

He sent His Son in the first place, "in a form like that of our own sinful nature" to condemn sin morally, and in the second place, He sent His Son "as a sacrifice for sin," to condemn sin vicariously.

Though "in the likeness of," the Lord Jesus Christ was not *sinful as* "sinful flesh" (Rom. 8:3 AV), for He was *without* sin, specifically *the only begotten* Son of God, conceived miraculously of the Holy Spirit in the womb of a virgin; "From the beginning He had the nature of God" (Phil. 2:6 WEYMOUTH). As opposed to the spiritually bankrupt stock of the first and fallen Adam, who being "ignorant of the righteousness provided by God" sought "to establish their own," the Second and Last Adam had the righteousness of God inherently in Him, "for the consummation of Law in Christ" (Rom. 10:3—4 WEYMOUTH).

Every demand made by the Law in righteousness found its complete fulfillment in the person of the Lord Jesus Christ; there was no point at which the Law could accuse Him! In the beginning *with* God, and as its author *as* God, Christ was the Law's *fulfillment* in righteousness; as "utter man" He satisfied His own demands as utter God, and His utterness was given utterance in utter righteousness! He was the *Word* through whom God *speaks*, and what He has to say at first condemns you!

It is quite obvious that the righteousness of Christ's life

may be equated with the righteousness demanded by God's Law. This being so, what can the life He lived *then*, nineteen hundred years ago, do for you *now*?

If the life He lived *then* simply demonstrated the righteousness demanded by the Law, all that His life *then* can do for you *now*, is what the *Law* can do for you *now*! And we know what the Law *cannot* do; it cannot make you perfect! The Law condemns you and proves you guilty! "Now we know that what things soever the law saith, it saith to them who are under the law: that every mouth may be stopped, and all the world may become guilty before God. Therefore by the deeds of the law shall no flesh be justified in his sight: for by the law is the knowledge of sin" (Rom. 3:19–20).

His life also condemns you and proves you guilty!

Compare your life with the demands which the Law makes upon you, and your mouth will be stopped, your sin exposed, and you will be proved guilty! Compare your life with the demands which Christ's life makes upon you, and your mouth will be stopped, your sin exposed, and you will be proved guilty! Whether you try to fulfill the Law or imitate His life, both will condemn you morally! By two equally absolute standards of measurement, you will be exposed for the sinner you are, for you have "come short of the glory of God" (Rom. 3:23).

The plumb line may show me that the wall in my garden is crooked, but it will not put it straight, and had Jesus Christ come into this world simply to demonstrate a sinless life and leave us with a matchless example, He would have left us to wallow in the squalor of our own inadequacy; the "good news" of the gospel would have been a message of despair— to mock us, without being able to mend us!

The life He lived on earth condemns you—for He *could*, but you *can't!* Why did He live *then* a life that can only condemn you *now?* Because

The Life He Lived Qualified Him
for the Death He Died

The Lord Jesus Christ could not have died the death He died, had He not lived the life He lived! He could have suffered a martyr's death, a prophet's death, a preacher's death—the death of a noble idealist, the champion of some lofty cause, or as the hero of some courageous enterprise destined to bless mankind, but *not a Saviour's death!* "For Christ, the Messiah, [Himself] died for sins once for all, the Righteous for the unrighteous—the Just for the unjust, the Innocent for the guilty—that He might bring us to God" (1 Peter 3:18 AMPLIFIED NEW TESTAMENT).

> Because the sinless Saviour died,
> My sinful soul is counted free;
> And God the Just is satisfied,
> To look on Him, and pardon me!

God sent His Son into the world not only "in a form like that of our own sinful nature" to condemn sin *morally*, but "as a sacrifice for sin," to condemn sin *vicariously.*

"For he hath made him to be sin for us, who knew no sin; that we might be made the righteousness of God in him" (2 Cor. 5:21).

The Bible leaves us absolutely in no doubt about the significance of the death of Christ; He died in your place and mine, incurring for our sakes a penalty that He did not deserve. This was no sentimental gesture, but a deliberate act of redemption! Apart from His death, His life could only condemn us, like the Law which His life fulfilled; but His death added *grace to truth:*

G ... God's
R ... Riches
A ... At
C ... Christ's
E ... Expense

Truth declared by the Law and fulfilled by His life convicts sinners of their sins and tells them to be sorry; but *grace* provided by His death tells sinners who are sorry how they may be saved! "For the law was given by Moses, but grace and truth came by Jesus Christ" (John 1:17).

Without a sinless life, the Lord Jesus Christ could never have suffered a vicarious, substitutionary, and atoning death. To deny the supernatural nature of His birth is to deny His deity; to deny His deity is to deny His sinlessness, and to deny His sinlessness is to deny the atonement; and to deny *that*, is to deny that God has *done* what the Law could not *do!*

Have you accepted Christ as your Redeemer? Do you know that for His dear sake your sins are forgiven? You may know this just as soon as you say, "Thank You, Lord! Be it unto me according to Your Word! Redeem my soul, cleanse my heart, and wash me in the blood of the Lamb, the Lamb of God that taketh away the sin of the world!"

> In peace let me resign my breath,
> And Thy salvation see;
> My sins deserve eternal death,
> But Jesus died for me!

To know your sins are gone is joy indeed! The record cleansed and reconciled to God, heaven is now your home; but is that really all you need?

It is where you must *begin*, but it is not all you need!

Does the knowledge that your sins have been forgiven, *in itself*, impart to you any new capacity to live a different kind of life? The answer obviously is—No!

There may have been created within you a genuine desire to serve God, out of a sincere sense of gratitude to Christ for dying for you; you may be impelled out of a sense of duty as a Christian, to seek conformity to some pattern of behavior that has been imposed upon you as the norm for Christian living; you may be deeply moved by the need of others all around you, and holy ambitions may have been stirred within your heart, to count for God; if, however, all that has happened is that your sins have been forgiven, because you have accepted Christ as the Saviour who died for you, leaving you *since* your conversion only with those resources which you had *before* your conversion, then you will have no alternative but to "Christianize" the flesh and try to teach it to "behave" in such a way that it will be godly!

That is a sheer impossibility!

The nature of the flesh never changes. No matter how you may coerce it or conform it, it is rotten through and through, even with a Bible under its arm, a check for missions in its hand, and an evangelical look on its face! You need something more than forgiveness, and *what* you need is the *big news* of the gospel! This is the very heart of the message, for if the life that Christ lived qualified Him for the death that He died, then

The Death That He Died Qualifies You for the Life That He Lived!

The moment you are redeemed through the atoning death of Christ upon the Cross (see chart 1, chapter 6), you receive the Holy Spirit within your human spirit, represented by the horizontal shading in the small circle at the top of figure D. You have "passed from death to life"—raised from the dead—and the life that has been imparted to you by the Holy Spirit is the very life of Christ Himself; "He made us alive together in fellowship *and* in union with Christ.—He gave us the very life of Christ Himself, the same new life with which He quickened Him" (Eph. 2:5a AMPLIFIED NEW TESTAMENT).

The life that the Lord Jesus Christ lived *for* you nineteen hundred years ago—condemns you; but the life that He now lives *in* you—saves you! The Christian life is the life that He lived *then*, lived *now* by Him *in* you. As He behaved in the sinless humanity that the Father had prepared for Him then, so He wants to behave in your humanity presented to Him now.

He wants your mind placed at His disposal through the indwelling Holy Spirit; your emotions, your will, all that you are and have, made available to the Lord Jesus Christ as a living member of His new corporate body on earth, which is called the church.

This is the new law in action, the law of the Spirit of life in Christ Jesus, re-establishing the "faith-love" relationship between your soul and God, making it possible for you to "declare" the Son, as once the Son "declared" the Father. Your "behavior mechanism" will be once more wholly "deo-centric" instead of "ego-centric," "so that the commandment of the law may find fulfillment" in you, whose conduct, no longer under the control of your lower nature, "is directed by the Spirit." A radical change of government!

We see then certain principles evolving, and I would like to summarize them in four simple sentences:

1. He had to come as He did (miraculous birth)
   to be what He was (perfect).
2. He had to be what He was (perfect)
   to do what He did (redeem).
3. He had to do what He did (redeem)
   that you might have what He is (life).
4. You must have what He is (life)
   to be what He was (perfect).

He Had to Come as He Did (Miraculous Birth) to Be What He Was (Perfect)

His supernatural birth qualified Him for the sinless life He lived—the Word incarnate, never less than God in what He *was*, but never more than man in what He *did!* Completely empty of sin, always *filled* with the Spirit and *led* by the Spirit and *empowered* by the Spirit (Luke 4:1, 14).

Could He not have chosen His own path and made His own decisions? As God, yes! As man, no! Did He have no power of His own? As God, enough to create the universes, to throw them into space, and keep them there "by the word of His power"! As man, none! "Then answered Jesus and said unto them, Verily, verily, I say unto you, The Son can do nothing of himself, but what he seeth the Father do: for what things soever he doeth, these also doeth the Son likewise" (John 5:19).

He Had to Be What He Was (Perfect)
to Do What He Did (Redeem)

Only by virtue of His own sinlessness could He die *vicariously* for those whose sin His life had condemned *morally*. God has done what the Law could not do!

> He knew how wicked man had been,
> He knew that God must punish sin;
> So out of pity Jesus said:
> I'll bear the punishment instead!

He Had to Do What He Did (Redeem)
That You Might Have What He Is (Life)

Here is the "much more" of your salvation! Christ in the present tense! Not what He was—that would condemn you; and not just what He will be—that would only tantalize you, but all the overwhelming adequacy of all that He *is right now*, for every step of the way, and for every bend in the road! "For if, when we were enemies, we were reconciled to God by the death of his Son, much more, being reconciled, we shall be saved by his life" (Rom. 5:10).

You Must Have What He Is (Life)
to Be What He Was (Perfect)

For godliness is not the consequence of your capacity to imitate God, but the consequence of His capacity to reproduce Himself in you; not self-righteousness, but Christ-righteousness; the righteousness which is by faith—a faith which by renewed dependence upon God releases His divine action, to restore the marred image of the invisible God. It is not inactivity, but Christ-activity; God in action accomplishing the divine end through human personality—never reducing man to the status of a cabbage, but exalting man to the stature of a king! "For if by one man's offense death reigned by one; much more they which receive abundance of grace and of the gift of righteousness shall reign in life by one, Jesus Christ" (Rom. 5:17).

At first sight this might seem to offer to you the possibility of sinless perfection as the result of spiritual regeneration, but this is far from being the case; for it is only your faith and your obedience which allow Him to be in you *now* what He was *then* (perfect)—and you will be what He was *then* only to the degree in which you allow Him to be in you what He is *now* (perfect)!

All of the Father was available to all of the Son, because by His faith-love relationship, all of the Son was available to all of the Father, and this constituted His perfect manhood; and the availability of the Son to you will be in the degree of your availability to the Son, because of *your* faith-love relationship to Him!

Had you *perfect* faith and *perfect* love, you could enjoy His *perfect* life—but these you do not have; for although you have been restored to life by the presence of the Holy Spirit within your human spirit, there is no eradication of the flesh, which as you will see represented in figure D (chart 1, chapter 6) by the smaller, inner circle containing the I, is still operative within the human soul. The wrong man still clings tenaciously to his seat at the keyboard of the Grand Piano, and resists every attempt on the part of the Right Man to take over!

This is the problem of the "carnal Christian," who

although indwelt by the Holy Spirit is still dominated to a large degree by the flesh; the image of the invisible God is only partially restored as indicated by the marginal ring around figure D, half solid—representing still the "works of the flesh" and half unshaded—representing the "fruits of the Spirit." Only in certain areas of the carnal Christian's life, and to a limited degree, is the Lord Jesus allowed to "be Himself" and to *express* Himself through the "behavior mechanism" of the believer placed only spasmodically at His disposal.

In other words, though you may be redeemed and regenerate, God never deprives you of your moral capacity to choose. The *act* of changing our mind about Adam's change of mind, which constituted your conversion, and which brought about your reconciliation to God through faith in Christ, must be followed by an *attitude* which perpetuates the change of mind, if you are to enter experientially into all the good of the new life in Christ, of whose divine nature you have become a partaker (2 Peter 1:4).

If the initial *act* of faith was genuine by which you were redeemed (and you will only *be* redeemed if the initial act of faith *was* genuine) your subsequent *attitude* will never change the consequences of the *act*—you will remain redeemed by His "one sacrifice for sins for ever" (Heb. 10:12) and irrevocably "sealed with that Holy Spirit of promise" (Eph. 1:13), by whom God "[has also appropriated and acknowledged us as His], putting His seal upon us and giving us His (Holy) Spirit in our hearts as the security deposit *and* guarantee [of the fulfillment of His promise]" (2 Cor. 1:22 AMPLIFIED NEW TESTAMENT); but your subsequent attitude *will* determine *on the way to heaven*, how far it will be possible for the Lord Jesus Christ to implement in you that for which He has redeemed you!

It is your inherent right to choose, which enables you to enter into this unique relationship with Christ—or to reject

Him; but you reject Him at your peril! It has been magnificently demonstrated in the film "City of the Bees," produced by the Moody Bible Institute of Science, that there is an interlock between instinct and the behavior patterns of this tiny instinct, as in the case of every other form of animal life, only man excepted; upon the efficiency of this interlock its very existence and survival depends. Remove the interlock, and order would be swallowed up in chaos; the social, logistic, structural, and administrative problems of a bee society would be way and beyond the mental capacity of the most progressive individual bee! Anarchy would inevitably precede disaster and extinction!

No such interlock exists between man and *his* behavior patterns, for God created man to be a moral being, to enter into all the hidden depths of this amazing mystery—the mystery of godliness! The only interlock is an interlock of love, faith, and obedience to God, which allows *Him* to reproduce *Himself* in man; and make man *man* after the immaculate image of his Maker!

Remove *this* interlock, and little wonder that across the rubble of a wrecked society of men, a lonely cross has cast its shadow; the shadow of a lonely God, waiting for men to be made *men* again, as God intended men to be; and it takes God to be a *man!*

That is why it takes Christ to be a Christian—for Christ in a Christian puts God back into the man!

Chapter X

How Much Are You Worth?

And that he died for all, that they which live should not henceforth live unto themselves, but unto him which died for them, and rose again. (2 Cor. 5:15)

Christ died to kill death dead, and to swallow it up in victory! He drew its sting—for "the sting of death is sin" (1 Cor. 15:56), and "he appeared to put away sin by the sacrifice of himself" (Heb. 9:26b). This He did for all men, without exception, "not willing that any should perish, but that all should come to repentance" (2 Peter 3:9b).

Never allow anyone to deceive you into believing that God has placed an arbitrary limitation upon the efficacy of the blood of Christ, or that there are those who cannot repent, even if they would, simply because God has deliberately placed them outside the scope of His redemptive purpose! This blasphemes the grace, the love, and the integrity of God, and makes Him morally responsible for the unbelief of the unbeliever, for the impenitence of the impenitent, and saddles Him squarely with the guilt of the guilty—as an aider and abettor of their sin!

Such is not the teaching of the Bible, for the Lord Jesus Christ made it abundantly clear that the reluctance is on *man's* part, not on God's! "O Jerusalem, Jerusalem, the city that murders the prophets and stones the messengers sent to her! How often have I longed to gather your children, as a hen gathers her brood under her wings, but you would not let me" (Luke 13:34 NEB).

It is equally clear from the Saviour's lips, that the wrath of God abides on those who do not believe and that these will not see life, for "this is the condemnation, that light is come into the world, and men loved darkness rather than light, because their deeds were evil" (John 3:19); and whether men love light or love darkness, God or the Devil, heaven or hell, love can only be expressed by the exercise of a free will.

Without freedom of choice it is equally impossible to obey or to disobey—to be condemned for the one or to be commended for the other! I cannot blame my typewriter for the spelling mistakes it makes, nor congratulate it for its beautiful prose—it is an impersonal machine! It neither offers its services nor withholds them, for it has no capacity to choose; yet it is precisely at this point that men are held morally responsible to God, who will take "vengeance on them that know not God, and that obey not the gospel of our Lord Jesus Christ: who shall be punished with everlasting destruction from the presence of the Lord, and from the glory of his power" (2 Thess. 1:8–9).

Some would have you believe that only those can obey the gospel and accept Christ as their Saviour, to whom God has given the ability to obey as a purely arbitrary, mechanical act on His part, leaving no option in the matter to any individual either way! On the basis of this strange hypothesis, the fearful judgment of God is to fall upon those who have remained in their rebellious state of unbelief, only because they have been unable to exercise an ability to obey the gospel, which only God can give, and which He has refused to give them! Needless to say, such an idea can only serve to bring the righteousness and judgment of God into contempt and disrepute.

The revelation that God has given to us by His Holy Spirit through the apostles is delightfully clear: "If any man sin, we have an advocate with the Father, Jesus Christ the righteous: And he is the propitiation for our sins: and not for ours only, but also for the sins of the whole world" (1 John 2:1b–2); "Who gave himself a ransom for all" (1 Tim. 2:6a); "that he by the grace of God should taste death for every man" (Heb. 2:9c).

It is your inherent right to choose which is at the very heart of the mystery, both of the mystery of *godliness* and of the heart of *mystery*, for as we began to see in chapter 4, it is man's ability to say "yes" to God in a faith-love relationship of total dependence, producing godliness, which gives him alternatively the ability to say "no" to God in independence—to become a soul dominated by the flesh and producing iniquity.

The Cross involves for all men everywhere a personal decision that cannot be avoided; for God "now commandeth all men everywhere to repent: Because he hath appointed a day, in the which he will judge the world in righteousness by that man whom he hath ordained; whereof he hath given assurance unto all men, in that he hath raised him from the dead" (Acts 17:30–31).

This is the compelling love of Christ; God's command to *all men everywhere* to repent is an invitation to life! He does not mock men who are sorry for their sin, nor does He command men to repent of their sin who cannot be sorry! "For the love of Christ constraineth us; because we thus judge, that if one died for all, then were all dead" (2 Cor. 5:14)—the fact that the Lord Jesus Christ died for all, is ample corroboration of the fact that "in Adam" all die, spiritually dead, "alienated from the life of God"—lamps that are out! How thrilling and wonderful to know, however, that "as in Adam all die, even so in Christ shall all be made alive" (1 Cor. 15:22)!

You can know the indwelling presence of the risen Lord, resident within your human spirit by His Holy Spirit, from the very moment that you receive Christ as your Redeemer! You are then no longer *waiting* for the resurrection—you are enjoying it!

It is true, of course, that there will be a physical resurrection of the body, for "this perishable nature must clothe itself with the imperishable, and this mortality must clothe itself with immortality" (1 Cor. 15:53 WEYMOUTH) but this is only incidental compared with the priceless privilege of sharing *now* the very life of the Lord Jesus Christ Himself!

Consider further with me, however, this important passage in 2 Corinthians 5:15, "And He died for all, so that all those who live might no longer live to *and* for themselves, but to *and* for Him Who died and was raised again for their sake" (AMPLIFIED NEW TESTAMENT). When the apostle refers to "all those who live," he is speaking of those who have already been raised from the dead spiritually; they are no longer "in Adam"—dead; they are "in Christ"—alive! He goes on to explain to what end God has raised them to life again. It is that they may no longer live "to and for themselves," but "to and for Him Who died and was raised again for their sake"!

In other words, there is to be a remarkable change of attitude and outlook; for Christ died and rose again from the dead to introduce an entirely new principle of human behavior!

To live "to and for yourself" is to "walk after the flesh"!

To live "to and for Christ" is to "walk after the Spirit"!

These are the two principles of human behavior. It is not just a matter of *degree*, it is a matter of *kind*; to be dominated by the flesh is to be dominated by the Devil; and to be dominated by the Spirit is to be dominated by God.

Two men doing identically the same thing may at the same time, by their identical act, be demonstrating two different principles of behavior which are diametrically opposed to each other.

Both Cain and Abel brought an offering to the Lord (Gen. 4:3-8); and to the undiscerning, it would appear that both were engaged in a sincere act of worship; yet Cain and his offering were both rejected, and God had no respect for them.

Was it the *act* which God rejected and which made Cain unacceptable? No—it was the principle which governed the act! A principle which made the otherwise innocent act as sinful as the principle which prompted it! He was still living "to and for himself"!

Sin was still lying at the door—the flesh was still dominant; Cain was still convinced of his own superior judgment as to what was good for him, and for that matter, as to what was good for God! He "brought of the fruit of the ground an offering unto the Lord" (Gen. 4:3)—the ground that God had cursed! (Gen. 3:17). Cain "was of that wicked one [the Devil], and slew his brother. And wherefore slew he him? Because . . ." *in the very act of "worship"* "his own works were evil, and his brother's righteous" (1 John 3:12b).

To bring an offering to the Lord was for Cain just another way of letting "that wicked one" give expression to his undying hatred of God, and to his unremitting hostility to the Son, for the offering that he brought was in deliberate defiance of the spiritual significance of the lamb that Abel offered. An "act of worship" ended up in an act of cold-blooded murder, but though there may have been some difference in degree between the acts, there was absolutely no difference in kind; it was the Devil himself and no other who as we have already seen "was a murderer from the beginning" (John 8:44), who inspired both the "act of worship" and the act of killing Abel; there was death in his religion! When God called his bluff, he was furious and exposed himself for the Devil's dupe he was!

It would not really matter whether as a professor in a theological seminary you denied the Virgin Birth of Christ, as a pastor from the pulpit you discredited the atoning efficacy of the blood He shed, or as a church member you participated in those apostate forms of Christless "Christianity" which repudiate His deity and His sinlessness, or drove the nails into His hands and feet upon the cross—all would be equally satisfying to the Devil!

Abel on the other hand, through faith "offered to God a more acceptable sacrifice than Cain, and through this faith he had witness borne to him that he was righteous, God bearing witness by accepting his gifts" (Heb. 11:4 WEYMOUTH). It was certainly not the monetary value of the lamb which made either Abel or his gift acceptable, for this may well have been far less than the value of the offering which Cain had brought.

Wherein, then, lay his acceptability?

It was in the principle which governed his act, a principle which demanded total obedience *to* God out of an attitude of total dependence *on* God.

By faith Abel appropriated the spiritual significance of the little lamb, as the symbol of the Lamb of God that taketh away the sin of the world. In humble anticipation he sheltered beneath the "faith-shadow" of a future cross upon which the Prince of Peace would die to kill death dead, and bring him, Abel, back to life again! "And the LORD had respect unto Abel and to his offering" (Gen. 4:4).

What is the principle that governs *your* behavior?

I am not asking you the *nature* of your behavior, I am asking you the *principle* from which it springs!

You will remember that we have seen sin defined in the Bible as independence: "whatsoever is not of faith is sin" (Rom. 14:23b), an attitude of "lawlessness" (1 John 3:4);

what then does repentance involve? It involves stepping out of *independence* back into *dependence*—and the measure of your *repentance* will be the measure of your *dependence!*

Every area of your life in which you have not learned to be dependent, is an area of your life in which you have not as yet repented.

Perhaps you are a businessman, and you imagine that once you have crossed the threshold of your office—you are the boss! Everything you say goes! This is your little kingdom—perhaps even a mighty empire—but you congratulate yourself upon the fact that you have just what it takes to outbid your competitor or to outsmart your opponents; you need Christ for your Sunday school class, and you need Christ for some of the other church responsibilities which you shoulder, but right there in the city amidst the stern demands of modern commerce, you are out on your own! It is sink or swim by the might of your own right arm.

Sir! That is just the area in your life where you have *not yet repented!*

Maybe you are a mother, and if there is one thing for which you consider yourself to be completely adequate, it is for the business of rearing a family! What you have not learned about child psychology is hardly worth knowing, and the discipline of a well-planned family life leaves you little opportunity to get upon your knees. Bathwater and baby powder have stronger claims upon your time than prayer, and pride of house takes precedence over humility of heart!

Madam! This is just the area of your life in which you have *not yet repented!*

The words flow like water running down a mountain stream when you stand up in the pulpit and intoxicate your congregation with your latest verbal masterpiece; the logic is supreme and the anecdotes are apt, whilst a dignified deportment gives added point to weighty utterances already underlined by gentle gestures with the hands! Aunt Agatha was right when she said that you would one day be a preacher—but she did not know how *fine* a preacher you would be! You have all that it takes to build a thriving church!

Preacher! The pulpit is the place! The place where you have *not yet repented!*

Is it your beautiful voice or your musical talent? Is it your athletic skill or your academic gift? In what part of your life are you adequate *without* Christ—where to lose *Him* would be to lose *nothing?* That is it! Right there!

That is the place in your life where you have *not yet repented!*

You have been "made alive" in Christ to be exclusively at His disposal, so that by the Holy Spirit He may monopolize your total personality and give expression to Himself through you in your behavior.

That is what it means to be "filled with the Spirit" (Eph. 5:18) or to be "godly" as represented by figure E in chart 1 (chapter 6). The capital I is on the cross, and as indicated by the unshaded margin at the circumference of figure E, all that you *do* is what Christ *does,* and creates in you the image of all that Christ *is!* "I have been crucified with Christ, and it is no longer I that live, but Christ that lives in me; and the life which I now live in the body I live by faith in the Son of God who loved me and gave Himself up for me" (Gal. 2:20 WEYMOUTH).

The image will never be perfect or complete down here on earth, but the degree in which by your free consent, you live to *and* for Christ, is the degree of your spirituality; the degree in which you still live to and for yourself is the degree of your carnality—and the degree in which you have not as yet repented!

It may be, however, that until now your experience as a

Christian has been one of consistent defeat; you are baffled and bewildered at your own impotence and almost in despair of any possibility of improvement. Sometimes you cry from your heart:

> I find therefore this rule, that when I desire to do what is right, evil is there with me. In my inmost self all my sympathy is with the Law of God; but I discover in my faculties a different law, at war with the law of my understanding, and leading me captive to the law which is in my faculties—the law of sin. Unhappy man that I am! Who will rescue me from this body of death? (Rom. 7:21–24 WEYMOUTH)

There is war in your soul, and you will always be baffled and perplexed until you recognize what I have constantly reiterated, that within the soul of every regenerate person there are two powerful forces at work; the constant down-drag of the old, Adamic nature and the mighty liberating power of Christ the Lord. "So then I myself serve with my understanding the Law of God, but with my lower nature the law of sin" (Rom. 7:25 WEYMOUTH).

There are two "appetites" at work within you: one insatiably hungry for all that is evil and hostile to God and the other insatiably hungry for all that is pure and noble, wholesome and true; the one has its origin in the Devil, the other in God.

To be in ignorance of this fact or to act in defiance of it, will make you as foolish as the Galatian Christians, to whom the apostle Paul put the following question: "Are you so foolish *and* so senseless *and* so silly? Having begun [your new life spiritually] with the (Holy) Spirit, are you now reaching perfection [by dependence] on the flesh?" (Gal. 3:3 AMPLIFIED NEW TESTAMENT).

Having received the very life of Christ through the Spirit, the only source of godliness, these foolish Galatians then tried to live the Christian life in the energy of the flesh, which is only the source of iniquity. They tried to make the leopard change its spots!

Is this what *you* have been doing? Having received *everything* which God can give you *in Christ*, have you been living as though God had given you *nothing*—as though everything depended on *you*?

It is as though you were born with a battered, old Ford car in the garage, with broken springs, faulty brakes, and dirty plugs—the flesh! Then you are born again, and there is a brand new Cadillac—the Spirit—alongside the rusty old Ford in the garage. But instead of going out in the brand new Cadillac, you drive around in your old tin crate—honking, snorting, puffing, and blowing in a cloud of smoke, "giving your testimony," and telling folk about your lovely new car!

Your testimony would be as flat as your tires! You would spend all your time asking God for spares: "O God, please give me new springs; and please God, give me new plugs!" And God would do nothing of the sort! He would say, "Stick it in the dump! It's only fit for the scrap heap—so bury it! Go out in the brand new Cadillac I have given you—it has power enough and to spare!" For "it is the spirit that quickeneth; the flesh profiteth nothing" (John 6:63a).

The death of Christ upon the Cross accomplished something much more than your redemption from the penalty of sin. It put your *pride* on the scrap heap and *you* in the dump!

However little we may be able to explain it, "We know that our old (unrenewed) self was nailed to the cross with Him in order that [our] body, [which is the instrument] of sin, might be made ineffective *and* inactive for evil, that we might no longer be the slaves of sin" (Rom. 6:6 AMPLIFIED NEW TESTAMENT).

In other words, as illustrated by the center circle in figure

E (chart 1, chapter 6), there must not only be a cross on the hill, but a Cross in your heart!

The "self" that sin makes of you was taken by the Lord Jesus Christ into death with Him—that you might be delivered not only from sin's penalty, but also from its power. Your soul is released from sin's evil influence, so that you may become the "self" that Christ makes of you—"a new creature: old things are passed away; behold, all things are become new" (2 Cor. 5:17b).

The "I" has been crucified with Christ so that God may "have right of way" into every area of your personality, at liberty to reproduce Himself once more in you, and transform you into His own likeness—and that is *godliness!*

We were buried therefore with Him by the baptism into death, so that just as Christ was raised from the dead by the glorious [power] of the Father, so we too might habitually live *and* behave in newness of life. For if we have become one with Him by sharing a death like His, we shall also be [one with Him in sharing] His resurrection [by a new life lived for God]. (Rom. 6:4–5 AMPLIFIED NEW TESTAMENT)

However, just as the death of Christ *for* you is only *potential* until by a deliberate and voluntary *act* of faith you appropriate its efficacy for your redemption, so *your* death *with* Christ is only potential unless by a deliberate and voluntary *attitude* of faith you appropriate its efficacy for your sanctification—enabling God to put you once more to that intelligent use for which He created you, and for which Christ has now redeemed you.

For by the death He died, He died to sin [ending His relation to it] once for all, and the life that He lives He is living to God—in unbroken fellowship with Him. Even so consider yourselves also dead to sin *and* your relation to it broken, but [that you are] alive to God—living in unbroken fellowship with Him—in Christ Jesus. (Rom. 6:10–11 AMPLIFIED NEW TESTAMENT)

You are to live exclusively "to and for Christ," and to consider yourself "alive to God" only by virtue of what you are "in Him."

You cannot *accomplish* your own redemption, and you cannot *accomplish* your own sanctification! It is "according as his divine power hath given unto us all things that pertain unto life and godliness, through the knowledge of him that hath called us to glory and virtue" (2 Peter 1:3): *faith takes* what *God gives*, and *God gives* what *man needs! All* that he needs!

All that God *gives*, which is all that you *need*, He gives to you in Christ, "That no flesh should glory in his presence. But of him are ye in Christ Jesus, who of God is made unto us wisdom, and righteousness, and sanctification, and redemption" (1 Cor. 1:29–30).

The degree to which by a deliberate, voluntary attitude of faith you are reckoning yourself to be dead "with Christ" to all that you were "in Adam" and *alive* to God in all that you are "in Christ"—is the degree to which the redemptive purpose of God has been wrought out in your life—and this is the only valid estimate of your worth! Everything else is a *dead loss!* "Consequently, from now on we estimate *and* regard no one from a [purely] human point of view—in terms of natural standards of value" (2 Cor. 5:16a AMPLIFIED NEW TESTAMENT).

Pointing to an affluent looking gentleman coming into the church, I might say to you (if I were mischievous enough), "How much is he worth?" and maybe you would reply, "If he's worth a dollar, he's worth a million!" And I would say to you, "I did not ask *how much money he had in the bank!* I simply asked you how much he was *worth!*"

A man could have all the money in all the banks in all the world and be worth *nothing*—so far as God is concerned, if he were still living "to and for himself"! The measure of a man's worth is the measure in which he no longer lives "to and for himself," but "to and for Jesus Christ." *No more and no less!*

How much are *you* worth?

You tell me that you have just completed your church building program, and that the board has just appointed a new minister; that's fine, but pardon me for asking—how much is he worth? "Why," you say, "he has a most distinguished academic record," and you begin to enlarge upon the letters after his name, but you will forgive me if I interrupt, I am sure. It is excellent that a man should take the trouble to be highly qualified, but I did not ask you *how clever he was at mastering facts or in passing examinations*, I simply asked how much he was *worth!*

A man's worth is not primarily a matter of *scholarship*, it is essentially a matter of *relationship*—relationship to Jesus Christ. It is, of course, perfectly possible and perfectly legitimate to have both, and this is to be commended—but we should always remind ourselves that—

> The foolishness of God is wiser than men, and the weakness of God is stronger than men. For consider, brethren, your own calling. Not many worldly-wise, not many influential, not many of noble birth have been called. But God has chosen the foolish things of the world in order to shame its wise men; and God has chosen the weak things of the world in order to shame what is strong; and the mean and despised things of the world—things that are nothing—God has chosen in order to bring to nothing things that are; to prevent any mortal man from boasting before God. (1 Cor. 1:25–29 WEYMOUTH)

How much *are* you worth?

There was a time when Paul the apostle, as Saul of Tarsus, hated Christ and persecuted the church, and he had done so because he had still regarded Christ from a purely human point of view—in terms of natural standards of value.

Had these "natural standards of value" been spiritually

valid, Saul of Tarsus would have been right and Paul the apostle would have been wrong!

To Saul, according to all the facts as he knew them, and as they were commonly accepted by all the "people that mattered," Jesus Christ was the illegitimate child of an unfaithful woman, so that by all normally accepted standards of society, He was an outcast! Socially, how much was He worth? Nothing!

Born of peasant stock, His schooling was negligible, sufficing only to equip Him for the humble duties of a common craftsman. Professionally, how much was He worth? Nothing!

A fanatical street preacher and a rabble rouser, He was totally repudiated by all the ecclesiastical dignitaries of His day, and having had absolutely no theological training whatever, was looked upon with supreme contempt by all that called itself scholarship amongst those who searched the Scriptures. Ecclesiastically, theologically, and intellectually how much was He worth? Nothing!

His financial standing was such that He even had to borrow a coin for one of His farfetched illustrations! He was an incorrigible "scrounger" by all "natural standards of value," for He had no home of His own. Born in a borrowed stable, He lived and dined in borrowed homes; He rode upon a borrowed donkey, was crucified on a borrowed cross, and buried in a borrowed tomb! He was bankrupt from the start! Financially, how much was He worth? By all "natural standards of value"—nothing!

Shall we be angry with Saul of Tarsus? Was his judgment insincere? Were the conclusions to which he came not entirely reasonable?

If the Lord Jesus Christ were to appear in the world today under similar circumstances, what congregation would call Him to be their pastor? What university or Bible college or training institute would appoint Him to their faculty? What missionary organization would invite Him on their board or even send Him to the field? Who would make Him chairman of the building committee?

Maybe our standards of value are as wrong today as were those of Saul in his day!

Something happened, however, which changed Saul of Tarsus completely; the old standards of value went by the board, and everything assumed an entirely new perspective!

The *values themselves* had not changed! It was simply that in a dazzling encounter on the road to Damascus, Saul of Tarsus saw "the glory of God in the face of Jesus Christ" (2 Cor. 4:6b). He looked into the face of a *man* and saw *God*, and was blinded by the sight—for he saw "the perfect imprint *and* very image of [God's] nature" (Heb. 1:3 AMPLIFIED NEW TESTAMENT).

In one blinding, crushing moment of humiliation, his own utter worthlessness was exposed to the stubborn heart of this proud enemy of the faith! "Circumcised the eighth day, of the stock of Israel, of the tribe of Benjamin, an Hebrew of the Hebrews; as touching the law, a Pharisee; Concerning zeal, persecuting the church; touching the righteousness which is in the law, blameless" (Phil. 3:5–6), by all "natural standards of value" this man was worth *everything*—and had already outstripped many of his Jewish contemporaries in his boundless devotion to the traditions of his ancestors (Gal. 1:14 NEB), but in the light of this new discovery of God, he could only say:

> But all such assets I have written off because of Christ. I would say more: I count everything sheer loss, because all is far outweighed by the gain of knowing Christ Jesus my Lord, for whose sake I did in fact lose everything. I count it so much garbage, for the sake of gaining Christ and finding myself incorporate in him, with no righteousness of my own, no legal rectitude, but the righteousness which comes from faith in Christ, given by God in response to faith. (Phil. 3:7–9 NEB)

Saul of Tarsus suddenly discovered that a man is worth only as much *as can be seen of God in him;* and that he was in the presence of the man in whom (to use his own description) "the whole fulness of Deity (the Godhead), continues to dwell in bodily form—giving complete expression of the divine nature" (Col. 2:9 AMPLIFIED NEW TESTAMENT), and that this *man* was *Jesus Christ* whom he was persecuting!

From that moment on, nothing else mattered! Saul of Tarsus stopped being Saul of Tarsus, and became Paul the apostle! He was *out* of Adam, and he was *in* Christ, and the "law of the Spirit of life" began to operate, introducing the new principle of human behavior which made him a "new Creature"!

Paul had found reality in God, and the "show" was over! He could afford to discard his makeup, and lay aside the musty costumes of a religious performance! Neither the pompous self-esteem of a godless society nor the honors it could bestow upon its servile devotees impressed him!

The apostle was emancipated! He was released from the hollow art of living in a fool's paradise of faulty values; a world of artificial standards anchored to a cloud and blown by every wind of fashion!—"God forbid," he said, "that I should glory, save in the cross of our Lord Jesus Christ, by which the world is crucified unto me, and I unto the world" (Gal. 6:14)!

Losing his life—he found it! Dying to self and buried with Christ he found himself alive again—*in God;* for in that blinding flash of glory on the Damascus Road, the whole *mystery of godliness* had become an *open secret* in the face of Jesus Christ!

He had discovered how much he was worth—*nothing!*

To discover that, is to discover how much Christ is worth—*everything!*

When you are willing to *obey* what you have *discovered,*

and let the Truth *behave*, then the Lord Jesus Christ will fill what you are—nothing, with what He is—everything, and that indeed will be something!

With the wrong man out, and the Right Man in, how wealthy God will have made you! Good friend, before you lay this book aside embrace by faith these great and precious promises, and commit yourself to Christ for all that which He is committed to in you; He waits to fill you with Himself and share with you the secret of the mystery! "Even the mystery which hath been hid from ages and from generations, but now is made manifest to his saints. To whom God would make known what is the riches of the glory of this mystery among the Gentiles; which is *Christ in you*, the hope of glory" (Col. 1:26–27, emphasis added).